Portraits
Political & Personal

by Leon Trotsky

PATHFINDER PRESS   NEW YORK

D1342584

Edited by George Breitman and George Saunders
Copyright © 1977 by Pathfinder Press, Inc.
All rights reserved
Library of Congress Catalog Card Number 77-50342
ISBN 0-87348-503-3 cloth; 0-87348-504-1 paper
Manufactured in the United States of America
First edition 1977

The publisher acknowledges with gratitude the permission of the following to use materials by Leon Trotsky in this book: Harvard University Press, Cambridge, Massachusetts, for excerpts on Natalia Sedova from *Trotsky's Diary in Exile, 1935,* copyright © 1958 by the President and Fellows of Harvard College. *Intercontinental Press,* New York, for speech on Adolf Joffe, copyright © 1975 by *Intercontinental Press. International Socialist Review,* New York, for speech on Liebknecht and Luxemburg, copyright © 1971 by *International Socialist Review;* and for permission to reprint from its predecessors: *The New International,* articles on Engels, Yenukidze, and Krupskaya, and *Fourth International,* articles on Plekhanov, Sverdlov, Herriot, and Zinoviev and Kamenev. *Life* magazine, New York, for article on Stalin, copyright © 1939 and 1967 by Time, Inc. *The Militant,* New York, for article on Tsintsadze, and for permission to reprint from its predecessor, *Socialist Appeal,* article on Lenin. G.P. Putnam's Sons, New York, for article on Wells from *Lenin,* copyright © 1971 by G.P. Putnam's Sons. University of Michigan Press, Ann Arbor, for Chapter IV, "The Tsar and the Tsarina," from *The History of the Russian Revolution,* volume 1, copyright © 1932, 1933, 1960 by the University of Michigan.

Pathfinder Press, Inc.
410 West Street, New York, N.Y. 10014

CONTENTS

Introduction *by the editors* 5
Karl Liebknecht and Rosa Luxemburg 14
Karl Kautsky 28
Georgi Plekhanov 34
Vera Zasulich 41
Vladimir Ilyich Lenin 48
H.G. Wells 55
Mikhail Glazman 64
Yakov Sverdlov 69
Adolf Joffe 78
Nicholas and Alexandra Romanov 81
Kote Tsintsadze 93
Charolambos 98
Anatoli Lunacharsky 104
Natalia Sedova 109
Friedrich Engels 126
Édouard Herriot 145
Maxim Gorky 160
Grigori Zinoviev and Lev Kamenev 164
Abel Yenukidze 174
Leon Sedov 189
Nadezhda Krupskaya 204
Joseph Stalin 207
Glossary 222
Index 234

INTRODUCTION

Leon Trotsky (1879-1940) is most widely remembered as a political figure—a central leader of the Russian revolutions of 1905 and 1917, founder of the Red Army, Marxist theoretician, chief opponent of the Stalinist degeneration of the Soviet Union, and organizer of the Fourth International. He was also a historian, biographer, essayist, cultural critic, and journalist—in the opinion of some, one of the best writers of the century[1]—and this collection of portraits written during the last third of his life is worth reading first of all because it contains some of his finest writing.

It also merits attention because it offers lively and concrete treatments from a Marxist viewpoint of the connection between the personal and political. When Marxism first appeared in the nineteenth century, it had to contend against "great man" theories of history in its attempts to establish the primacy of social and economic forces in the development of humanity. In some cases the heat of argument led supporters of Marxism to bend the stick too far back, leaving the impression that they denied the importance of the individual. Some sought to explain all social phenomena in terms of impersonal or supra-personal factors. Trotsky was one of those who helped to correct this imbalance.

Trotsky had no quarrel with those who did psychological studies of personality, as long as they were not "parlor

---

1. See, for example, the comment of Michael Foot, a British social democratic opponent of Trotsky's views: "He is, probably in all history, the greatest man of action who was also a very great literary genius." From "Trotsky's Diary—A Poignant Document," in the left Labourite weekly, *Tribune,* June 17, 1959.

psychologists" inclined toward "belletristic irresponsibility."[2] He had a high regard for Freud and was acquainted with the psychoanalytic movement during his years in Vienna (1907-14); although he disagreed with the Freudians in many respects, he regarded the psychoanalytic method as compatible with dialectical materialism and as a fruitful working hypothesis, even if it lent itself to being used in capricious and arbitrary ways. Much of Trotsky's own writing, as can be seen in this volume, reflects the partial influence of psychoanalysis; but he borrowed from it selectively, and organically merged what he took with the overall historical and philosophical method of Marxism. In 1925, while a leader of the Soviet ruling party, which still enforces the Stalin-era prohibition against the psychoanalytical line of inquiry, Trotsky wrote: "We have no grounds and no right to put a ban on the [Freudian] procedure." But he was disdainful of "sham Freudianism as an erotic indulgence or piece of naughtiness,"[3] as well as of "those unrelated psychological researches which are now so often substituted for social and historical analysis" and those "historians and biographers of the psychological tendency [who] not infrequently seek and find something purely personal and accidental where great historical forces are refracted through a personality."

"We do not at all intend to deny the significance of the personal in the mechanics of the historic process, nor the significance in the personal of the accidental," he wrote. "We only demand that a historic personality, with all its peculiarities, should not be taken as a bare list of psychological traits, but as a living reality grown out of definite social conditions and reacting upon them. As a

---

2. That was how Trotsky characterized Emil Ludwig, a popularizer of the "psychological" school who specialized in portraits of great men of the past and of such 1930s leaders as Mussolini, Roosevelt, and Stalin. To Ludwig's uncritical dialogues with his "subjects," which pretended to follow Freudian technique but actually served the interests of diplomacy and politics, Trotsky contrasted the unsparing methods of the founder of psychoanalysis. Freud made a "heroic break with all kinds of conventions" and "was bothered least of all about the prestige of his patient." See Trotsky's 1932 essay "On Lenin's Testament" in *Lenin's Fight Against Stalinism* (Pathfinder, 1975), pp. 30-31.

3. See the essay "Culture and Socialism" in Trotsky's *Problems of Everyday Life and Other Writings on Culture and Science* (Pathfinder, 1973), especially pp. 233-234.

rose does not lose its fragrance because the natural scientist points out upon what ingredients of soil and atmosphere it is nourished, so an exposure of the social roots of a personality does not remove from it either its aroma or its foul smell."

Accidental characteristics had, for Trotsky, "the interest only of historic anecdotes. Infinitely more important are those traits of character which have been grafted, or more directly imposed, on a person by the mighty force of conditions, and which throw a sharp light on the interrelation of personality and the objective factors of history."

He was particularly alert to "just where in a personality the strictly personal ends—often much sooner than we think—and how frequently the 'distinguishing traits' of a person are merely individual scratches made by a higher law of development."

He found this to be especially true when people came under great pressure. "Similar (of course, far from identical) irritations in similar conditions call out similar reflexes; the more powerful the irritation, the sooner it overcomes personal peculiarities. To a tickle, people react differently, but to a red-hot iron, alike. As a steam-hammer converts a sphere and a cube alike into sheet metal, so under the blow of too great and inexorable events resistances are smashed and the boundaries of 'individuality' lost."[4]

Because this was a major theme in Trotsky's "theory" of personality, some commentators have taken it to be his only theme, while others have held that his character sketches were political or intellectual rather than really personal.[5] These views seem to us to miss the point. Trotsky was a political activist and thinker, and the people he wrote about were almost all political figures too; there is a political dimension even in his essay on the non-political fisherman Charolambos, his guide in the sea around Prinkipo. "But politics develops by and through people," he

---

4. See Trotsky's *History of the Russian Revolution,* volume 1 (U. of Michigan, 1957), pp. 52, 92-93, 94, 95.

5. James T. Farrell, the American novelist, wrote: "He [Trotsky] saw in everyone the representative of a class or of a social group, and in everyone's ideas he perceived their political consequences. His estimates of character, despite the charges of his critics, were generally not personal: they were political and intellectual. His brilliant character vignettes in *The History of the Russian Revolution* are actually social studies in miniature." From "Leon Trotsky," *Partisan Review,* September-October 1940.

wrote, "and nothing that is human is foreign to politics."[6] The personal traits that interested him most were those that explained or illuminated political tendencies—which doesn't necessarily make them less personal than the other character traits—and he concentrated on them in much the way that a good novelist does.

His memoir of Yakov Sverdlov, first president of the Soviet government, mentions that Sverdlov "invariably walked around encased in leather from head to toe, from his leather cap to his leather boots . . . which somehow corresponded with the character of those [civil war] days," but this is done in a sentence or two; the emphasis is, correctly, on Sverdlov's organizational genius and revolutionary optimism. Trotsky did not have a gossip columnist's curiosity about the details of the divorce of Karl and Luise Kautsky, but he finds in the different reactions of Karl Kautsky and Friedrich Engels to that divorce much that is significant for an understanding of their characters, which he then relates to the different kinds of politics they represented. When he recalls Stalin's demand for a regular supply of wine in the Kremlin during the bitter years of civil war and famine, it is not in order to pass judgment on Stalin's personal tastes or habits but to trace the beginnings of bureaucratic privilege in the new Soviet state.

This collection disposes of another misconception, fathered by Bernard Shaw[7]—that Trotsky's interest in his opponents was exclusively intellectualistic and did not extend beyond proving they were politically wrong on whatever issue was in dispute. On the contrary, toward some opponents, especially those on the other side of the class barricades, he could be quite merciless. His portraits of the last Russian tsar and tsarina, scrupulously based on facts about these monarchs' barbarism, superstition, and moral emptiness, are devastating antidotes to the romantic figures depicted in the recent widely distributed book and film

---

6. See the article entitled "The Expulsion of Zinoviev and Kamenev" in *Writings of Leon Trotsky (1932)* (Pathfinder, 1973), pp. 245-56.

7. Shaw wrote: "Like Lessing, when he [Trotsky] cuts off his opponent's head, he holds it up to show that there are no brains in it; but he spares his victim's private character. . . . He leaves [his victim] without a rag of political credit; but he leaves him with his honor intact." From "Trotsky, Prince of Pamphleteers," in *The Nation and the Athenaeum* (London), January 7, 1922.

entitled *Nicholas and Alexandra.* Trotsky was more restrained as well as more "political" in his dissection of Edouard Herriot, the leading French politician between the two world wars, a spokesman for the middle classes and a preacher of moderation who somehow always ended up in the service of the capitalist class and reaction; but it will be difficult for many readers of this essay to retain any respect for the advocate of the Golden Mean as either person or politician. H.G. Wells, who fancied himself an enlightener and a progressive, comes off as a smug ass under Trotsky's pen. In none of these cases was Trotsky in the least concerned about sparing his subjects' private characters or honor.

On the other hand, Trotsky manifestly strove to be fair to many of his political opponents, calling attention to their earlier contributions and positive aspects at the same time that he strongly condemned their degeneration or decline. The sole personal anecdote he offers about Plekhanov, the founder of Russian Marxism who ended up as an enemy of the Russian revolution, shows him at an important meeting charming all present by his erudition and wit. Trotsky's obituary about his former associate Lunacharsky stresses the strengths as well as the weaknesses of that gifted Bolshevik intellectual who adapted himself to Stalinism without a single objection, and concludes, "Neither friend nor honest opponent will deny respect to his shade." His memoir of Vera Zasulich is affectionate, although their political paths coincided for only a year or two, and his brief obituary for Krupskaya sums up the historical and the personal, the great and the tragic, at the end of an important life. And while Trotsky never had much that was favorable to say about Gorky's politics in any phase of his career, he wrote, on Gorky's death, about "the great writer and great man," of whom "we take leave . . . without a note of intimacy, without exaggerated praise, but with respect and gratitude."

Conversely, Trotsky's admiration for Lenin—whom he regarded as the greatest figure of modern times and as his teacher—did not prevent him from writing the rigorously objective portrait of Lenin as an orator that is included in this volume. It captures only certain aspects of Lenin's personality, about which Trotsky wrote a great deal elsewhere, but it captures them quite vividly.

Trotsky's favorite quotation was from Spinoza: "Neither to laugh nor to cry, but to understand." Intended by this was an appeal to reason, not an Olympian injunction against laughter or tears. In any case, Trotsky was no more capable of concealing strong emotions in his writing than in his relations with other people. His pamphlet about his son and comrade, Leon Sedov, written immediately after Sedov's death at the hands of Stalinist assassins, is one of the most moving pieces of political literature ever written. Deep feelings of grief and indignation are mingled in his tribute to Kote Tsintsadze, the stern and incorruptible revolutionary from the Caucasus, whose death from tuberculosis was hastened by Stalin's denial of appropriate medical treatment, and whom Trotsky holds up as a model for revolutionary youth everywhere. And that much abused word, love, seems the only correct one to describe the emotion that invests his writings here about his companion, Natalia Sedova, written in his diary thirty-three years after he first met her, and about Marx's collaborator and friend Engels, written in the form of a book review forty years after Engels's death.[8]

There are, in addition, the materials here of a self-portrait. Every painter puts something of himself into his pictures, and the attentive reader can glean much in this collection about Trotsky's own character, if only by noticing the traits he likes or dislikes in others. Some of this self-revelation is undoubtedly premeditated, but some is not.

---

8. After reading *Trotsky's Diary in Exile, 1935* (Atheneum, 1963), in which Natalia Sedova is discussed, Erich Fromm, the psychoanalyst with an interest in the personalities of all the revolutionary Marxist leaders, wrote: "No doubt Trotsky as an individual was as different from Marx, Engels and Lenin as they were among themselves and yet in being permitted to have an intimate glimpse of the personal life of Trotsky, one is struck by all that he has in common with these productive personalities. Whether he writes about political events, or Emma Goldman's autobiography, or Edgar Wallace's detective stories, his reaction goes to the roots, is penetrating, alive and productive. Whether he writes about his barber, the French police officials or Mr. Henri Spaak, his judgment is profound and to the point. . . In the midst of insecure exile, illness, cruel persecution of his family, there is never a note of self-pity or despair. There is objectivity and courage and humility. This is a modest man; proud of his cause, proud of the truths he discovers, but not vain or self-centered. The words of admiration and concern in which he expresses himself about his wife are deeply moving. Just as was the case with Marx, here was the concern, understanding and sharing of a deeply loving man which shines through Trotsky's diary." From "An Estimate of Trotsky," *Dissent,* Spring 1959.

The twenty-two selections in this book, presented here in chronological order, date from 1919 to 1939, from a little more than a year after the revolution of which Trotsky was the chief military-political organizer to a year before he was assassinated in Mexico by an agent of Stalin, whom Trotsky called the gravedigger of that revolution. The first three are from the period before Lenin's death in 1924, when Trotsky was commissar of war and a member of the Communist Party's powerful Political Bureau. The next six are from the period when Stalin and his allies in the new bureaucracy were tightening their grip on the party and government and campaigning to drive Trotsky and other Left Oppositionists from the positions they still held, which culminated in Trotsky's expulsion from the Communist Party in 1927 and his deportation to Turkey in 1929. From Trotsky's last exile period, three of the selections are from Turkey, two from France, three from Norway, one from a tanker ship crossing the Atlantic, and four from Mexico.

The nature, form, and timing of many of these selections were obviously affected by the dramatic and violent events they deal with. Two are actually speeches rather than articles—one delivered before an official Soviet meeting in Petrograd mourning the murder of the German Marxists Liebknecht and Luxemburg; the other at an unauthorized public rally of Left Oppositionists, held in a Moscow cemetery to mourn the suicide of Trotsky's friend Joffe. Others were written after the suicide of Trotsky's secretary Glazman, the Moscow trial and execution of Old Bolsheviks Zinoviev and Kamenev, the execution without a public trial of the Old Bolshevik Yenukidze, and the murder of Leon Sedov. The portrait of Stalin was written soon after Stalin signed the sensational pact with Hitler that opened the way to World War II.

Most of these articles, then, were meant to be political acts, completed rapidly in response to political events, and, from 1929 on, most of them found publication only in the journals of the Left Opposition and Fourth International, whose readers were few in number but shared or understood the premises from which Trotsky wrote and usually did not need the kind of exposition required by the general reading public. But there were important exceptions, influenced by the fact that in exile Trotsky had to earn his living by writing for periodicals which, unlike the "movement" journals, would pay him for his articles and books. For such articles and their much broader audiences he took more time and wrote in a more popular vein. Examples in this collection are the essays on Nicholas and Alexandra Romanov (from *The History of the Russian Revolution*), Engels, Herriot, Yenukidze, and Stalin, although not all of these essays were accepted by the large-circulation periodicals to which they were submitted.

Trotsky undoubtedly had a liking for the "portrait" style of writing. Many of those he wrote were collected in his 1926 book, *Political Silhouettes,* of which the first third was translated in England as *Political Profiles* in 1972. In the middle of his work on *The History of the Russian Revolution* in January 1931, he wrote from Turkey to Max Eastman, then his literary agent as well as translator, of his plan to write a book of political portraits, but this project was never completed.[9] In December 1937 he wrote from Mexico to a friend in the United States who was helping to market his articles there and had suggested that Trotsky do an article about Stalin. Trotsky thought the suggestion inopportune, but added: "But I could write a series of portraits of the most important Soviet personalities: Zinoviev, Kamenev, Bukharin, Tukhachevsky, Rakovsky, Chicherin, Lunacharsky, etc. I would give psychological portraits and the ambient milieu with manifold little stories and anecdotes: in one word, a very 'human'

---

9. "In a few words I want to let you know about a new book I am writing in the interval between two volumes of *The History of the Russian Revolution.* The book will perhaps be called *They or We* or *We and They* and will include a whole series of political portraits: representatives of bourgeois and petty-bourgeois conservatism on the one hand, proletarian revolutionaries on the other. For instance: Hoover and Wilson from the Americans; Clemenceau, Poincaré, Barthou, and certain other Frenchmen. From the English: Baldwin, Lloyd George, Churchill, MacDonald, and the Labourites in general. From the Italians I would take Count Sforza, Giolitti, and the old man Cavour. Of the revolutionaries: Marx, Engels, Lenin, Luxemburg, Liebknecht, Vorovsky, Rakovsky. Probably Krasin as a transitional type. I've been working on this book throughout the past month. From that, you can see that it hasn't yet gotten very far forward, but its general physiognomy is already clear to me. . . . Its character will be determined by a most serious study of all these figures in the context of the political conditions surrounding them, etc. . . . When will this book be ready? That depends on how soon I must deliver the second volume of my history of the revolution. If the second volume is postponed for about eight months I might finish the book of portraits in the next four months." From Max Eastman's introduction to Trotsky's *The Young Lenin* (Doubleday, 1972).

and very 'American' kind of article without any political tendency." But when he submitted the first article of this kind (on Yenukidze) three weeks later, the American publishers to whom it was offered had their own opinions about its alleged lack of "political tendency" and they rejected it.

Each selection is preceded by an editorial preface telling something about the subject and why Trotsky wrote about it at the time he did, as well as information about the translations and their sources. Changes have been made in some of the translations in order to achieve uniformity in style, spelling, and punctuation and to correct or improve word choices. A glossary in the back presents additional data about people, groups, periodicals, and concepts mentioned in Trotsky's texts.

In regard to the forms of Russian first names used in this book: Where there is a customary English (or Westernized) form it has been used—e.g., Leon Sedov, Joseph Stalin, Nicholas and Alexandra Romanov. Otherwise the Russian name has been transliterated directly: Yakov Sverdlov, Lev Kamenev.

The Editors
August 1976

KARL LIEBKNECHT
AND ROSA LUXEMBURG

*Karl Liebknecht and Rosa Luxemburg were both born in 1871—
he in Germany, she in Russian-dominated Poland—and both
became socialists in their teens. By World War I they were leaders
of the left wing of the powerful German Social Democratic Party
(SPD), fighting the reformists and bureaucrats in its dominant
right wing. Liebknecht was an SPD member of the Reichstag
(German parliament), well known for his organizing activity
among young people and soldiers. Luxemburg was a journalist,
pamphleteer, and educator.*

*With the war the Second International collapsed when most of
its affiliates, including the SPD, violated their antiwar pledges
and socialist principles and supported the imperialist governments of their own countries. Liebknecht and Luxemburg led a
small, persecuted movement eventually called the Spartacus
League, which issued illegal literature against the war and the
SPD leadership. In 1914 Liebknecht broke SPD discipline by
voting against war credits in the Reichstag. He was arrested in
1916 for organizing an antiwar May Day demonstration at
Potsdam Square in Berlin, and when he began serving a four-
year sentence that year, his name was famous internationally as
a symbol of revolutionary struggle against imperialist war. For
her antiwar activity Luxemburg spent most of the conflict in
prison.*

*From their separate prison cells, they hailed the Bolshevik-led
seizure of power by the soviets in Russia in November 1917
(called the October revolution according to the old Russian
calendar). Germany's turn came one year later when sailors
revolted, strikes began, and workers' and soldiers' councils,
similar to the soviets in Russia, spread to all the big cities. On
November 9 a general strike forced the government to abdicate,
the monarchy was abolished, and a democratic republic was
proclaimed. To keep things from going too far, Friedrich Ebert,
the SPD right-wing leader, was brought in as chancellor.*

Liebknecht and Luxemburg were released from prison, and an armistice ended the war.

In the following weeks Germany seemed to be on the verge of a soviet revolution. Most of the conditions were present, except one—there was no German party of the Bolshevik type, able to supply the leadership needed to overthrow capitalism. Moving quickly to fill the gap, the Spartacists called a national congress at the end of December and established the new Communist Party, whose program of action was written by Luxemburg. But the Ebert government, supported by the capitalists and the army general staff, moved faster. When an insurrectional strike movement, not organized but supported by the CP, began in January 1919, the government launched a reign of terror against the revolutionaries. Liebknecht and Luxemburg were arrested on January 15 and, in the custody of government troops, were murdered on the way to prison.

The news was a severe blow to the Bolsheviks. They had conceived of their own revolution as the first step in the world revolution, doomed to failure unless it was followed by successful uprisings against capitalism in the industrially advanced countries, Germany above all. The November 9 revolution had offered hope that the beleaguered Russian workers, fighting a desperate civil war, would soon receive significant aid from their German brothers and sisters; the January defeat tended to undermine that hope and urgently needed to be explained to the Russian people. So mass memorial meetings were organized in several cities, the biggest being held on January 18 by the Petrograd Soviet, with Trotsky and Zinoviev the chief speakers.

Trotsky, then commissar of war, was chosen partly because he had personally known and worked with Liebknecht and Luxemburg during his prewar exile. His speech was designed to inspire his audience with the heroic conduct of the martyred revolutionaries and to convince it that while the German revolution had suffered a bad setback, the final showdown in Germany was still to come. To this end, he drew parallels between the Germany of 1918-19 and the Russia of 1917, with which his audience was familiar and could identify. Today's readers may find parts of the speech old-fashioned in style or regret that its judgments of Liebknecht and Luxemburg are exclusively uncritical. But Trotsky was speaking in 1919, when rhetorical styles were somewhat different, and he was speaking not to college students in a classroom long after the events but to an audience primarily of unsophisticated working people three days after the murders, in the midst of a civil war where news of a tragic blow had just been received. He was to write better-balanced appraisals later, in the 1930s.

Although Liebknecht was the better known of the two in 1919, the situation has since become reversed, thanks to growing interest in Luxemburg's books and pamphlets. There are two biographies in English: Rosa Luxemburg: Her Life and Work *by Paul Frölich (1940), and* Rosa Luxemburg *by J.P. Nettl (1966).* Rosa Luxemburg Speaks *(1970) is the most representative collection of her political writings and speeches.* Liebknecht's Militarism and Anti-Militarism *is also back in print.*

The translation from the Russian by John Fairlie and Tom Scott was first published, under the title "Karl Liebknecht, Rosa Luxemburg: Martyrs of the Third International," in International Socialist Review, *January 1971. It is reprinted here with some revisions by George Saunders.*

We have sustained, at one blow, two heavy casualties, and together they fuse into one great and terrible loss. Two of our leaders have been struck down from our ranks. Their names are entered forever in the great book of the proletarian revolution: Karl Liebknecht and Rosa Luxemburg. They have perished. They have been killed. They are no longer with us.

The name of Karl Liebknecht, famous even earlier, acquired immediate worldwide significance from the first months of the terrible European slaughter. It sounded like a name of revolutionary honor, like a promise of future victory. In those first weeks, when German militarism was celebrating its first orgies, rejoicing over its first mad victories; in those weeks when German regiments were marching through Belgium, sweeping away Belgian fortresses like houses of cards; when the 420 mm German cannon seemed to threaten all Europe with subjugation and enslavement to Wilhelm; in those days and weeks, when the official German Social Democracy, headed by Scheidemann and Ebert, was bending its patriotic knee to German militarism, to which—it seemed then—everything had succumbed: both externally—crushed Belgium, and France, where the North had been seized—and internally: not only the German Junkers, not only the German bourgeoisie, not only the chauvinistic petty bourgeoisie, but also the officially recognized party of the German working class—in those dark, terrible, base days, there resounded in Germany the stormy voice of protest, indignation, denunciation—this was the voice of Karl Liebknecht. And it sounded throughout the world!

In France, where the mood of the broad masses was weighed down by the German invasion; where the ruling party of the French social patriots was proclaiming to the proletariat the necessity of a fight not for life, but to the death—how could it be otherwise, when in Germany the "whole nation" was striving to seize Paris!—even in France the sober, warning voice of Liebknecht sounded, tearing down the barriers of lies, slander, and panic. One felt that Liebknecht alone spoke for the stifled masses.

In fact, though, he was no longer alone, even then. For hand in hand with him from the first day of the war was the courageous, unhesitating, heroic Rosa Luxemburg. Arbitrary German bourgeois parliamentarism denied her the opportunity of sounding her protest from the parliamentary platform, as Liebknecht had done—thus less was heard from her. But her share in arousing the best elements of the German working class was no less than the share of her co-fighter in the struggle and in death, Karl Liebknecht. These two fighters, so different in nature and yet so alike, complemented each other, strove unyieldingly for the common goal, met death at the same time, and will go down together in history.

Karl Liebknecht represented the true, complete incarnation of the unbending revolutionary. During the last days and months of his life countless legends grew up about him. Some were senselessly malicious—made up by the bourgeois press; some heroic—circulating by word of mouth among the working masses.

In private life Karl Liebknecht was—alas, already we must say *was!*—the incarnation of kindness, simplicity, and brotherhood. I first met him more than fifteen years ago. He was a charming person, attentive and sympathetic. You could say that in his character there was an almost feminine tenderness, in the best sense of the word. But along with this womanly tenderness he was distinguished by an exceptional temper of revolutionary will, an ability to fight for what he considered just and true, to the last drop of his blood. His spiritual independence was shown even in his youth, when he dared more than once to insist on his own opinion against the indisputable authority of Bebel. His work among young people was distinguished by great courage, as was his struggle against the Hohenzollern military machine. Finally, he revealed his true worth when he raised his voice against the unity of the bellicose bourgeoisie and the treacherous Social Democracy in the German Reichstag, where the whole atmosphere was permeated with the stench of chauvinism. He revealed the full measure of his personality when, as a soldier, in Berlin's Potsdam Square he raised the banner of open insurrection against the bourgeoisie and its militarism. Liebknecht was arrested. Prison and penal servitude did not break his spirit. In his cell he waited and confidently predicted. Liberated by the revolution of November last year, Liebknecht immediately took his place at the head of the best, the most decisive elements of the German working class. A Spartacus appeared in the ranks of the Spartacists and died with their banner in his hands.

The name of Rosa Luxemburg is less well-known in other countries, and even here in Russia. But it can be said with great confidence that her nature was in no way less than that of Karl Liebknecht. Small in height, frail, with a noble cast of face and beautiful eyes which shone with intelligence, she was striking for the courage of her thought. She had such perfect command of the Marxist method that it almost seemed a physical part of her. One could truly say that Marxism had entered into her very blood.

I have said that these two fighters, so different in temperament, complemented each other. I want to underline and clarify this. If the inflexible revolutionary Liebknecht had a feminine tenderness in his personal manner, then this frail woman had a manly power of thought. Ferdinand Lassalle once spoke of the physical power of thought, the tense force with which it exerts itself as it seemingly overcomes the physical obstacles in its path. That was precisely the impression you got, chatting with Rosa, reading her articles, or hearing her speak from the rostrum against her enemies. And she had many enemies! I remember once at a party conference—in Jena, it would be—how her high-pitched voice, tense as a violin string, cut through the stormy protests of the Bavarian, Baden, and other opportunists. How they hated her! And how she scorned them! Small in height and frail in build, she dominated the congress from the rostrum, like the incarnation of proletarian revolutionary thought. By the force of her logic and the power of her sarcasm she silenced her most inveterate enemies. Rosa knew how to hate the enemies of the proletariat and for that very reason she could arouse their hatred of her. She was marked out by them beforehand.

From the first day, no, from the first hour of the war, Rosa Luxemburg started a campaign against chauvinism, against the orgy of patriotism, against the vacillation of Kautsky and Haase, against the centrist avoidance of any clear position, for the revolutionary independence of the proletariat, for internationalism, for the proletarian revolution.

Yes, they complemented one another!

In the force of her theoretical thinking and in her capacity for generalization, Rosa Luxemburg was head and shoulders above not only her enemies, but also her comrades. She was a genius. Her style—terse, exact, brilliant, merciless—was, and will ever remain, a true mirror to her thought.

Liebknecht was not a theoretician. He was a man of direct action. Impulsive and passionate by nature, he possessed exceptional political intuition, a sense of the masses and of circumstance, and finally, an incomparably courageous revolutionary initiative.

An analysis of the internal and international situation in which Germany found herself after November 9, 1918, and also a revolutionary prognosis, one could have, indeed should have, expected first of all from Rosa Luxemburg. A summons to direct action, and—at a certain moment—to armed uprising, would probably have come first from Liebknecht. These two fighters complemented each other in a way that could not be bettered.

Luxemburg and Liebknecht were scarcely out of prison when they took each other's hand, that indefatigable revolutionary man and that unyielding revolutionary woman, and went together, at the head of the best elements of the German working class—to meet the new battles and trials of the proletarian revolution. And on the first steps of this path a treacherous blow has cut them down on one and the same day.

Indeed, reaction could have chosen no worthier victims. What a well-aimed blow! And no wonder: reaction and revolution knew each other well, for reaction this time was embodied in the persons of the former leaders of the former party of the working class, Scheidemann and Ebert, whose names will forever be inscribed in the black book of history as the shameful names of the organizers responsible for this treacherous murder.

True, we have received the official German communication

which describes the murder of Liebknecht and Luxemburg as a chance incident, as a street "misunderstanding," due, perhaps, to the insufficient watchfulness of the guard in the face of the enraged crowd. A court of inquiry has even been set up to investigate. But you and I know only too well how these "spontaneous" onslaughts against revolutionary leaders are arranged by reaction; we well remember the July days, experienced by us here, within the walls of Petrograd; we remember only too well how the Black Hundreds, summoned by Kerensky and Tsereteli to fight against the Bolsheviks, systematically annihilated the workers and slaughtered their leaders, making short work of individual workers in the streets. The name of the worker Voinov, murdered by way of a "misunderstanding," is remembered by most of us. We managed to save Lenin then, but only because he did not fall into the hands of the enraged Black Hundreds. There were at that time among the Mensheviks and the SRs some pious people indignant because Lenin and Zinoviev, who had been accused of being German spies, were not going to appear in court to refute the slander. They were especially reproached for this. But what court was this? A court, on the road to which they would have arranged for Lenin to "flee," as Liebknecht did? And if Lenin had been shot or stabbed, the official communication of Kerensky and Tsereteli would have said that the Bolshevik leader had been killed by the guard while trying to escape. No, now, after the terrible Berlin experience, we have tenfold grounds for being pleased that Lenin did not then appear in that kangaroo court, and, still more, that he did not risk punishment without trial.

But Rosa and Karl did not go into hiding. The enemy hand held them firm. And this hand strangled them! What a blow! What a misfortune! And what treachery! The best leaders of the German Communist Party are no more—our great comrades are no more among the living. And their murderers stand under the banner of the Social Democratic Party, and have the effrontery to trace their descent from none other than Karl Marx! What a perversion! What mockery! Just think of it, comrades: this "Marxist" Social Democracy, leader of the Second International, is the same party that betrayed the interests of the working class from the first days of the war, that supported unbridled German militarism during the rout of Belgium and the seizure of the northern provinces of France; the same party that betrayed the October revolution to German militarism after the Brest truce; the party whose leaders, Scheidemann and Ebert, are now organizing gangs of thugs to murder the heroes of the International, Karl Liebknecht and Rosa Luxemburg!

What a monstrous historical perversion! Looking far back through the centuries, you can see a certain parallel with the historical fate of Christianity. The evangelical teaching of slaves, fishermen, toilers, the oppressed, everyone on earth crushed by slave society—this teaching of the poor, which had its roots in their history—was later taken over by the monopolizers of riches, kings, aristocrats, metropolitans, moneylenders, patriarchs, bankers, and the Roman pope, and became an ideological cover for their crimes. However, there can be no doubt that between the teachings of original Christianity, as it took shape from the consciousness of the lower classes, and official Catholicism or Orthodoxy, there is nothing like the gap that exists between the teachings of Marx, which are the kernel of revolutionary thought and revolutionary will, and those despicable offshoots of bourgeois ideas on which the Scheidemanns and Eberts of all countries live and prosper. Through the Social Democratic leaders, the bourgeoisie has made an attempt to rob the proletariat of its spiritual property, and to conceal its brigandage under the banner of Marxism. But it is to be hoped, comrades, that this foul crime will be the last for which the Scheidemanns and Eberts will be responsible. The German proletariat has suffered much from those who were placed at its head; but this will not pass unnoticed. The blood of Karl Liebknecht and Rosa Luxemburg will cry out. This blood will cause the pavements of Berlin to speak, and the bricks of that same Potsdam Square on which Liebknecht first raised the banner of insurrection against the war and capital. And one day sooner or later on Berlin's streets, barricades will be raised from those bricks against the real grovellers and chained dogs of bourgeois society, against the Scheidemanns and the Eberts!

In Berlin now the butchers have crushed the Spartacist movement, the German Communists. They have killed the two best inspirers of that movement, and perhaps today they are even celebrating victory. But there has been no real victory there, for there has not yet been a direct, open, all-out fight; there has not yet been an uprising of the German proletariat in the name of the conquest of political power. This was only a big reconnaissance operation, a deep reconnoitering of the opponent's encampment. Reconnaissance precedes battle, but it is not yet battle. The German proletariat needed this reconnaissance in depth, just as we needed it in our July days. The unfortunate thing is that in the reconnaissance two of the best commanders fell. It is a cruel loss, but it is not a defeat. The fight is still to come.

We shall understand what is going on in Germany better if we take a look at our own situation of yesterday. You remember the course of events and its inner logic. At the end of February, Old Style, the masses threw the throne of the tsars off their backs. For the first few weeks there was a feeling that the main thing had already been accomplished. The new people coming forward from the opposition parties, which had never been in power in our country, enjoyed for the first period the trust or partial trust of the popular masses. But this trust quickly began to develop cracks in it. Petrograd was in the lead at the second stage of the revolution too, as was to be expected. In July, just as in February, it was the vanguard of the revolution and had gone far ahead of the rest. This vanguard, which summoned the popular masses to open warfare against the bourgeoisie and the conciliators, paid heavily for the deep reconnaissance which it carried out.

In the July days the Petrograd vanguard came into collision with the Kerensky government. This was not yet the insurrection we went through in October. It was a skirmish by the vanguard, the historical significance of which the broad masses in the provinces did not yet fully realize. In this clash the Petrograd workers showed the popular masses not only of Russia, but of all countries, that behind Kerensky there was no independent army; that the forces supporting him were the forces of the bourgeoisie, the White Guard, the counterrevolution.

At that time, in July, we suffered a defeat. Comrade Lenin had to go into hiding. Some of us were in prison. Our newspapers were silenced. There was a clampdown on the Petrograd Soviet. The presses of the party and the Soviet were broken up, the working-class buildings and rooms were sealed. Everywhere the violence of the Black Hundreds was raging. In other words, what was happening was what is happening now on the streets of Berlin. And nonetheless, not one of the real revolutionaries then had a shadow of doubt about the fact that the July days were only a prelude to our triumph.

A similar situation has arisen in the last few days in Germany. Like Petrograd here, Berlin has gone out ahead of the rest of the popular masses; as they did here, all the enemies of the German proletariat have been howling that the dictatorship of Berlin cannot be tolerated; that Spartacist Berlin is isolated; that a constituent assembly must be called and moved from Red Berlin, corrupted by the propaganda of Karl Liebknecht and Rosa

Luxemburg, to a more healthy provincial town of Germany! Everything the enemy did here, all the malicious agitation, all the base slanders we heard here, all this—in German translation—has been fabricated by the Scheidemanns and Eberts and spread around Germany, against the Berlin proletariat and its leaders, Liebknecht and Luxemburg. True, the German proletariat's reconnaissance developed wider and deeper than ours in July, and there are more victims there, and more important ones—all that is true. But this is explained by the fact that the Germans are going through an episode which we have already gone through once; their bourgeoisie and military have learned from our July and October experiences. But the main thing is that the class relations there are incomparably more clearly defined than ours; the possessing classes are incomparably more tightly knit, cleverer, more active—and that also means more ruthless.

In our country, comrades, there were four months between the February revolution and the July days; the Petrograd proletariat needed a quarter of a year to feel the incontrovertible necessity of coming out onto the streets and attempting to shake the pillars on which the Kerensky-Tsereteli temple of state rested. After the defeat of the July days it took another four months for the heavy reserves of the provinces to support Petrograd, and it was with confidence of victory that we were able to declare a direct attack on the bastions of private property in October 1917.

In Germany, where the first revolution, which overthrew the monarchy, broke out only at the beginning of November, our July days are already taking place at the beginning of January. Does this not indicate that in its revolution the German proletariat is following an abbreviated calendar? Where we needed four months, they need only two. And one may hope that this scale will be kept up. It may be that from the German July days to the German October not four months will pass, as here, but less. Perhaps two months will be enough, or even less. But however events proceed, one thing is certain: those shots fired into Karl Liebknecht's back have echoed powerfully throughout Germany. And that echo sounded a death knell in the ears of the Scheidemanns and Eberts, German and otherwise.

And so a requiem has been sung here for Karl Liebknecht and Rosa Luxemburg, leaders who have perished. We shall never again see them alive. But how many of you comrades ever saw them when they were alive? A tiny minority. Nevertheless, Karl

Liebknecht and Rosa Luxemburg have lived among you constantly for the past several months and years. At meetings and congresses you have elected Karl Liebknecht honorary chairman. He himself has not been here (he never managed to get to Russia), but he was still in your midst, sitting as a guest of honor at your table, as one of you, as your own kith and kin. For his name has become not just the name of an individual man. No, it has become for us a word for all that is good, brave, noble, in the working class. If any one of us had to imagine a man wholeheartedly devoted to the downtrodden, tempered like steel from head to foot, a man who never dipped his standard before the enemy, the name of Karl Liebknecht would immediately come to mind. He has entered the consciousness and memory of the peoples forever by the heroism of his actions. In the frenzied camp of the enemy, when triumphant militarism was sweeping all before it and crushing everything, when all those who should have been protesting were silent, when there seemed to be no fresh-air vent anywhere—he, Liebknecht, raised his fighter's voice. He said: You, you reigning tyrants, martial butchers, aggressors; you, you servile lackeys, conciliators, you are trampling Belgium, you are threatening France, you want to crush the whole world, you think you can evade justice—but I say to you: we, the few, are not afraid of you; we are declaring war on you, and we shall arouse the masses and fight this war to the end!

It is that kind of bold decisiveness, that heroism of action, that makes the figure of Karl Liebknecht unforgettable for the world proletariat.

And at his side stands Rosa, a warrior of the world proletariat equal to him in spirit. Their tragic death—at their combat posts—joins their names with a special link, unbreakable forever. From now on they will always be named together: Karl and Rosa, Liebknecht and Luxemburg!

Do you know the basis for the legends about the eternal life of saints? It is the need of people to preserve the memory of those who stood at their heads, who in one way or another led them; the striving to eternalize the personality of the leaders in an aura of sanctity. We, comrades, have no need of legends, have no need to transform our heroes into saints. For us the reality in which we are living now is enough, for that reality is itself legendary. It is awakening miraculous forces in the spirit of the masses and of their leaders, it is creating magnificent figures which tower over the whole of humanity.

Karl Liebknecht and Rosa Luxemburg are such eternal figures. We sense their presence among us with a striking, almost physical, immediacy. In this tragic hour we are one in spirit with the best workers of Germany and the whole world, thrown into sorrow and mourning by the terrible news. We here feel the sharpness and bitterness of the blow just as much as our German brothers. We are just as much internationalists in our sorrow and mourning as we are in all our struggles.

Liebknecht for us is not only a German leader. Rosa Luxemburg for us is not only a Polish socialist who stood at the head of the German workers. No, for the world proletariat they are both our own, our kin, we are all linked with them by a spiritual, indissoluble bond. To their last breath they belonged not to a nation, but to the International!

For the information of Russian working men and women, it must be said that Liebknecht and Luxemburg were especially close to the Russian revolutionary proletariat, and in the most difficult times too. Liebknecht's flat was the headquarters for the Russian exiles in Berlin. When a voice of protest had to be raised in the German parliament against the services the German rulers were rendering to the Russian reaction, we turned first of all to Karl Liebknecht, and he knocked on every door and on every skull, including the skulls of Scheidemann and Ebert, to make them protest against the crimes of the German government. And we invariably turned to Liebknecht when it was necessary to give some comrade material aid. Liebknecht was tireless in the service of the "Red Cross" of the Russian revolution.

At the German Social Democratic congress in Jena already mentioned, which I attended as a guest, the presidium, on Liebknecht's initiative, proposed that I speak on the resolution, likewise proposed by Liebknecht, denouncing the violence of the tsarist government in Finland. Liebknecht prepared himself with the greatest care for his own speech, collected figures and facts, questioned me in detail on the customs relations between tsarist Russia and Finland. But before it was time for him to speak (I was to speak after Liebknecht) the news came by telegraph of the assassination of Stolypin in Kiev. This wire message produced a great effect on the congress.

The first question which occurred to the leaders was whether it was proper for a Russian revolutionary to speak at a German congress at a time when some other Russian revolutionary had just assassinated the Russian prime minister. This thought swayed even Bebel. The old man, although he stood three heads taller than the other members of the Vorstand [central committee], nevertheless did not like "unnecessary" difficulties. He immediately sought me out and put me through an interrogation: What was the meaning of the assassination. What party could be responsible for it? Did I not think that under the circumstances my speaking would merely draw the attention of the German police to me? "You are afraid," I asked the old man carefully, "that my speech might produce certain difficulties?" "Yes," replied Bebel, "I admit I would prefer you not to speak." "In that case," I replied, "there can of course be no question of my speaking." On that we parted.

A minute later Liebknecht literally came running over to me. He was extremely agitated. "Is it true that they suggested you shouldn't speak?" he asked me. "Yes," I replied, "I've just settled the matter with Bebel." "And you agreed?" "How could I not agree?" I answered, trying to justify myself, "I'm not the host here, I'm a guest." "It's an outrageous thing for our presidium to do, it's a disgrace, it's an unheard-of scandal, it's contemptible cowardice!" etc., etc. Liebknecht gave vent to his indignation in his speech, in which he mercilessly attacked the tsarist government, despite behind-the-scenes warnings from the presidium, which tried to persuade him not to cause "unnecessary" difficulties in the form of insults to His Majesty the tsar.

From the years of her youth Rosa Luxemburg stood at the head of the Polish Social Democratic Party, which has now joined together with the so-called Lewica, i.e., the revolutionary section of the Polish Socialist Party, in founding the Communist Party. Rosa Luxemburg spoke excellent Russian, had a profound knowledge of Russian literature, followed Russian political life day by day, was connected by the closest bonds to the Russian revolutionaries, and lovingly explained in the German press the revolutionary steps of the Russian proletariat. In her second homeland, Germany, Rosa Luxemburg, with her special talent, acquired not only a perfect command of the German language, but also a full knowledge of German political life, and she took up one of the most prominent places in the old Social Democracy of Bebel's time. There she invariably remained in the extreme left wing.

In 1905 Karl Liebknecht and Rosa Luxemburg lived through

the events of the Russian revolution, in the real sense of the word. Rosa Luxemburg left Berlin for Warsaw in 1905—not as a Pole, but as a revolutionary. Freed on bail from the citadel of Warsaw, she came illegally to Petrograd in 1906, and there under a false name she visited several of her friends in prison. Back in Berlin, she redoubled the fight against opportunism, opposing to it the methods and techniques of the Russian revolution.

Together with Rosa we went through the greatest misfortune ever to fall upon the working class. I am speaking of the shameful bankruptcy of the Second International in August 1914. Together with her we raised the banner of the Third International. And now, comrades, in our day-to-day work we shall remain faithful to the legacy of Karl Liebknecht and Rosa Luxemburg; if today in a Petrograd still cold and starving we are raising the edifice of a socialist state, we are acting in the spirit of Liebknecht and Luxemburg; if our army advances on the fronts, it is defending with its blood the legacy of Liebknecht and Luxemburg. What a bitter thing it is that it was unable to defend them too!

In Germany there is no Red Army, for power there is still in the hands of the enemy. We already have an army; it is growing and becoming stronger. And in expectation of the day when the army of the German proletariat will rally around the banner of Karl and Rosa, all of us will consider it our duty to bring to the awareness of the Red Army who Liebknecht and Luxemburg were, what they died for, and why their memory must be held sacred by every Red Army soldier, by every worker and peasant.

It is an unbearably hard blow that has been struck against us. Still we look forward, not only with hope, but with confidence. Despite the fact that today in Germany there is a flood of reaction, we do not for a minute lose confidence in the fact that there a Red October will soon be at hand. The great fighters have not perished in vain. Their deaths will be avenged. Their spirits will get satisfaction. Turning to those dear spirits, we may say, "Rosa Luxemburg and Karl Liebknecht, you are no longer in the land of the living; but you are present among us; we can sense your powerful spirit; we shall fight under your banner; our fighting ranks will be inspired by your moral grandeur! And each of us swears—if the time comes and the revolution demands it—to die without flinching, under the same banner you died under, friends and comrades-in-arms, Rosa Luxemburg and Karl Liebknecht!"

KARL KAUTSKY

Karl Kautsky, the son of a Czech father and an Austrian mother, was born in Prague in 1854. As a student in Vienna he joined the Austrian Social Democratic Party in 1875, but did not become a Marxist until 1880, when he came under the influence of Eduard Bernstein in Zurich. The following year he met Marx and Engels in London, and he worked there for five years, 1885-90, in close contact with Engels. (Trotsky deals with their relations in his essay on Engels, later in this book.)

In 1883 Kautsky founded the monthly magazine Die Neue Zeit *(a weekly after 1890), which became the most influential journal of the Second International and which he edited until 1917. In 1887 he published an internationally popular book,* The Economic Doctrines *of Karl Marx. In 1891 he gained further attention by writing the "theoretical part" of the first important program that any Marxist party had adopted—the Erfurt program of the German Social Democratic Party (SPD), which served as a model for other parties of the Second International. After Engels's death in 1895, he was generally recognized as the most authoritative representative of Marxism in the world. He moved to Berlin in the 1890s.*

Kautsky defended "orthodox Marxism" against Bernstein's attempts in 1899 to scrap the revolutionary content of Marxism ("revisionism"), and the SPD leaders sided with Kautsky, but neither they nor he took note of the fact that behind the cloak of such affirmations the SPD continued in practice increasingly to adapt itself to reformism and opportunism. By 1910 Kautsky, the leader of the SPD's "Marxist center," was attacking the party's left wing, led by Luxemburg and others who wanted a really revolutionary policy.

Kautsky's centrism became more manifest with the outbreak of World War I when he took a pacifist position against both the SPD right wing, which supported the German government, and the Spartacists, who advocated revolutionary action against the war. This put him to the right of all the genuinely revolutionary elements in and around the International (including Nashe Slovo, *the Russian daily paper edited by Trotsky in Paris in the early part of the war, to which he refers in the opening sentence of his article on Kautsky). When the SPD split in 1917, Kautsky joined the centrist Independent Social Democratic Party (USPD), and when centrists left the Second International and formed the Two-and-a-Half International in 1921, Kautsky joined that too. After the German revolution in November 1918, he became secretary of state for foreign affairs in the SPD-USPD coalition government that kept the revolution from going beyond bourgeois limits.*

The October revolution in Russia produced among other things a series of books by Kautsky denouncing it as a betrayal of Marxism and predicting its inevitable collapse. In 1923 Kautsky also helped to merge the remnants of the USPD back into the SPD in Germany, and to reestablish the Second International on a wholly reformist basis. In 1924 he moved to Vienna, where he remained until the Nazi occupation of Austria in 1938. Then he fled to Amsterdam, where he died the same year.

There is no biography in English. Many of his early historical works are still in print, such as Foundations of Christianity, Thomas More and His Utopia, *and* Communism in Central Europe in the Time of the Reformation *(English title of his* Precursors of Socialism). *Kautsky's 1919 book* Terrorism and Communism *was answered by Trotsky with a book of the same title in 1920, and Lenin in 1918 wrote a work called* The Proletarian Revolution and the Renegade Kautsky.

Trotsky's article was dated March 18, 1919, and was expanded or revised April 24, 1922. It has been translated for this book by George Saunders from the Russian text in Trotsky's collection War and Revolution, *volume 1 (1922).*

Nashe Slovo had to settle accounts with Kautsky among others. His international authority, on the eve of the imperialist war, was still very great, though not nearly what it had been at the turn of the century and especially at the time of the first Russian revolution.

Kautsky was undoubtedly the foremost theoretician of the Second International, and for the better part of his conscious life he represented and gave generalized expression to the *best* aspects of the Second International. A propagandist and popularizer of Marxism, Kautsky saw his principal theoretical mission as the reconciling of reform and revolution. But he achieved intellectual maturity in an era of reform. Reform was for him the reality. Revolution was a theoretical generalization and a long-term historical prospect.

The Darwinian theory of the origin of species encompasses the entire span of development of the plant and animal kingdoms. The struggle for survival and the processes of natural and sexual selection proceed continuously and uninterruptedly. But if one could observe these processes with ample time at one's disposal— a millennium, say, as the smallest unit of measure—one would undoubtedly discover with one's own eyes that there are long ages of relative equilibrium in the world of living things, when the laws of selection operate almost imperceptibly, and the different species remain relatively stable, seeming the very embodiment of Plato's ideal types. But there are also ages when the equilibrium between plants, animals, and their geophysical environment is disrupted, epochs of geobiological crisis, when the laws of natural selection come to the fore in all their ferocity, and evolution passes over the corpses of entire plant and animal species. On this gigantic scale Darwinian theory stands out above all as the theory of critical epochs in the plant and animal development.

Marx's theory of the historical process encompasses the entire history of human social organization. But in ages of relative social equilibrium the fact that ideas depend upon class interests and the property system remains masked. The age of revolution is Marxism's school of advanced study. Then the struggle of classes resulting from systems of property assumes the character of open civil war, and the systems of government, law, and philosophy are stripped bare and revealed as instruments in the service of classes. Marxist theory itself was first formulated in a prerevolutionary period, when the classes were searching for a new orientation, and it achieved its final form through the experiences of revolution and counterrevolution in 1848 and the following years.

Kautsky did not have this irreplaceable living experience of revolution. He accepted Marxism as a ready-made system and popularized it like a schoolmaster of scientific socialism. The heyday of his activity came in the middle of the deep trough between the crushing of the Paris Commune and the first Russian revolution. Capitalism expanded with invincible might. The working class organizations grew almost automatically, but the final goal, i.e., the social revolutionary task of the proletariat, became separated from the movement itself and led a purely academic existence. This is the source of Bernstein's notorious aphorism, "The movement is everything, the final goal nothing." As the philosophy of a workers' party this was banal nonsense. But as the reflection of the actual spirit of the German Social Democracy during the last quarter century before the war, Bernstein's utterance was highly indicative: the day-to-day struggle for reforms assumed a self-sufficient quality: the final goal was left to Kautsky's department.

Kautsky untiringly defended the revolutionary essence of Marx and Engels's doctrine, although the initiative in repelling revisionist sallies was not usually his, but was taken by the more decisive elements (Luxemburg, Plekhanov, Parvus). In the political arena, however, Kautsky made total peace with the Social Democracy in the form it had acquired, never commenting on its profoundly opportunist nature and never responding to the efforts to make the party's tactics more resolute. As far as that went, the party, i.e., the ruling bureaucracy, also made peace with Kautsky's theoretical radicalism. This combination of practical opportunism with revolution in principle found its highest expression in August Bebel, the brilliant skilled worker (a turner), who became the undisputed leader of the party for almost half a century. Bebel supported Kautsky in the realm of theory and remained for Kautsky the court of last appeal in questions of policy. Only Luxemburg sometimes tugged Kautsky farther left than Bebel wanted him to go.

The German Social Democracy had the leading place in the Second International. Kautsky was its acknowledged theoretician and, it seemed, its inspirer. He emerged the victor from the battle with Bernstein. French socialist ministerialism (Millerandism) was condemned in 1903 at the Amsterdam congress in a resolution introduced by Kautsky. Thus Kautsky seemed to have become the acknowledged theoretical lawgiver of international socialism. This was the period of his greatest influence. Opponents and enemies called him the "pope" of the International. Sometimes he was given that grand title by friends, too, though in an affectionate way. As I recall, Kautsky's old mother, a writer of didactic novels, which she dedicated to her "son and teacher," on her seventieth birthday received a greeting from Italian socialists that read *alla mamma del papa* ("to the mother of the pope").

Then came the outbreak of the 1905 revolution [in Russia]. It immediately strengthened the radical tendencies in the international workers' movement and greatly reinforced Kautsky's authority as a theoretician. In the internal disputes on questions of the revolution he took a resolute position (though, to be sure, later than others) and forecast a revolutionary Social Democratic government in Russia. Bebel would joke in private about how "Karl has gotten carried away," and smile out of the corner of his thin mouth. In the German party things went as far as a discussion on the general strike and the adoption of a radical resolution. This was Kautsky's high point. After that came the decline.

I first met Kautsky in 1907, after my flight from Siberia. The defeat of the revolution was not yet evident. Luxemburg's influence on Kautsky was very great at that time. His authority was beyond question for all the factions of the Russian Social Democracy. It was not without emotion that I walked up the steps of his neat little home in Friedenau, a suburb of Berlin. He gave an "otherworldly" impression—a white-haired little old man with clear blue eyes who welcomed me in Russian: "Zdravstvuite." With what I already knew of Kautsky from his scholarly works, which had taught us all a good deal, this seemed to complete a very charming personality. The thing that appealed to me most was his lack of vanity, which, as I discovered later, was the result of his unchallenged authority and the inner confidence it gave him. One got very little, however, out of personal conversation with Kautsky. His mind was too angular and dry, too lacking in nimbleness and psychological insight. His judgments were schematic, his jokes trite. For the same reason Kautsky was extremely weak as an orator.

In Russia the revolution was beaten down and the proletariat thrown back. Socialism was shattered and driven underground. The liberal bourgeoisie sought reconciliation with the monarchy on the basis of an imperialist program. A wave of disillusionment with revolutionary methods swept through the International. Opportunism took its revenge. At the same time the tension in international relations between the major capitalist countries kept mounting. The denouement grew nearer. And each socialist party was obliged to make its position completely clear: Was it

with its own national state or against it? It was necessary either
to draw the appropriate conclusion from revolutionary theory or
to carry practical opportunism to its logical end. Yet all of
Kautsky's authority rested on the reconciliation of opportunism
in politics with Marxism in theory. The left wing (Luxemburg
and others) demanded direct answers. The entire situation
demanded them. From the other direction the reformists took the
offensive all along the line. Kautsky grew less and less sure of
himself, he fought the left wing more and more determinedly,
drew closer and closer to the Bernstein people, while vainly
trying to maintain the appearance of loyalty to Marxism. He was
no longer himself during this time, even in outward appearance.
His clear-eyed calm disappeared. Anxiety flickered in his glance.
Something was pitilessly gnawing at him from within.

The war brought things to a head, exposing the utter falsity
and rottenness of Kautskyism from its very first day. Kautsky's
advice was either to abstain from voting for the war credits to
Wilhelm or to vote for them "with reservations." Then a polemic
went on for several months during which it became clear exactly
what Kautsky was advising. "The International is an instrument
of peace, not of war." Kautsky grabbed at this empty phrase like
a drowning man at a straw. Having criticized the excesses of
chauvinism, Kautsky began to prepare the way for a general
reconciliation with the social patriots after the war. "We are all
human; everyone makes mistakes; nevertheless, the war will
pass; and we will make a fresh start."

When the German revolution broke out, Kautsky became
something of a foreign minister for the bourgeois republic. He
preached a break with Soviet Russia ("No matter, it will fall in a
few weeks") and, giving Marxism a new twist along Quaker lines,
he groveled on all fours in front of Wilson.

How savagely the dialectic of history has dealt with one of its
own apostles!

GEORGI PLEKHANOV

Georgi V. Plekhanov, the founder of Russian Marxism, was born in Russia in 1856 and became a revolutionary as a student at the age of nineteen. He was a member of the Narodnik (populist) movement, and when it split in 1879, he became a leader of the wing that stressed revolutionary propaganda, rather than terrorism. In 1880 he emigrated to Western Europe, where he lived until the 1917 revolution that overthrew tsarism. Study and acquaintance with the European labor movements led him to break with Narodism and to become a Marxist. In 1883 he organized the Emancipation of Labor Group, which translated into Russian and published many of the works of Marx and Engels, developed the Marxist refutation of Narodism, and laid the theoretical foundations for the Marxist movement that arose in Russia in the 1890s. Plekhanov participated in the congresses and work of the Second International from its formation in 1889.

Plekhanov met Lenin in Switzerland in 1895, leading to collaboration between the Emancipation of Labor Group and the illegal Marxist organizations in Russia. Together they founded and edited the newspaper Iskra *and the magazine* Zaria *and helped prepare the Second Congress of the Russian Social Democratic Labor Party, held in Brussels and London in 1903. This was the congress which ended in a split between the Bolsheviks headed by Lenin and the Mensheviks headed by Martov. At the congress Plekhanov aligned himself with Lenin, but before the year was out he went over to the Mensheviks.*

When the 1905 revolution broke out, he advocated that the rebellious workers should ally themselves with the bourgeois liberals, instead of antagonizing them, and condemned the armed uprising in Moscow. In 1914 he became a defender of the tsarist war effort, and after his return to Russia in 1917 he supported the Provisional Government and bitterly opposed its overthrow by the Soviets. He died in 1918 an opponent of the revolution he had foreseen and helped to prepare.

Despite this, Lenin retained a high opinion of Plekhanov's theoretical contributions. "One cannot become an intelligent, a real *Communist unless one has studied—and I mean* studied— *everything Plekhanov has written on philosophy, for it is the best in world Marxist literature,"* he said, and he urged that *Plekhanov's work in this field be included in a series of standard textbooks on communism. The best collection of Plekhanov in English is his* Selected Philosophical Works *published in Moscow, no date, of which only the first volume has been published; it includes* The Development of the Monist View of History. Plekhanov: The Father of Russian Marxism *is a biography by Samuel H. Baron (1963).*

Trotsky was only twenty-three when he first met Plekhanov in 1902 and relations between them were never personally friendly. But in a Moscow speech made a few days after Plekhanov's death, he said that the leaders of the revolution remembered Plekhanov as "the one from whom we learned the alphabet of revolutionary Marxism" and that they would "go on making use of the best part of the spiritual legacy which Plekhanov has left us." The article that follows was written on April 25, 1922, four years after Plekhanov's death.

The translation from the Russian by Margaret Dewar was first published, under the title "A Note on Plekhanov," in Free Expression *(London), November 1942, and was reprinted in* Fourth International, *March 1943. It has been revised here by George Saunders. The Russian text erroneously referred to the Second International's "Zurich congress of 1893"; in the third from last paragraph the translator corrected this to the International's founding congress, in Paris in 1889.*

The war has drawn the balance sheet on an entire epoch of the socialist movement; it has weighed and appraised the leaders of this epoch. Among those whom it has mercilessly liquidated is also to be found G.V. Plekhanov. This was a great man. It is a pity to think that the entire young generation of the proletariat today who joined the movement since 1914 is acquainted with Plekhanov only as a protector of all the Alexinskys, a collaborator of all the Avksentievs, and almost a co-thinker of the notorious Breshkovskayas—that is to say, they know Plekhanov only as the Plekhanov of the epoch of "patriotic" decline. This was a truly great man. And it is as a great figure that he has gone down in the history of Russian social thought.

Plekhanov did not create the theory of historical materialism; he did not enrich it with new scientific achievements. But he introduced it into Russian life. And this is a merit of enormous significance. It was necessary to overcome the homegrown revolutionary prejudices of the Russian intelligentsia, in which the arrogance of backwardness found its expression. Plekhanov "Russianized" Marxist theory and thereby denationalized Russian revolutionary thought. Through Plekhanov it began to speak for the first time in the language of real science; established its ideological bond with the world working class movement; opened real possibilities and perspectives for the Russian revolution by finding a basis for it in the objective laws of economic development.

Plekhanov did not create the materialist dialectic, but he was its convinced, passionate, and brilliant crusader in Russia from the beginning of the eighties. And this required the greatest penetration, a broad historical outlook, and a noble courage of thought. These qualities Plekhanov combined also with lucidity of expression and an endowment of wit. The first Russian crusader for Marxism wielded his sword superbly. How many wounds he inflicted! Some of them, like those he inflicted on the talented epigone of Narodism, Mikhailovsky, were of a fatal nature. In order to appreciate the force of Plekhanov's thought one has to have an understanding of the density of that atmosphere of populist, subjectivist, and idealist prejudices which prevailed in the radical circles of Russia and the Russian emigration. And these circles represented the most revolutionary force to emerge from Russia in the second part of the nineteenth century.

The spiritual development of today's advanced working class youth proceeds (happily!) along entirely different paths. The greatest social upheaval in history sets us apart from the period when the Beltov-Mikhailovsky duel took place.* That is why the form of the best—i.e., precisely the most brilliantly polemical— works of Plekhanov has become dated, just as the form of Engels's *Anti-Dühring* has become dated. For a young, thinking worker, Plekhanov's viewpoint is incomparably more understandable and familiar than the viewpoints that he demolishes.

---

*Under the pseudonym Beltov, Plekhanov in 1895 managed to get his most successful and brilliant work, *The Development of the Monist View of History*, past the tsarist censor.—L.T.

Consequently, a young reader has to give more attention and use more imagination to reconstruct in his mind the views of the Narodniks and subjectivists than to appreciate the force and accuracy of Plekhanov's blows. That is why his books cannot attain wide circulation today. But the young Marxist who has the opportunity to work systematically on broadening and deepening his world outlook will invariably turn to the original source of Marxist thought in Russia—to Plekhanov. For this it will be necessary each time to work oneself back into the ideological atmosphere of the Russian radical movement from the sixties to the nineties. No easy task. But in return, the reward will be a widening of one's theoretical and political horizons, and the esthetic pleasure that a successful effort toward clear thinking gives in the fight against prejudice, stagnation, and stupidity.

In spite of the strong influence of the French literary masters on Plekhanov, he remained entirely a representative of the old Russian school of publicists (Belinsky, Herzen, Chernyshevsky). He loved to write at length, never hesitating to make digressions and in passing to entertain the reader with a witticism, a quotation, another little joke. . . . For our "Soviet" era, which slashes words that are too long and compresses the pieces to make one word, Plekhanov's style seems out of date. But it reflects an entire era and, of its kind, it remains superb. The French school left its positive mark on his style, in the form of precision in formulation and transparent clarity in exposition.

As an orator Plekhanov was distinguished by the same qualities he possessed as a writer, both to his advantage and disadvantage. When you read books by Jaurès, even his historical works, you get the impression of an orator's speech, transcribed. With Plekhanov it is just the reverse. In his speeches you hear the writer speaking. The writing of orators and the oratory of writers may reach very high levels. Nevertheless, writing and oratory are two different fields and two different arts. For this reason Jaurès's books tire one with their oratoric intensity. And for the same reason the orator Plekhanov often produced the secondhand—hence, dampening—effect of a skillful reader of his own articles.

He was at his peak in the theoretical disputes in which whole generations of the Russian revolutionary intelligentsia never tired of immersing themselves. Here the material of the controversy itself brought the art of writing and that of oratory closer together. He was weakest in speeches of a purely political nature, those which pursued the task of uniting the audience around practical, concrete conclusions, fusing their wills into one. Plekhanov spoke like an observer, like a critic, a publicist, but not like a leader. He was never destined to have the opportunity to directly address the masses, summon them to action, lead them. His weak sides come from the same source as does his chief merit: he was a forerunner, the first crusader of Marxism on Russian soil.

We have said that Plekhanov left hardly any works that could become theoretical tools in wide everyday use by the working class. The sole exception is, perhaps, the *History of Russian Social Thought*; but this work is far from irreproachable in point of theory; the conciliatory and patriotic tendencies of Plekhanov's politics of the last period succeeded—at least partly—in undermining even his theoretical foundations. Entangling himself in the insoluble contradictions of social patriotism, Plekhanov began to seek guidance outside the theory of the class struggle— now in national interests, now in abstract ethical principles. In his last writings he makes monstrous concessions to normative morality, seeking to make of it a criterion of politics ("the defensive war is a just war"). In the introduction to his *History of Russian Social Thought* he limits the sphere of action of the class struggle to the field of domestic relations; in international relations he replaces the class struggle by national solidarity.* This, however, is no longer according to Marx, but rather according to Sombart. Only those who know what a relentless struggle Plekhanov waged for decades against idealism in general, normative philosophy in particular, and the school of Brentano, with its pseudo-Marxist falsifier Sombart—only they can appreciate the depth of Plekhanov's theoretical downfall under the pressure of national patriotic ideology.

But this downfall was prepared: Plekhanov's misfortune came from the same source as his immortal merit—he was a forerunner. He was not a leader of the proletariat in action but

---

* "The course of development of any given society divided into classes is determined by the course of development of those classes and their mutual relations, i.e., first, by their *mutual struggle* where the internal social order is concerned, and, secondly, by their more or less friendly *collaboration* where the question of the defense of the country from external attack arises." (G.V. Plekhanov, *History of Russian Social Thought,* Moscow, 1919, page 11, Russian edition.)—L.T.

only its theoretical precursor. He polemically defended the methods of Marxism but had no possibility of applying them in practice. Though he lived for several decades in Switzerland, he remained a Russian emigre. Opportunist, municipal, and cantonal Swiss socialism, with its extremely low theoretical level, scarcely interested him. There was no Russian party. For Plekhanov its place was taken by the Emancipation of Labor Group, i.e., a close circle of co-thinkers (composed of Plekhanov, Axelrod, Zasulich, along with Deutsch, who was doing hard labor in Siberia). Since he lacked political roots, Plekhanov strove all the more to strengthen the theoretical and philosophical roots of his position. As an observer of the European workers' movement, he very often left out of consideration the most colossal manifestations of political pettiness, pusillanimity, and conciliationism on the part of the socialist parties; but he was always on the alert in regard to theoretical heresy in socialist literature.

This imbalance between theory and practice, which arose out of the whole course of his life, proved fatal for him. In spite of his wide theoretical groundwork, he showed himself unprepared for great political events: even the 1905 revolution caught him unawares. This profound and brilliant Marxist theoretician oriented himself toward the events of the revolution by means of empirical, essentially rule-of-thumb appraisals; he felt unsure of himself, said as little as possible, and evaded definite answers, begging the question with algebraic formulas or witty anecdotes, for which he had such a great fondness.

I first saw Plekhanov at the end of 1902, i.e., in the period when he was concluding his superb theoretical campaign against Narodism and against revisionism, and found himself face to face with the political questions of the revolution. In other words, the period of decline had begun for Plekhanov. I only once had the opportunity to see and hear Plekhanov at full flower, so to speak, and in all his splendor: that was in the program commission of the Second Party Congress (July 1903, in London). The representatives of the *Rabocheye Delo* Group (Martynov and Akimov), the representatives of the Bund (Lieber and others), and a few of the provincial delegates were attempting to introduce amendments to the draft of the party program, mainly the work of Plekhanov, amendments that for the most part were incorrect theoretically and poorly thought out. In the commission discussions Plekhanov was inimitable and—merciless. On every question or even minor point that arose he quite effortlessly brought to bear his outstanding erudition and forced his listeners, even his opponents, to the realization that the problem only began precisely where the authors of the amendment thought it to end. With a clear, scientifically finished conception of the program in his mind, sure of himself, of his knowledge, his strength; with a merry, ironical twinkle in his eyes; with his whiskers bristling merrily too; with slightly theatrical but lively and expressive gestures, Plekhanov, who chaired the session, illuminated this heavily attended gathering like a human firework of erudition and wit. This was reflected in the admiration that lit up all faces, even those of his opponents, where delight struggled with embarrassment.

Discussing tactical and organizational questions at the same congress, Plekhanov was infinitely weaker and sometimes seemed quite helpless, producing bewilderment among the very delegates who had admired him on the program commission.

As early as the Paris International Congress in 1889 Plekhanov had declared that the revolutionary movement in Russia would conquer as a workers' movement or not at all. That meant that in Russia there was not and could not be a revolutionary bourgeois democracy capable of triumphing. But from this there followed the conclusion that the victorious revolution, achieved by the proletariat, could not end other than with the transfer of power into the hands of the proletariat. From this conclusion, however, Plekhanov recoiled in horror. Thus he politically denied his old theoretical premises. New ones he did not create. Hence his political helplessness and vacillations, crowned by his terrible patriotic fall from grace.

In the period of the war and in the period of the revolution, nothing remained for the true disciples of Plekhanov but to wage an irreconcilable struggle against him.

Since Plekhanov's death, his often surprising and invariably worthless admirers and adherents of his period of decline have brought together all of his worst writings and published them in a separate edition. By this they only helped to separate the false Plekhanov from the real one. The great Plekhanov, the true one, belongs entirely and wholly to us. It is our duty to restore to the young generation his spiritual figure in all its stature. These hasty lines do not of course represent even an approach to this task. But it must be accomplished and will be highly rewarding. Yes, it is high time a good book was written about Plekhanov.

VERA ZASULICH

Vera I. Zasulich, born in Russia in 1849, became a Narodnik in St. Petersburg at the age of nineteen. Because of her acquaintance with revolutionaries who had attracted police attention, she was arrested in 1869, held in prison for two years, and sent into exile for two more. In 1878, she shot and wounded General F.F. Trepov, the governor of St. Petersburg, for having ordered the flogging of a political prisoner who failed to remove his cap in the general's presence. A jury acquitted her, the government sought to arrest her again, and she was smuggled out of Russia by friends. Returning in 1879, she found the Narodnik movement splitting up, and adhered to the Plekhanov wing. A year later she emigrated to Switzerland, where she worked on behalf of Russian political prisoners, became a Marxist, and helped to found the Emancipation of Labor Group. She translated a number of Marxist works into Russian, wrote a history of the First International as well as many articles, and corresponded with Engels. Along with Plekhanov and Lenin she was a member of the Iskra *editorial board. She became a Menshevik in 1903, a supporter of Russian imperialism in World War I, and an opponent of the October revolution until her death in 1919.*

Selections from Zasulich's memoirs, including her account of the shooting of the hated general, are translated in Five Sisters: Women Against the Tsar, *edited by B.A. Engel and C.N. Rosenthal (1975).*

Zasulich was fifty-three and Trotsky twenty-three when they first met in 1902. After escaping from Siberia and arriving in London, he had gone straight to the home of Lenin and Krupskaya for a long discussion. Then Krupskaya helped him find a room to rent in the same building where Zasulich lived. Trotsky's reminiscences of Zasulich were written twenty-two years later, shortly after Lenin's death, as part of a memoir entitled "Lenin and the Old Iskra," which was included in his first book about Lenin (1924), translated into English under the title Lenin. This portrait of Zasulich has been composed out of several scattered excerpts and rearranged in a slightly different sequence than they appear in Trotsky's memoir. It has been translated from the Russian for this book by Donald Kennedy.

For lodgings, I was taken by Nadezhda Konstantinovna [Krupskaya] several blocks away, to the house where Zasulich, Martov, and Blumenfeld lived. The latter was in charge of *Iskra's* print shop. There a vacant room was found for me.

The apartments were arranged vertically, as is common in England, and not on the same floor, as in Russia: the lowest room was occupied by the landlady, and then came the tenants, one above another. There was in addition one common room, which Plekhanov christened "the den" after his first visit. In this room, thanks mostly to Vera Ivanovna Zasulich, but with assistance from Martov, great disorder reigned. There we had coffee, gathered for conversations, smoked, and so on; hence its name.

As regards Zasulich, the simplicity and cordiality in her attitude toward young comrades were truly beyond comparison. If one cannot speak in a literal sense of her hospitality, it is only because she was more in need of it herself than able to offer it to others. She lived, dressed, and ate like the most frugal of students. In the realm of material things, her greatest passions were tobacco and mustard. She used both in enormous quantities. When she would spread a very thin slice of ham with a thick layer of mustard, we used to say, "Vera Ivanovna is off on a binge."

It was not just her heroic past that had placed Vera Ivanovna in the front ranks. No, it was her penetrating mind, her extensive education, primarily in history, and a rare psychological insight. It was through Zasulich that the Emancipation of Labor Group had in the past kept in contact with the old Engels.

The editorial board of *Iskra* and *Zaria* consisted, as we know, of six people: three "old-timers" (Plekhanov, Zasulich, and Axelrod) and three young members (Lenin, Martov, and Potresov). Plekhanov and Axelrod lived in Switzerland. Zasulich was in London, with the younger members. Potresov was at that time somewhere on the Continent. This dispersion of personnel caused technical inconveniences, but Lenin did not feel at all burdened by them; quite the contrary. Before my visit to the Continent, while initiating me cautiously into the internal affairs of the editorial board, he told me that Plekhanov insisted on moving the whole editorial staff to Switzerland, but that he, Lenin, was against this, as it would make the work more difficult. It was then that I understood for the first time, but only dimly, that the editorial board remained in London not only because of considerations involving the police but also for organizational and personal reasons. In the day-to-day organizational and political work Lenin wanted the maximum independence from the "old" members and, first of all, from Plekhanov, with whom he had already had sharp conflicts, especially over the drafting of the party program. Zasulich and Martov were the mediators in these situations: Zasulich acted as Plekhanov's second, and Martov served in the same capacity for Lenin. Both mediators were of a very conciliatory disposition and, what is more, very friendly with each other. Only gradually did I learn about the sharp clashes that had occurred between Lenin and Plekhanov over the theoretical part of the program.

As far as I remember, according to the accounts of Martov and Zasulich, Lenin's original draft, which he counterposed to Plekhanov's, was severely criticized by the latter in the haughty and mocking tone that was characteristic of Georgi Valentinovich on such occasions. But it was impossible, of course, for Lenin to become either discouraged or intimidated by this. The struggle took on a very dramatic aspect. Vera Ivanovna, according to her own account, once told Lenin: "Georgi is a greyhound: he will shake you and shake you and then let you go; but you are a bulldog: you have a deadly grip." I remember this phrase very well, and also Zasulich's concluding remark: "This appealed to Lenin very much. 'A deadly grip?' he repeated with obvious delight." And Vera Ivanovna good-naturedly mimicked Lenin's intonation and accent.

During the London period, as in Geneva later, I met Zasulich and Martov much more often than Lenin. In London we lived in the same house, and in Geneva we usually had lunch or dinner in the same small restaurants, so Martov, Zasulich, and I met several times a day, while with Lenin, who lived a family life, every meeting apart from official gatherings was something of an event.

Zasulich was an exceptional person, with a special charm. She wrote very slowly, going through real torments of creation. "Vera Ivanovna doesn't write," Vladimir Ilyich once told me. "She composes a mosaic." And indeed, she would put her thoughts on paper one sentence at a time, pacing up and down the room, shuffling in her slippers, endlessly smoking hand-rolled cigarettes, disposing of cigarette butts, or simply half-smoked cigarettes, in all the corners and on all the window sills and tables, strewing ashes over her blouse, hands, manuscript, tea, and glass, and also, on occasion, her interlocutor. She was, and remained to the end, an old radical intellectual, on whom Marxism had been grafted by fate. Zasulich's articles show that she had assimilated the theoretical elements of Marxism splendidly. But at the same time the moral and political foundations of a Russian radical of the 1870s persisted in her, undiminished, to the end. In intimate conversations she would allow herself to grumble about certain methods or conclusions of Marxism. For her the concept "revolutionary" had a self-sufficient meaning independent of class content. I remember my conversation with her about her "Revolutionaries from among the Bourgeoisie." I used the expression "bourgeois-democratic revolutionaries." "But no," Vera Ivanovna responded with a trace of annoyance, or rather, chagrin. "Not bourgeois and not proletarian, but simply revolutionaries. You can, of course, say 'petty-bourgeois revolutionaries,'" she added, "if you count as petty-bourgeois all those you don't know what else to do with. . . ."

Germany was then the ideological center of the Social Democracy, and we were tensely following the struggle between the orthodox wing and the revisionists in the German Social Democratic Party. But Vera Ivanovna cared little for this, and would only say:

"Here's how it is. They will do away with revisionism, they will restore Marx, they will win the majority, and all the same they will live with the kaiser."

"Who are 'they,' Vera Ivanovna?"

"The German Social Democrats."

On this point, by the way, Vera Ivanova was not so mistaken as it seemed then, although everything happened differently, and for different reasons, than she thought.

"With Vera Ivanovna much is based on morals, on feelings," Lenin said to me one day. He then told how she and Martov had been inclined toward individual terror when Val, the governor of Vilna, ordered the flogging of workers who took part in a demonstration. Traces of this temporary "deviation," as we would now call it, can be found in one of the issues of *Iskra.* This, it seems, is how it happened. Martov and Zasulich were putting out an issue without Lenin, who was on the Continent. The news agencies carried a report of the flogging in Vilna. This awoke in Vera Ivanovna the heroic radical who shot Trepov for ordering the whipping of political prisoners. Martov backed her up. Lenin, when he received the new issue of *Iskra,* was indignant: "This is the first step toward capitulation to the Social Revolutionary doctrine." Simultaneously a letter of protest was received from Plekhanov. This episode took place before my arrival in London, so there may be some factual inaccuracies in this account, but I remember well the essence of the affair. "Naturally," Vera Ivanovna explained to me, "it is not a question of terror as a system; but it seems to me that terror might teach them not to flog people. . . ."

Zasulich never engaged in real debate; even less was she skilled in public speaking. She never answered her opponent's argument directly, but would work on some thought deep inside herself and then, catching fire, would rapidly pour out a string of phrases, choking on the words and addressing not the one who had disagreed with her, but the one who, she hoped, was able to understand her. If there was a formal discussion, with a chairperson, Vera Ivanovna never put her name on the speakers' list, because the only way she could say anything was to burst out with it. And when that happened she would hold forth without paying any attention to the speakers' list, which she treated with utter contempt; she always interrupted both the speaker and the chair and kept talking until she had said what she wanted to say. In order to understand her, it was necessary to follow her train of thought closely. But her ideas—whether right or wrong—were always interesting and entirely her own. It is not hard to imagine what a contrast Vera Ivanovna—with her diffuse radicalism, her subjectivity, and her untidiness— presented to Vladimir Ilyich. It was not that there was a lack of sympathy between them so much as a feeling of deep organic dissimilarity. With her psychological insight, Zasulich sensed Lenin's strength, and viewed it with a shade of hostility even then. That was expressed in her phrase about the deadly grip.

Vera Ivanovna Zasulich felt the approach of the revolution, I suspect, more directly than all the other old members. Her knowledge of history—lively, free from pedantry, and richly intuitive—helped her in this. But her sense of the revolution was that of an old radical. She was convinced to the depths of her soul that we already had all the elements of the revolution, with the exception of "genuine," self-confident liberalism, which should take the leadership into its hands, and that we, the Marxists, by our premature criticism and "baiting" of them, were only frightening the liberals and thereby playing, in essence, a counterrevolutionary role. In the press, of course, Vera Ivanovna never said this. Even in personal conversations she did not always express it fully. Nevertheless, this was her heartfelt conviction.

After one of the editorial meetings in the Café Landolt . . . , Zasulich, in the shy but insistent voice peculiar to her on such occasions, began to complain that we were attacking the liberals "too much." That was a sore point with her.

"Just look how hard they are trying," she said, gazing past Lenin, though she was addressing him primarily. "In the last issue of *Ozvobozhdenie* Struve holds up the example of Jaurès to our liberals and calls on them not to break with socialism; otherwise they will be threatened with the pitiful fate of German liberalism. He says they should take their cue from the French Radical Socialists."

Lenin stood by the table with his soft straw "imitation Panama" hat on (the meeting had already ended, and he was preparing to leave).

"It's all the more necessary to attack them," he said, smiling gaily and seemingly teasing Vera Ivanovna.

"So that's how it is," she exclaimed in utter despair. "They move toward us, and we attack them!"

"Exactly. Struve tells his liberals: Against our socialism we must use, not crude German methods, but the subtler French ones. We must lure, cajole, deceive, and corrupt in the manner of the French left Radicals who are flirting with Juarèsism."

I remember that it was a spring day (or perhaps, already early summer?), the sun was shining brightly, and Lenin's guttural laugh was cheerful. I remember his whole appearance—calm, mocking, self-assured, and "solid"—yes, solid, although Vladimir Ilyich was then much thinner than in the last period of his life. Vera Ivanovna, as always, was fidgeting, turning now to one person, now to another. But no one, it seems, intervened in the argument, which, moreover, lasted only a short time as the meeting was breaking up.

I returned home with her. Zasulich was depressed, feeling that Struve's ace had been trumped. I could offer her no consolation. None of us, however, foresaw then to what extent, in what superlative degree, the aces of Russian liberalism had indeed been trumped in that little dialogue at the door of the Café Landolt.

VLADIMIR ILYICH LENIN

Vladimir Ilyich Lenin was born in the Volga region of Russia in 1870 and became involved in politics under the impact of his older brother's arrest and execution for a terrorist plot against the tsar in 1887. He became a Marxist in the late 1880s and a few years later was writing serious studies of capitalist development in Russian agriculture and polemicizing against Narodnik views. In St. Petersburg he helped organize the League of Struggle for the Emancipation of the Working Class, whose activities led to his arrest and exile in Siberia (1897-1900). Emigrating to Western Europe, he spent the next three years working, in collaboration with Plekhanov and others, to create a nationwide socialist newspaper and to consolidate the Russian Social Democratic Labor Party as a unified and effective instrument of revolution. The party was reorganized at a congress in 1903, which ended with sharp differences over perspectives and a split between the Bolsheviks and the Mensheviks.

The Bolshevik tendency, which Lenin led until his death (and which changed its name to Communist Party in 1918), was the first to show the kind of party needed to lead a working class revolution. At the turn of the century, with the coming of the age of imperialism, it was Lenin who most effectively revived Marxism as the theory and practice of revolution after it had been debased by the opportunists, revisionists, and fatalists of the Second International. He was also the first Marxist to fully understand and explain the central importance of colonial and national struggles. He led the first victorious workers' revolution in 1917 and served as head of the Soviet government until his death. He played the central role in founding the Communist International and helped elaborate its principles, strategy, and tactics. In 1922 he began a struggle against the bureaucratization of the Soviet state and of the Communist Party, but illness and death cut short his effort.

The portrait of Lenin included here had a limited purpose—to show Lenin as a public speaker at the height of his powers at the head of the revolution. Trotsky was greatly interested in the oratorical styles and abilities—and idiosyncrasies—of the political leaders he depicted. Here he captures the particular features of Lenin's speaking style with great vividness.

This portrait offers only a sampling of the vast amount Trotsky wrote about Lenin. He projected a full biography of the Bolshevik leader but managed to complete only the first volume, finally published in English in 1972 as The Young Lenin. *Extensive passages about Lenin will also be found in Trotsky's* My Life *(1930) and* Stalin *(1941).*

A forty-five-volume edition of Lenin's Collected Works *in English is in print from Moscow; although this edition contains Lenin material suppressed in Stalin's time, it continues to exclude other material which it considers politically unpalatable.*

The translation by John G. Wright from Trotsky's 1924 book on Lenin was first published, under the title "Lenin on the Platform," in Socialist Appeal, *January 25, 1941.*

After the October revolution many photographs of Lenin were taken and movies were also made. His voice was reproduced on phonograph records. His speeches were transcribed by stenographers and were then published. All the elements of Vladimir Ilyich are thus available. But they remain only—the elements. The living personality consists of the unreproducible and always dynamic combination of these elements.

I am trying to evoke Lenin in my mind with a fresh eye and fresh ear, as if seeing and hearing him on the platform for the first time, and I see a strong, pliant figure of medium height and I hear an even, fluent voice speaking very rapidly, with a slight lisp, without interruptions, almost without a pause and, in the initial stages, without any special inflection.

The introductory phrases are, as a rule, general, the tone is that of probing; the speaker's entire figure seems not to have found its equilibrium as yet; the gesture has yet to take shape, the eyes seem to gaze inward; the expression on the face appears sullen and even annoyed—the idea is probing for an approach to the audience. This introductory phase lasts for a longer or shorter period of time, depending upon the audience, the topic, the speaker's mood. But now the speaker has found the trail. The theme begins to unfold. The upper part of his body tilts forward, the thumbs slide under the armpits into the vest. And this twofold movement immediately causes the head and elbows to protrude. The head does not, in and of itself, seem large on this strong but not tall, well-knit, and balanced body. But the forehead and the ridges on the bald skull appear enormous. The hands are very agile but not fidgety or nervous. The wrists are broad, chunky, "plebeian," strong. They, like the entire body, suggest dependability and virile good nature. Before this can be perceived, however, the speaker must catch fire internally, as he exposes an opponent's cunning ruse, or himself succeeds in laying a trap. Then from beneath the mighty canopy of forehead and skull the Lenin eyes appear (which were just barely caught by a lucky photograph taken in 1919). Even an indifferent listener catching this glance for the first time would snap to and sit up in expectation. At such moments the angular cheekbones were illumined and softened by tremendously perceptive tolerance, behind which could be sensed a vast knowledge of men, of interrelationships and situations reaching to the nethermost depths of things. The lower part of the face with its reddish-gray growth seemed to remain in the shadows. The voice became softer, more flexible and—at times—slyly ingratiating.

But now the speaker brings up an opponent's possible objection or cites a vicious quotation from an enemy's article. Before he proceeds to analyze the hostile idea, he gives you to understand that the objection is groundless, superficial, or false. He disengages his fingers from behind the vest, tilts his body back a little, retreats a few short paces, as if to make room for a running start and—either ironically, or with a look of despair—shrugs his thickset shoulders, spreads his hands with the thumbs expressively extended. He always prefaces a refutation by condemning his opponent, deriding or disgracing him—depending on the opponent and the circumstances. It is as if the listener were forewarned what sort of proof to expect, and how to attune his mind. Then, the logical offensive is launched. The left hand again seeks out either the vest or, more frequently, the trouser pocket. The right accompanies the logic of the exposition and sets the rhythm. When necessary, the left hand lends assistance. The speaker moves toward the audience, strides to the very edge of the platform, leans forward, and with rounded gestures of his hands molds his words. This means that the central idea, the main point of the entire speech, has been reached.

If opponents are present in the audience, the speaker is greeted from time to time with critical or hostile heckling. Nine times out of ten these remain unanswered. The speaker intends to say what he has to say: say it to those whom he is addressing, in whatever way he feels it must be said. He is not to be sidetracked by chance remarks. Hasty wit is alien to his concentrated thought. Following hostile exclamations his voice only becomes more harsh, his sentences more compact and aggressive, the formulations grow sharper, the gestures more abrupt. He catches up the hostile heckle only if it coincides with the general trend of his thought and can aid him in reaching the necessary conclusions more quickly. Then his answers are entirely unexpected and annihilating in their simplicity. Point-blank, he lays bare a situation which, according to all expectations, he should have sought to camouflage. The Mensheviks went through this experience more than once during the initial period of the revolution when charges of violations of democracy still had a ring of novelty. "Our newspapers have been shut down!" "Of course! But unfortunately not all of them as yet. They will all be shut down presently. The dictatorship of the proletariat will destroy at its very roots this shameful traffic in bourgeois opium!" The speaker has straightened up. Both hands are in the pockets. There is not even a hint of posing, in the voice not a trace of oratorical modulation—instead the entire figure, the angle of the head, the compressed lips, the cheekbones, the slightly hoarse timbre of the voice all radiate an indomitable confidence in his correctness and his truth. "If you want to fight, then come on, let's really fight."

Whenever the speaker lashes out not at an enemy but at one of "his own," it can be felt both in the gestures and the voice. The most violent attack in such cases still preserves the tone of trying to "bring one to one's senses." Occasionally the speaker's voice breaks off on a high note. This happens whenever he swoops down on "a friend," exposes him, tries to put him to shame, proves that the opponent understands exactly nothing and is unable to adduce so much as a scintilla in support of his objections. It is on these "exactly nothings" and "scintillas" that the voice now and then rises to a falsetto and breaks off, and this unexpectedly invests the angriest tirade with a semblance of good nature.

The speaker has completely thought out his idea in advance down to the last practical conclusion—the idea, but not the presentation, not the form of presentation, with the exception perhaps of the most succinct, most pertinent, and juiciest expressions and coined words, which thereupon enter into the political life of the party and of the country as the ringing medium of exchange. The construction of the sentences is as a rule massive; clause accumulates on clause like geological strata, or, on the contrary, a clause imbeds itself in the previous one. These constructions are a trial to the stenographers and then to the editors. But through these massive phrases the intense and imperious idea cuts a strong and reliable highway for itself.

Is it really true that the speaker is a profoundly educated Marxist, a theoretician and an economist, a man of enormous erudition? Why, it seems, at least every now and then, that some extraordinary self-educated person is speaking, one who arrived at these conclusions through his own efforts, pondered all this in his own brain, in his own way, without any scientific equipment, without scientific terminology, and is now presenting it in his own manner. Why? Because the speaker has thought out the problem not only for himself but also for the masses; in his imagination, he has thought through the experience of the masses and has completely removed from his presentation the theoretical scaffolding, which he had himself utilized when first approaching the problem.

It so happens, by the way, that on occasion the speaker ascends too swiftly up the ladder of his thoughts, skipping two and three rungs at a time. This happens whenever a particular conclusion is all too clear to him, is of great practical urgency, and the audience must become acquainted with it as quickly as possible. But now he has sensed that the listeners cannot keep up with him, that the bond between him and the audience has been disrupted. He immediately takes himself in hand and with a single leap descends in order to begin his ascent anew but this time with a more tranquil and measured stride. The voice itself, free of any extra strain, becomes altered and subtly persuasive. The construction of the speech naturally suffers from this duplication. But is a speech designed for its construction? Is there any worthwhile logic in a speech other than the logic which compels action?

And when the orator arrives for a second time at his conclusion, this time bringing all his listeners along, not losing a single one on the way, a rejoicing at the satisfactory culmination of the intense labor of the collective mind can be physically felt in the hall. It remains to nail down the conclusion with two or three good taps in order to reinforce it; give it simple, lucid, and pictorial expression for memory's sake; and then it is permissible to take a breathing spell, joke and laugh a little, so that the collective mind is better able in the interim to absorb its new conquest.

Lenin's oratorical humor is as simple as all his other devices, if it is possible to speak of devices in this connection. In Lenin's speeches there is no self-sufficient wit or wordplay, but there is the joke, salty and accessible to the masses—folk humor in the real sense of the term. If there is nothing too alarming about the political situation, if the audience is predominantly "his own," then the speaker is not averse to a little "horseplay" in passing. The audience heartily welcomes the sly-simple adage, the good natured–merciless characterization, sensing that this, too, is intended not as a flourish, but to serve the same goal.

When the speaker is about to jest, the lower part of his face becomes more prominent, especially the mouth capable of infectious laughter. The lines of forehead and skull seem to soften, the eyes stop boring like gimlets and twinkle with a merry light, the lisp becomes more pronounced, the stern intensity of thought is softened with humaneness and love of life.

In Lenin's speeches, as in all his work, the outstanding trait is purposefulness. The speaker is not engaged in constructing a speech but in guiding toward a specific conclusion—action. He approaches his audience in diverse ways; he explains, he reasons, he shames, he jokes again, he reasons and once again explains. What unifies his speech is not a formal plan but a clear, practical goal, rigidly delineated for the current period, which must imbed itself in the consciousness of the audience as a splinter enters the flesh. His humor is likewise subordinated to this. The joke is utilitarian. The colorful newly-coined word has its practical purpose: to spur on some, to curb others. Among these are *khvostism* (tail-endism) and *peredyshka* (breathing spell), *smychka* (alliance with the peasantry), *drachka* (inner-party squabble), and *komchvanstvo* (communist boastfulness), and scores of others which have not been perpetuated. Before he gets to such a word the speaker circles around as if in search of a suitable spot. Once that is located he affixes the nail, gauges the distance properly, takes a full swing and brings the hammer down on the head once, twice, ten times until the nail is driven in so firmly that it becomes difficult to dislodge it even after the necessity for it no longer exists. When that occasion arises, Lenin will, uttering an adage, have to tap this nail from the right and from the left in order to loosen it, and tear it out and cast it into discard among the archives—to the great sorrow of those who had grown accustomed to it. But now the speech is coming to its end. The balance sheet has been drawn, the conclusions have been driven home securely. The speaker looks like a worker who is tired but whose job has been completed. From time to time he passes his hand over the naked skull beaded with perspiration. The voice loses its intensity, like a fire dying down. The speech may now be concluded. But one need not expect a peroration, without which it would seem hardly possible to leave the platform. Others could not do it, but Lenin can. He does not conclude his speech oratorically. He finishes his work and puts a period. Not infrequently, the closing sentence goes like this: "If we understand this, if we do it, then we shall surely conquer." Or, "This is what we must set as our goal, not in words but in action." And sometimes, simply, "This is all I wanted to say to you." And nothing more. And such a conclusion is in complete harmony with the nature of Lenin's eloquence and with Lenin's own nature, and it in no way chills the audience. On the contrary, it is precisely after such an "ineffective," "drab" ending that the audience seems once again to grasp in a single eruption everything that Lenin gave in his speech, and bursts into stormy, grateful, ecstatic applause. But having quickly picked up his slips of paper Lenin has already left the platform in order to escape the inevitable. His head is slightly drawn into his shoulders, chin down, the eyes withdrawn behind the brows, the mustache bristling almost angrily on an upper lip which curls upward in dissatisfaction. The applause mounts wave upon wave. Long live . . . Lenin . . . leader . . . Ilyich . . .   The never-to-be-duplicated head shimmers in the electric light amid the wild waves of applause. And when it seems that the whirlwind of enthusiasm has reached its highest intensity, suddenly through the roar, the tumult and the handclaps, some youthful, shrill, happy and ecstatic voice cuts like a siren through a storm: Long live Ilyich! And somewhere from the trembling innermost depths of solidarity, love, and enthusiasm a veritable cyclone rises in answer with every voice mingled inseparably in a roof-splitting, shouting cry: LONG LIVE LENIN!

H.G. WELLS

Herbert George Wells was born in England in 1866 and worked as a journalist and teacher before achieving popularity and influence as a writer. He belonged to the Fabian Society. He produced forty volumes of fiction and science fiction along with a greater number of volumes of sociological and political prophecy, history, and his Experiment in Autobiography *(1934). He died in 1946.*

In 1920 Wells visited the Soviet Union and was granted an interview by Lenin. Wells's account of the interview entitled "The Dreamer in the Kremlin," was printed in the Sunday Express *(London), November 28, 1920. Trotsky ran across the article in a Russian anthology printed shortly after Lenin's death in January 1924, the same month that the first government headed by the British Labour Party ("Wells's party") had taken office. Trotsky's article, dated April 6, 1924, was written in the Caucasus where he had gone for medical treatment.*

The translation by Tamara Deutscher first appeared, under the title "The Philistine and the Revolutionary," in Trotsky's Lenin *(1971).*

In one of the many anthologies on Lenin I found an essay by the English writer H.G. Wells under the title "The Dreamer in the Kremlin." The editors of the volume remark in the preface that "even such progressive people as Wells had not understood the meaning of the proletarian revolution which occurred in Russia."

This, it would seem, was not a sufficient reason for including Wells's essay in a volume devoted to the leader of that revolution. But I do not want to be quarrelsome; in any case I personally have read not without interest Wells's few pages. This, however, as will be seen later, has not been due to the author.

I vividly remember Wells's visit in Moscow. This was during

the cold and hungry winter of 1920-21. There was in the air an anxious presentiment of the difficulties which awaited us in the spring. Starving Moscow lay buried in thick snow. The economic policy was on the eve of a sharp change. I remember very well the impression which the talk with Wells made on Lenin: "What a petty bourgeois! What a philistine!" he kept on repeating, raising both his arms, laughing and sighing in a way characteristic of him when he felt inwardly ashamed for another man. "Oh, what a philistine!" he repeated, recalling the conversation.

We were both waiting for the opening of a session of the Politburo, and in fact Lenin said nothing more about Wells, except what I have just quoted. But this was quite enough. I admit I have read little of Wells, and I have never met him. But I could well imagine the personality of this English drawing-room socialist, one of the Fabians, a novelist, and the author of fantastic and utopian stories, who had journeyed to Moscow to take a look at the communist experiment. Lenin's exclamations, and quite especially their tone, completed and enlivened the picture.

Now, Wells's essay, which providence in its mysterious ways introduced into a Lenin anthology, not only evoked in my memory Lenin's exclamation, but filled it with living content. Although there is hardly a trace of Lenin in Wells's essay about him, there is in it the whole of Wells himself as clearly seen as the back of one's hand.

Let us start from the beginning, from the first complaint made by Wells: poor man, do you know it took him quite some time and some effort to get an appointment with Lenin and this was "tedious and irritating" to him. Why should it have been? Had Lenin invited Wells there? Did he promise to see him? Perhaps Lenin had too much time on his hands? On the contrary, during these difficult days every minute of Lenin's time was taken up; it was not easy for him to carve out one hour in which to receive Wells. This should have been plain even to a foreigner. The trouble was that Wells, as an illustrious foreigner and for all his "socialism" a rather conservative Englishman of imperialist habits, was absolutely convinced that in fact he was by his visit conferring a great honor on this barbarian country and its leader. His whole article, from first to last, oozes this quite groundless conviction.

The characterization of Lenin begins, as one might have expected, from a great discovery. You see, Lenin "is not a writer."

Who, in fact, should know this better than Wells, a professional man of letters? "The shrill little pamphlets and papers issued from Moscow in his name, full of misconceptions of the labor psychology of the West . . . display hardly anything of the real Lenin mentality. . . ." The honorable gentleman does not know, of course, that Lenin is the author of a whole series of fundamental works on the agrarian question, on economic theory, on sociology and philosophy. Wells knew only the "shrill little pamphlets"; he also remarked that they were issued "in his name," hinting perhaps that they were written by other people. The real "Lenin mentality" reveals itself not in the dozens of volumes which he had written, but in the hour-long conversation into which the eminent visitor from Great Britain so generously deigned to enter.

One would have expected Wells to give at least an interesting description of Lenin's physiognomy. For a single well-observed, well-rendered feature we would have been ready to forgive him all his Fabian trivialities. But there is nothing of the kind in the essay.

"Lenin has a pleasant, quick-changing brownish [!] face with a lively smile. . . ." Lenin "is not very like the photographs you see of him. . . ." "he gesticulated a little with his hands during our conversation. . . ." Wells did not go beyond the banalities of a commonplace reporter, who has to fill a column of his capitalist paper. In addition Wells discovered that Lenin's head resembled the "domed and slightly one-sided cranium" of Arthur Balfour, and that, generally speaking, Lenin is a "little man: his feet scarcely touch the ground as he sits on the edge of his chair." As far as Arthur Balfour's skull is concerned, we can say nothing about this worthy object and we are ready to believe that it is domed. But all the rest! What indecent trash! Lenin had a reddish-blond complexion and one could not by any means describe him as "brownish." He was of medium height, or a little below that; but that he looked a "little man," whose feet hardly touched the floor, might have been only the impression of a Wells who arrived feeling like a civilized Gulliver on a journey to the land of northern communist Lilliputians. Wells also noticed that Lenin, whenever there was a pause in the conversation, was "screwing up one eye"; this habit, explains the shrewd writer, "is due perhaps to some defect in focusing." We know this gesture of Lenin's well. It was always there when Lenin had before him a stranger with whom he had nothing in common: covering his eyes, he used to throw a rapid glance through his fingers and the "defect in focusing" consisted in no more than that he saw through his interlocutor, saw his self-satisfied vanity, his narrow-mindedness, his "civilized" conceit and his "civilized" ignorance. Long afterwards, remembering the occasion, Lenin would shake his head: "What a philistine! What an awful petty bourgeois!"

Comrade Rothstein was present during the talk and Wells en passant made the discovery that this fact was "characteristic for the present condition of Russian affairs." Rothstein, you see, controls Lenin on behalf of the Commissariat of Foreign Affairs in view of Lenin's extreme frankness and his "dreamer's imprudence." What can one say about such a priceless observation? Wells went to the Kremlin, his mind stuffed with all the rubbishy information purveyed by the international bourgeoisie, and with his penetrating eye—without any "defect of focusing"—found in Lenin's office the confirmation of what he had earlier fished out of the pages of *The Times* or from some other source of respectable and genteel gossip.

But what then was the conversation about?

Here Wells conveys to us some hopeless platitudes which only show what a pitiful and hollow echo Lenin's thought evokes in some other heads whose one-sidedness incidentally we have no reason to question.

Wells turned up "expecting to struggle with a doctrinaire Marxist," but in fact he "found nothing of the sort." This should not surprise us. We have already learned that "the real Lenin mentality" has been revealed not during the more than thirty years of his political and literary activity, but in his conversation with the citizen from England. "I had been told that Lenin lectured people; he certainly did not do so on this occasion." How, indeed, to lecture a "gentleman" so full of self-importance? That Lenin liked to lecture people or to teach them was quite untrue. It was true that one could learn a good deal from a conversation with him. But this happened only when Lenin was of the opinion that his interlocutor was able to learn something. In such cases Lenin spared no time and no effort. After two or three minutes in the company of the wonderful Gulliver who by a lucky chance found himself in the office of the "little man," Lenin must have become firmly convinced that the inscription at the entry to Dante's hell—"Abandon all hope!"—was quite appropriate in this situation.

The conversation touched upon the problem of big cities.

Precisely in Russia, as Wells himself said, a remarkable idea occurred to him, namely, that the outlook of a city is determined by the trade in the shops and in the marketplaces. He shared this revelation with Lenin. Lenin "admitted" that under communism cities might become much smaller. Wells "pointed out" to Lenin that the renovation of cities and towns would constitute a gigantic task and that quite a few of the enormous buildings of Petersburg would retain their significance only as historical monuments. Lenin agreed with this original platitude. "I think it warmed his heart," added Wells, "to find someone who understood a necessary consequence of collectivism that many even of his own people fail to grasp."

Well, this gives you the measure of Well's level of thinking. He treats as proof of his extraordinary perspicacity the discovery that under a communist regime the existing huge urban concentrations will disappear and that our present monsters of capitalist architecture will preserve their significance as historic monuments only (unless they will be granted the honor of being demolished). Of course, how would poor communists ("the tiresome class-war fanatics") arrive at such discoveries, which, by the way, have a long time ago been described in a popular addendum to the old program of the German Social Democratic Party. We shall not mention that all this was quite familiar to the classical utopians of socialism.

Now you will understand, I hope, why Wells did not at all notice that famous laughter of Lenin about which he had been told so much. Lenin was in no mood to laugh. I even fear that he might have been a victim of quite the opposite temptation. But his versatile and clever hand, as usual, rendered him a service by concealing just in time an unkind yawn from a visitor preoccupied with his own person.

As you have learned, Lenin did not lecture Wells—for reasons which seem to us quite obvious. In return, however, Wells persisted in giving Lenin advice. He kept on impressing upon Lenin the completely new idea that for the success of socialism it is necessary to change not only the material side of life but also "the mentality of a whole people." He drew Lenin's attention to the fact that "the Russians are by habit and tradition traders and individualists"; he also explained to him that communism "was pressing too hard and too fast, and destroying before it was ready to rebuild," and so on, and so forth, all in the same spirit. "And that," relates Wells, "brought us to our essential difference—the difference of the collectivist and Marxist." By "evolutionary collectivism" one should understand a brew of the Fabians which consists of liberalism, philanthropy, a stingy social legislation together with Sunday meditations about a brighter future. Wells himself thus formulates the essence of "evolutionary collectivism": "I believe that through a vast sustained educational campaign the existing capitalist system could be civilized into a Collectivist world system." Wells does not make it clear, however, who is going to introduce this "vast sustained educational campaign" and who will be subjected to it: are we to suppose that English milords with "domed" heads will exercise it over the English proletariat, or, on the contrary, that the English proletariat will subject milords' heads to this education? Oh, no, anything but the latter. For what purpose do we have in this world the educated Fabians, the intellectuals, with their altruistic imagination, the gentlemen and the ladies, the Messrs. Wellses and Mmes. Snowdens, if not that they should, by a planned and prolonged process of sharing what they themselves carry concealed in their own heads, civilize capitalist society and transform it into a collectivist one, with such a sensible and happy gradualness that even the British monarchy will not notice this transformation?

All this Wells went on expounding to Lenin, and Lenin sat listening. "For me," Wells graciously remarked, "it was very refreshing" to talk to "this amazing little man." And for Lenin? Oh, long suffering Ilyich! He certainly had quite a few expressive and racy Russian words on his tongue. He did not utter them aloud nor did he translate them into English, not only because his English vocabulary would not stretch that far, but also because he was much too polite for this. But he could not limit himself to a polite silence alone.

"He [Lenin] had to argue . . . " relates Wells, "that modern capitalism is incurably predatory, wasteful and unteachable." Lenin quoted facts and figures published, inter alia, in the new book of [Leo] Chiozza Money [*The Triumph of Nationalization,* 1920], and showed how capitalism destroyed the English shipyards, how it prevented a sensible exploitation of coal resources, and so on. Lenin knew the language of facts and figures. "I had, I will confess," Mr. Wells unexpectedly concluded, "a very uphill argument." What did this mean? Wasn't this the beginning of a capitulation of evolutionary collectivism before the logic of Marxism? No, no. "Abandon all hope."

This admission, which on first sight seems unexpected, is not at all fortuitous, but forms an integral part of the typically Fabian evolutionary and didactic system. It was, in fact, addressed to the English capitalists, bankers, peers, and their ministers. Wells was telling them: You see, you behave so stupidly, so greedily, so selfishly, that you make it extremely difficult for me to defend the principles of my evolutionary collectivism in the discussions with the dreamer in the Kremlin. Listen to reason, take part in the Fabians' Sunday ritual ablutions, civilize yourself, march on to the road of progress.

Wells's melancholy admission was not the beginning of a critical revision of his views, but a continuation of that educative work of the same capitalist society, which, after the imperialist war and the Versailles treaty, has so much improved, so much moralized and fabianized itself.

Not without condescending sympathy, Wells remarks that Lenin "has an unlimited confidence in his work." With this statement we shall not quarrel. Indeed, Lenin had faith enough in the justice of his cause. What is true is true. This faith was also, incidentally, the source of the patience with which Lenin entered into conversations, during these harsh months of the blockade, with any foreigner who could serve as a contact, albeit indirectly, between Russia and the West. So Lenin met Wells. He talked a quite different language with English workers who used to visit him. With them he entered into a lively exchange; he taught them and he learned from them. With Wells the intercourse could not have anything but a strained, diplomatic character. "Our . . . argumentation ended indecisively," sums up the author. In other words, the match between evolutionary collectivism and Marxism this time ended in a draw. Wells returned to Great Britain, Lenin remained in the Kremlin. Wells wrote up his pompous "correspondence" for his bourgeois public, and Lenin, shaking his head, kept on repeating: "What a petty-bourgeois! Aye, aye, what a philistine!"

One may ask why and for what purpose I have given so much attention to an insignificant article by H.G. Wells, four years after its publication. The fact that the article was included in one of the anthologies brought out in connection with Lenin's death is not a valid reason. Nor is it a sufficient justification to say that I wrote these lines in Sukhum, where I was undergoing medical treatment. But I had more serious considerations too.

Just now in England, Wells's party is in power. At the head of the party we see the enlightened representatives of evolutionary collectivism. It seemed to me—perhaps not quite unreasonably—that Wells's words devoted to Lenin may perhaps better than anything else reveal to us the spirit of the leaders of the Labour Party. After all, Wells was by no means the worst of them.

How terribly these people lag behind, pressed down by the leaden weight of their bourgeois prejudices. Their pride, which is nothing else but a timeworn reflex of their historical role in the past, prevents them from penetrating, as they should, the minds of other nations, from examining new ideological phenomena, new historical processes which all pass them by. Routine-ridden, narrow-minded empiricists, with blinkers of their bourgeois public opinion over their eyes, these gentlemen carry with them all over the world their own prejudices; they have a peculiar talent for noticing nothing around them—except themselves. Lenin had lived in various countries of Europe, had learned foreign languages, read, studied, listened, pondered matters deeply, compared, generalized. At the head of a great revolutionary country, he never missed an opportunity to inform himself, attentively and conscientiously, to inquire, to learn. He never ceased to follow the events of the entire world. He read and spoke German, French, and English fluently, and he could read Italian too. In the last years of his life, overloaded with work, stealthily, during the Politburo's meetings, he studied a Czechoslovak grammar in order to have a more direct contact with the working class movement of that country. Sometimes we used to "catch him out," and, embarrassed, he would laugh and try to excuse himself. Beside him Wells was the embodiment of those pseudo-educated, narrow-minded bourgeois who look without seeing, who do not want to learn anything because they feel so comfortable behind their barrier of inherited prejudices. Then you have Mr. MacDonald, a more solid and gloomy variety of the same type, reassuring public opinion in England: We have fought against Moscow and we have won.

Have *they* won? They are indeed poor "little men" even if they have grown tall in size. Even now, after all that has happened, they still have no inkling of what the future has in store for them. Liberal and conservative businessmen easily manipulate these pedantic "evolutionary" socialists now in power, deliberately preparing not only the downfall of their government but their political debacle as well. At the same time, however, only unknowingly, they prepare the path to power for English

literally devoured work. It would be good to
he number of working hours Glazman put in
ars' service to the revolution: They would be
for twenty years in the lives of many, very

ked to join our military train as a stenographer
t is, the same month the train was being fitted
ampaign. From that time on there was hardly
azman and I were not together. His life and
life was summed up in his work—went on
ecame my closest collaborator. The authority
y person, with his quiet movements and
oned voice, was recognized by everyone. It
moral strength, revolutionary duty, honesty,
ness. Even Glazman's stenographic work,
mstance, took on the nature of a heroic feat:
compelled to take most of his shorthand in
ain going full tilt. I can still see his thin,
he desk in our car. The train is rocking so
to keep one's feet in front of the swaying
he ceiling. Glazman is glued to his chair;
small, thin hand are barely detectible. But
bed in his work. And so he remains—for
y, sometimes all night, even more often,
cles, orders, conversations over the open
hrough his hands. When he would bring
ials to be checked and signed, it was rare
erstanding, or omission appeared. Glaz-
ll conscientiousness; he greatly disliked
e fall victim to an error.

stenographer and secretary. He was a
nd not in the figurative, but in the most
se. He knew how to use a rifle, a pistol,
and use them well. He was obliged to
nment in combat and under fire. At
ts, when the troop detachment of the
plug a hole in the front, Glazman
ssion to go with the detachment." And
left without him, one could not refuse.
ha, sat ludicrously on this small and
The triple-bore rifle seemed out of
e and sunken chest. The pince-nez

Marxists. Yes, precisely for the Marxists, for those "tiresome class-war fanatics." The English social revolution too will proceed according to the laws defined by Marx.

Wells, with his peculiar humor so much like a stodgy English pudding, once threatened to cut off Marx's "doctrinaire" head of hair and his beard, to anglicize him, to make him more respectable and to "fabianize" him. But nothing came of this project, and nothing will ever come of it. Marx will remain Marx, just as Lenin will remain Lenin, even after subjection to Wells's blunt razor blade for more than a full tiresome hour. We dare to venture a forecast that in the not too distant future in London, perhaps in Trafalgar Square, there will appear, next to each other, two monuments in bronze: one of Karl Marx and the other of Vladimir Lenin. And English workers will say to their children: "What a good thing it was, that the little men of the Labour Party did not manage either to cut the hair or to shave the beards of these two giants."

Awaiting this day, which I hope to be alive to see, I shut my eyes for a second and I see clearly Lenin's figure in the same chair in which Wells saw him, and I hear—after Wells's visit or perhaps a day later—the slighty mournful yet good-natured voice: "What a petty bourgeois! What a philistine!"

MIKHAIL GLAZMAN

Mikhail S. Glazman was a stenographer who joined the Bolshevik Party in 1918, served throughout the civil war as a secretary to Trotsky on the military train that functioned as the mobile headquarters of the Commissar of War, became senior secretary to the chairman of the Military Revolutionary Council of the Republic after the civil war, heiped edit some volumes of Trotsky's collected works, and committed suicide in 1924 after being expelled from the party. Other biographical data are lacking.

Glazman was one of thousands in the Communist Party who supported Trotsky when the Stalin-Zinoviev-Kamenev majority of the Political Bureau unleashed a campaign against "Trotskyism" in 1923, but he was the first to lose his life for that reason. Like other rank-and-file Left Oppositionists, he was undoubtedly pressured and cajoled to break with Trotsky. Instead, he worked closely with Trotsky in 1924 to help publish the book 1917, which contained "Lessons of October," the first major counter-attack against the Stalinists (reprinted in The Challenge of the Left Opposition *[1975]). For this "crime" he was brought up on charges (the specific accusation remains obscure) and was expelled. According to Trotsky, the Central Committee ruled that the expulsion was an error after Glazman took his life. According to Max Eastman, in* Since Lenin Died *(1925), "The custom of suicide among party members has grown to such proportions since the beginning of this campaign [against 'Trotskyism'] that a special investigation was conducted, and a report made to the Central Committee recommending means to combat it. (See* Pravda *for October 9, 1924.)"*

Stalin bore a special animosity toward Trotsky's secretaries; in a typically bureaucratic way he seemed to think that he could silence Trotsky by depriving him of his closest assistants. Glazman was the first of a series of Trotsky secretaries whom

*Stalin's agents hound
and thirties.*

*Trotsky's tribute,
written in the Cauc
press in Moscow bu
volume of Trotsky'
has been translat
Saunders.*

Today is alre
hung over all t
death. Glazm
despite his ph
Glazman has

He was e
Commission.
expulsion ar
course. But
error, Glazi
possession
proved m
Glazman
reversed.

Glazm
Party d
and a
attenti
It was
that a
appre
cons
attit
him
He
nes
pe
ar
n
u

phlegmatically, h
have a count of
during his six ye
enough to accoun
many, other peopl
Glazman was as
in August 1918, tha
out for the Kazan c
a moment when Gl
his work—and his
before my eyes. He
of this small, sick
weak, always even-t
was the authority of
and supreme selfless
through force of circu
for three years he wa
a railroad car on a tr
bony back bent over t
badly that it is hard
map suspended from t
the movements of his s
he is completely absor
hours, sometimes all da
all day and night. Arti
wire—everything went t
a stack of decoded mater
that a mistake, misund
man was all attention, a
errors. Fate willed that

Glazman was not only
soldier of the revolution, a
immediate and literal sen
and an automatic pistol,
carry out many an assig
especially difficult momer
train had to disembark t
would say: "Request permi
though it was difficult to be
The tall fur hat, the *papak*
always close-cropped head
proportion to his small si

beneath the *papakha* violated military appearances even more. But this was a true soldier, a quiet, calm, even-tempered hero, unaware of his heroism.

Slowly, it would almost seem phlegmatically, he descended the steps of the train. But after a week or two he would be back. And once again his hand would trace out the ever so tiny hieroglyphics at the desk in the railroad car rushing along at sixty miles an hour.

Glazman was for a long time the secretary of the Military Revolutionary Council. He would sit motionless as though indifferent to the proceedings. But he heard everything, grasped the essence of everything, understood everything. The necessary information was always in his hands the minute it was needed. He would catch up suggestions on the fly. He worked noiselessly and without talking, but with what remarkable accuracy!

A countless number of tasks passed through his hands, involving party, military, personal, or incidental matters. How many assignments he was given during congresses, conferences, and other gatherings! He noted down everything, and carried it out or saw to its completion—and in every task and every assignment he displayed remarkable sensitivity and personal tact, and always distinguished correctly between what was important and what was not, what was true and what false. Each time information of a party nature was needed, I was astonished anew to see how well he remembered all the resolutions and discussions of party congresses and how closely he followed party literature.

Surely it will not be out of place for me to say how much of my own work was linked with the labors of this inestimable friend and comrade-in-arms. All my literary work of the past six years was done in constant collaboration with Glazman. His part in this collaboration went far beyond mere stenographic transcription. No, he was always at the heart of the matter, collecting materials, finding sources, references, quotations. With what endearing shyness he would give his suggestions, invariably well thought out, serious, and valuable.

Recently he did a great deal of work on preparing for publication my two-volume book *1917*. He dug untiringly through newspapers and archival material, discovering unsigned articles and resolutions, checking and comparing. I was struck by the accuracy of his judgment, the rightness of his guesses. He looked terribly exhausted, but he did not wish to leave for a vacation until he had brought the work to completion. I left Moscow on August 20. The evening of September 2, I received from Glazman a list of questions on a number of literary matters. How far I was at the time from thinking that the author of those questions was no longer alive! The next day came a telegram: "Today Glazman committed suicide after learning of his expulsion from the party." That blow came as too much of a shock for him. An enemy bullet at the front he could expect; the further advance of his tuberculosis he could and did expect; but he did not and could not expect expulsion from the party. That was a blow he could not endure.

The expulsion of Glazman has been ruled an error by a higher party body. He was buried today—the day these lines are written—as a revolutionary, a party member, a Bolshevik, that is, as what he was in life.

To the grave has gone a priceless individual—pure, firm, never ingratiating or sly. One of those on whom the party could rely under the most trying circumstances. People like Glazman remain true to the end. What a loss! What sorrow to all who knew him! He has gone from us in such a terrible way—our dear, quiet, steady Glazman. Forgive us, young friend, that we did not protect and save you.

Marxists. Yes, precisely for the Marxists, for those "tiresome class-war fanatics." The English social revolution too will proceed according to the laws defined by Marx.

Wells, with his peculiar humor so much like a stodgy English pudding, once threatened to cut off Marx's "doctrinaire" head of hair and his beard, to anglicize him, to make him more respectable and to "fabianize" him. But nothing came of this project, and nothing will ever come of it. Marx will remain Marx, just as Lenin will remain Lenin, even after subjection to Wells's blunt razor blade for more than a full tiresome hour. We dare to venture a forecast that in the not too distant future in London, perhaps in Trafalgar Square, there will appear, next to each other, two monuments in bronze: one of Karl Marx and the other of Vladimir Lenin. And English workers will say to their children: "What a good thing it was, that the little men of the Labour Party did not manage either to cut the hair or to shave the beards of these two giants."

Awaiting this day, which I hope to be alive to see, I shut my eyes for a second and I see clearly Lenin's figure in the same chair in which Wells saw him, and I hear—after Wells's visit or perhaps a day later—the slighty mournful yet good-natured voice: "What a petty bourgeois! What a philistine!"

MIKHAIL GLAZMAN

Mikhail S. Glazman was a stenographer who joined the Bolshevik Party in 1918, served throughout the civil war as a secretary to Trotsky on the military train that functioned as the mobile headquarters of the Commissar of War, became senior secretary to the chairman of the Military Revolutionary Council of the Republic after the civil war, helped edit some volumes of Trotsky's collected works, and committed suicide in 1924 after being expelled from the party. Other biographical data are lacking.

Glazman was one of thousands in the Communist Party who supported Trotsky when the Stalin-Zinoviev-Kamenev majority of the Political Bureau unleashed a campaign against "Trotskyism" in 1923, but he was the first to lose his life for that reason. Like other rank-and-file Left Oppositionists, he was undoubtedly pressured and cajoled to break with Trotsky. Instead, he worked closely with Trotsky in 1924 to help publish the book 1917, which contained "Lessons of October," the first major counter-attack against the Stalinists (reprinted in The Challenge of the Left Opposition *[1975]). For this "crime" he was brought up on charges (the specific accusation remains obscure) and was expelled. According to Trotsky, the Central Committee ruled that the expulsion was an error after Glazman took his life. According to Max Eastman, in* Since Lenin Died *(1925), "The custom of suicide among party members has grown to such proportions since the beginning of this campaign [against 'Trotskyism'] that a special investigation was conducted, and a report made to the Central Committee recommending means to combat it. (See* Pravda *for October 9, 1924.)"*

Stalin bore a special animosity toward Trotsky's secretaries; in a typically bureaucratic way he seemed to think that he could silence Trotsky by depriving him of his closest assistants. Glazman was the first of a series of Trotsky secretaries whom

Stalin's agents hounded to death or murdered during the twenties and thirties.

Trotsky's tribute, entitled "In Memory of M.S. Glazman," was written in the Caucasus on September 6, 1924. It was sent to the press in Moscow but was not printed anywhere until 1926, in the volume of Trotsky's collected works called Political Silhouettes. *It has been translated for this book from that source by George Saunders.*

Today is already the fourth day that a nightmarish cloud has hung over all those who knew Glazman and have learned of his death. Glazman—firm and courageous, great in endurance despite his physical frailty, totally devoted to the revolution— Glazman has shot himself.

He was expelled from the party by the Moscow Control Commission. The Central Committee has already ruled the expulsion an error. The investigation into this error is taking its course. But between the expulsion and the acknowledgment of error, Glazman had time to shoot himself. Despite his firm self-possession, despite his exceptional moral courage, this error proved more than Glazman could bear. It was too monstrous. Glazman shot himself. This is something that no longer can be reversed.

Glazman joined—or rather, grew to be part of—the Bolshevik Party during the civil war. He was a stenographer by training and a fine one. But everything Glazman did he did well, attentively, accurately, conscientiously, and through to the end. It was this quality of his, the highest level of integrity in work, that attracted people to him, above all those who knew how to appreciate this precious quality. In Glazman's case, being conscientious about his work did not mean adopting an officious attitude. There was nothing of the time-server or chair-warmer in him, although a goodly half of his work was pure office routine. He was a revolutionist and a party activist. His conscientiousness in work expressed his sense of revolutionary duty, which permeated him through and through. Frail and infirm in appearance, Glazman was an unremitting worker. Not that he never grew tired. The ashen color of his face and dark circles under his eyes often told how terribly tired he was. But he refused to acknowledge fatigue. Unhurriedly and even, from the look of it, phlegmatically, he literally devoured work. It would be good to have a count of the number of working hours Glazman put in during his six years' service to the revolution: They would be enough to account for twenty years in the lives of many, very many, other people.

Glazman was asked to join our military train as a stenographer in August 1918, that is, the same month the train was being fitted out for the Kazan campaign. From that time on there was hardly a moment when Glazman and I were not together. His life and his work—and his life was summed up in his work—went on before my eyes. He became my closest collaborator. The authority of this small, sickly person, with his quiet movements and weak, always even-toned voice, was recognized by everyone. It was the authority of moral strength, revolutionary duty, honesty, and supreme selflessness. Even Glazman's stenographic work, through force of circumstance, took on the nature of a heroic feat: for three years he was compelled to take most of his shorthand in a railroad car on a train going full tilt. I can still see his thin, bony back bent over the desk in our car. The train is rocking so badly that it is hard to keep one's feet in front of the swaying map suspended from the ceiling. Glazman is glued to his chair; the movements of his small, thin hand are barely detectible. But he is completely absorbed in his work. And so he remains—for hours, sometimes all day, sometimes all night, even more often, all day and night. Articles, orders, conversations over the open wire—everything went through his hands. When he would bring a stack of decoded materials to be checked and signed, it was rare that a mistake, misunderstanding, or omission appeared. Glazman was all attention, all conscientiousness; he greatly disliked errors. Fate willed that he fall victim to an error.

Glazman was not only a stenographer and secretary. He was a soldier of the revolution, and not in the figurative, but in the most immediate and literal sense. He knew how to use a rifle, a pistol, and an automatic pistol, and use them well. He was obliged to carry out many an assignment in combat and under fire. At especially difficult moments, when the troop detachment of the train had to disembark to plug a hole in the front, Glazman would say: "Request permission to go with the detachment." And though it was difficult to be left without him, one could not refuse. The tall fur hat, the *papakha*, sat ludicrously on this small and always close-cropped head. The triple-bore rifle seemed out of proportion to his small size and sunken chest. The pince-nez

YAKOV SVERDLOV

Yakov M. Sverdlov was born in Russia in 1885, became a Social Democrat at the age of sixteen, and joined the Bolsheviks two years later. From 1902 to 1917 he specialized in the party's underground work as a sort of traveling organizer when he was not under arrest or in exile. He and Stalin lived together in exile for a while but did not get along well. He was coopted to the Bolshevik Central Committee in 1913 and elected to it at a congress in 1917, where he also became a secretary of the Central Committee; at another congress later that year he was elected head of the Central Committee's secretariat. He was a central leader of the October revolution, and in 1918 was elected chairman of the Central Executive Committee of the Soviets, which made him titular head of state. He died suddenly during an influenza epidemic in 1919.

Lenin, who was not given to exaggeration in such matters, said, "In the course of our revolution, in its victories, it fell to Sverdlov to express more fully and more wholly than anybody else the very essence of the proletarian revolution." And, "Only thanks to the fact that we had such an organizer as Sverdlov were we able in war times to work as though we had not one single conflict worth speaking of." And, "Such a man we can never replace, if by replacement we mean the possibility of finding one comrade combining such qualities. . . . The work which he did alone can now be accomplished only by a whole group of men who, following in his footsteps, will carry on his service." A secretariat of three persons was in fact elected to continue Sverdlov's organizational tasks in 1919; this was before the post of party general secretary had been invented.

Trotsky's tribute to Sverdlov, dated March 13, 1925, was written six years after Sverdlov's death, for an anniversary volume published by the Communist Party's Bureau of Party History, a few weeks after the Stalin-Zinoviev-Kamenev faction in the Political Bureau had forced Trotsky out of his post as Commissar of War. Informed readers at the time must have noticed the fact that Trotsky praised Sverdlov for many positive attributes that were lacking in Sverdlov's eventual successor in the party's leading organizational post, general secretary Stalin.

The translation by John G. Wright was first published in Fourth International, *November 1946.*

I became acquainted with Sverdlov only in 1917 at a session of the Bolshevik fraction of the First Soviet Congress. Sverdlov was presiding. In those days there were hardly any in the party who guessed the true stature of this remarkable man. But within the next few months he was to unfold himself fully.

In the initial period after the revolution the emigres, that is, those who had spent many years abroad, could still be told apart from the "domestic" and "native" Bolsheviks. In many respects the emigres possessed serious advantages because of their European experience, the broader outlook connected with the latter, and also because they had generalized theoretically the experience of past factional struggles. Naturally, this division into emigres and non-emigres was purely temporary and presently all distinctions became obliterated. But in 1917 and in 1918 it was in many cases something quite palpable.

However, there was no "provincialism" to be sensed in Sverdlov even in those days. Month by month he grew and became stronger so naturally, so organically, so seemingly without effort, so much in step with events and in such constant contact and collaboration with Vladimir Ilyich that to a superficial view it might have seemed that Sverdlov had been born an accomplished revolutionary "statesman" of the first rank. All questions of the revolution he approached not from above, that is, not from the standpoint of general theoretical considerations, but rather from below, through the direct impulses of life itself as transmitted by the party organism. When new political questions were under discussion, it might have seemed sometimes that Sverdlov—especially if he kept silent, which was not infrequently the case—was wavering or had not yet been able to make up his mind. In reality, in the course of the discussion he was engaged in mentally working out the problem along parallel lines, which might be sketched out as follows: Who is available? Where should he be assigned? How shall we broach the problem and bring it into harmony with our other tasks? And no sooner had the joint political decision been reached, no sooner was it necessary to turn to the organizational side of the problem and the question of personnel than it almost invariably turned out that Sverdlov was already prepared with far-reaching practical proposals, based on his encyclopedic memory and personal knowledge of individuals.

In the initial stages of their formation all the Soviet departments and institutions turned to him for personnel; and this initial and rough allocation of party cadres demanded exceptional resourcefulness and inventiveness. It was impossible to depend on an established apparatus, on files, archives, etc. For all this was still in an extremely nebulous shape, and at any rate provided no direct means of verifying to what extent the professional revolutionist Ivanov may be qualified to head a particular Soviet department, of which only the name was yet in existence. A special psychological intuition was required to decide such a question: one had to locate in Ivanov's past two or three focal points and thence draw conclusions for an entirely new situation. Therewith these transplantations had to be made in the most diversified fields—in a search for a People's Commissar, or for a manager of the *Izvestia* printing plant, or for a member of the Central Executive Committee of the Soviets, or for a commandant of the Kremlin, and so on ad infinitum. These organizational problems arose, naturally, without any consecutiveness whatever, that is, never from the highest post down to the lowest or vice versa, but in every which way, accidentally, chaotically. Sverdlov made inquiries, gathered or remembered biographical details, made phone calls, offered recommendations, gave out assignments, made appointments. At the present time I am at a loss to say exactly in what capacity he performed all this work, that is, just what his formal powers were. But at all events a considerable part of this work had to be performed on his own personal responsibility—with the support, naturally, of Vladimir Ilyich. And no one ever challenged it, such were the exigencies of the entire situation at the time.

Sverdlov accomplished a considerable part of his organizational work as president of the Central Executive Committee, utilizing the members of this committee for various appointments and for particular assignments. "Talk it over with Sverdlov," Lenin would advise in many cases whenever someone turned to him with a particular problem.

"I must talk it over with Sverdlov," a newly baked Soviet

"dignitary" would say to himself whenever he hit a snag with his collaborators. One of the ways to solve a major practical problem was—according to the unwritten constitution—"to talk it over with Sverdlov."

But Sverdlov himself of course did not at all favor this highly individualistic method. On the contrary, his entire work prepared the conditions for a more systematic and regularized solution of all party and Soviet problems.

In those days the need was for "pioneers" in all spheres, that is, people capable of operating on their own two feet amid the greatest chaos, in the absence of precedents, without any statutes and regulations. It was for such pioneers for all conceivable exigencies that Sverdlov was constantly on the lookout. He would recall, as I have already said, this or that biographical detail, of how so-and-so had conducted himself at such-and-such a time, and from this he would adduce whether or not this or that candidate would be suitable. There were of course many mistakes. But the astonishing thing is that there were not many more. And what seems most astonishing is how Sverdlov found it possible to even broach a problem in the face of the chaos of tasks, the chaos of difficulties and with a minimum of available personnel. It was much clearer and easier to approach each problem from the standpoint of principle and political expediency than to approach it from the organizational standpoint. This situation is to be observed among us to this very day, flowing, as it does, from the very essence of a period that is transitional to socialism. But in those days the discrepancy between a clearly envisaged goal and the lack of material and human resources made itself felt much more acutely than today. It was precisely when matters came to the point of practical solution that many of us would start shaking our heads in perplexity. And then someone would ask: "Well, and what do you say, Yakov Mikhailovich?"

And Sverdlov would offer his solution. In his opinion "the undertaking was quite feasible." A group of carefully selected Bolsheviks would have to be sent; and they should be properly briefed, and given the proper connections, and proper attention paid, and the necessary aid given—and it could be done. To gain successes on this path one must be completely imbued with confidence that it was possible to solve any task and to overcome any difficulty. An inexhaustible reserve of *optimism in doing* did indeed supply the subsoil for Sverdlov's work. Naturally this does not mean to say that each problem was in this way solved 100 percent. If it was solved 10 percent, that was good. In those days this already meant salvation because it made tomorrow secure. But after all, this was precisely the gist of all the work during those initial and hardest years: it was necessary to get food supplies somehow; it was necessary to equip and train the troops somehow; it was necessary to keep the transport functioning somehow; it was necessary to cope with the typhus somehow—*no matter what the price, the revolution had to be secured its tomorrow.*

Sverdlov's qualities became strikingly revealed in the most critical moments, for example, after the July days in the year 1917, that is, after the White Guardists had crushed our party in Petrograd; and again, during the July days in the year 1918, that is, after the Left Social Revolutionaries staged their insurrection. In both cases it was necessary to rebuild the organization, to renew connections or create them over again, checking up on those who had passed a great test. And in both cases Sverdlov was irreplaceable with his revolutionary calm, his farsightedness, and his resourcefulness.

On another occasion I have told the story of how Sverdlov came from the Soviet Congress at the Bolshoi Theater to Vladimir Ilyich's office at the very "peak" of the Left SR uprising. After greeting us with a smile he said, "Well, I suppose we shall again have to move from the Sovnarkom [Council of People's Commissars] to the Revkom [Revolutionary Military Council], what do you think?"

Sverdlov remained himself, as he usually was. In such days one really learns to know people. And Yakov Mikhailovich was truly beyond compare: confident, courageous, firm, resourceful—the best type of Bolshevik. It was precisely in those critical months that Lenin came to know and to appreciate Sverdlov. Time and again it happened that Vladimir Ilyich would pick up the phone in order to propose to Sverdlov a particular emergency measure and in most cases the answer he got was: "Already." This meant that the measure had already been adopted. We often made jokes on this topic, saying, "Well, in all likelihood, Sverdlov has it—already."

"You know," Lenin once remarked, "in the beginning we were against including him on the Central Committee. How we underestimated the man! There was a considerable dispute over it, but the rank and file corrected us at the congress, and they proved to be entirely correct. . . ."

Despite the fact that there never was, of course, even talk of intermixing the organizations, the bloc with the Left SRs did unquestionably tend to make the conduct of our party nuclei somewhat nebulous. Suffice it to mention, for example, that when a large group of activists was detailed to the Eastern front, simultaneously with the appointment of Muraviev as commander in chief of that area, a Left SR was elected the secretary of this group of several score, most of whom were Bolsheviks. In the various institutions and departments, the greater was the number of new and accidental members of our own party all the more indefinite were the relations between the Bolsheviks and the SRs. The laxness, the lack of vigilance and of cohesion among party members only recently implanted in the still fresh state apparatus is characterized quite strikingly by the single fact that the basic core of the uprising was constituted by the Left SR organization among the Cheka troops.

The salutary change occurred literally within two or three days. During the days of the insurrection engineered by one ruling party against another, when all personal relations were suddenly put in question, and when the functionaries in the departments began wavering, then the best and the most devoted Communist elements within all sorts of institutions quickly drew close to one another, breaking all ties with the Left SRs and combating them. The Communist nuclei became fused in the factories and in the army sections. In the development of the party and the state alike this was a moment of exceptional importance. Party elements, distributed and in part dispersed throughout the still formless framework of the state apparatus, whose party ties had become to a large extent diffused in departmental relations, now came instantly to the fore, closed ranks, and became welded together under the blows of the Left SR insurrection. Everywhere Communist nuclei took shape which assumed in those days the actual leadership of the internal life of all the institutions. One may say that it was precisely in those days that the party in its majority became for the first time really conscious of its role as a ruling organization, as the leader of the proletarian state, as the party of the proletarian dictatorship not only in its political but also in its organizational aspects. This process—which might be designated as the beginning of the party's organizational self-determination within the Soviet state apparatus created by the party itself—took place under the direct leadership of Sverdlov, whether the All-Union Soviet Executive Committee or a garage of the War Commissariat was involved. Historians of the October revolution will be obliged to single out and minutely study this critical moment in the evolution of the reciprocal relations between the party and the state, a moment that was to place its stamp on the entire period to come, down to this very day. Therewith the historian who takes up this question will lay bare the great role played by Sverdlov, the organizer, during this all-important turning point. All the threads of practical connections were gathered in his hands.

Even more critical were the days when the Czechoslovaks threatened Nizhny Novgorod, while Lenin was struck down, with two SR bullets in his body. On September 1 at Svyazhsk I received a coded telegram from Sverdlov:

"Return immediately. Ilyich wounded. How critically not known. Complete calm prevails. Sverdlov. August 31, 1918."

I left immediately for Moscow. The party circles in Moscow were in a stern, somber, but unwavering mood.

The best expression of this unwaveringness was Sverdlov. His responsibilities and his role increased manyfold in those days. The highest tension could be sensed in his nervous body. But this nervous tension meant only a greater vigilance—it had nothing in common with aimless bustling, and all the less so with jitteriness. During such moments Sverdlov made his stature felt completely.

The diagnosis of the physicians was hopeful. No visitors were allowed to see Lenin; no one was admitted. There was no reason to remain in Moscow. Shortly after my return to Svyazhsk I received a letter from Sverdlov dated September 8:
"Dear Lev Davidovich,

"I take this opportunity to write a few words. Things are going well with Vladimir Ilyich. I shall probably be able to see him in three or four days."

The rest of the letter deals with practical questions which it is unnecessary to bring up here.

Engraved sharply in my memory is the trip with Sverdlov to the Little Hills estate (Gorki), where Vladimir Ilyich was convalescing from his wounds. It was on my next trip to Moscow. Despite the terribly difficult situation at that time, a change for the better could distinctly be felt. At the Eastern front, which was then the decisive one, we had recaptured Kazan and Simbirsk. The attempt on Lenin's life served the party as a supreme political overhauling: the party felt more vigilant, more on guard, better prepared to beat back the enemy. Lenin was improving rapidly and making preparation to return to work soon. All this together engendered moods of strength and assurance. Since the party had been able to cope with the situation up until now, it would surely continue to do so in the future. This was exactly our mood as we made the journey to Gorki.

En route Sverdlov acquainted me with what had happened in Moscow during my absence. He had an excellent memory, as is the case with most individuals who have a great creative will. His account revolved, as always, around the axis of the most important things that had to be done, with the necessary organizational particulars, accompanied, in passing, with brief characterizations of individuals. In brief, it was an extension of Sverdlov's customary work. And beneath it all was to be felt an undercurrent of calm, but at the same time compelling, confidence.

Sverdlov had to preside a great deal. He was chairman of many bodies and at many meetings. He was an imperious chairman. Not in the sense that he shut off discussion, or curbed the speakers, and so on. Not at all. On the contrary, he never quibbled or insisted on formalities. His imperiousness as chairman consisted in this, that he always knew exactly what practical decision was before the body; he understood who would speak, what would be said, and why; he was quite familiar with the backstage aspects of the issue—and every big and complex issue has its own backstage; he was adept at giving the floor in time to speakers who were needed; he knew how to put the proposition to a vote in time; he knew what could be carried and he was able to carry what he wanted. These traits of his as chairman were bound up indissolubly with all his qualities as a practical leader, with his ability to appraise people in the flesh, realistically, with his inexhaustible inventiveness in the field of organizational and personnel combinations.

During stormy sessions he was adept at permitting the assembly to become noisy and let off steam; and then at the proper moment he would intervene to restore order with a firm hand and a metallic voice.

Sverdlov was of medium height, of dark complexion, thin and gaunt; his face, lean; his features, angular. His powerful and even mighty voice might have seemed out of consonance with his physique. To an even greater degree this might be said of his character. But such an impression could be only fleeting. And then the physical image became fused with the spiritual. Nor is this all, for this gaunt figure with its calm, unconquerable, and inflexible will and with its powerful but not flexible voice would then stand forth as a finished image.

"Nichevo—never mind," Vladimir Ilyich would sometimes say in a difficult situation. "Sverdlov will tell them about it in his Sverdlovian bass and the matter will be settled. . . ."

In these words there was affectionate irony.

In the initial post-October period the Communists were, as is well-known, called "leatherites" by our enemies, because of the way in which we dressed. I believe that Sverdlov's example played a major role in introducing the leather "uniform" among us. At all events he invariably walked around encased in leather from head to toe, from his leather cap to his leather boots. This costume, which somehow corresponded with the character of those days, radiated far and wide from him, as the central organizational figure.

Comrades who knew Sverdlov in the underground days remember a different Sverdlov. But in my memory Sverdlov remains clothed in leather as in an armor grown black under the blows of the first years of the Civil War.

We were gathered at a session of the Political Bureau when Sverdlov, who was burning up with fever at home, took a turn for the worse. E.D. Stasova, then secretary of the Central Committee, came in during the session. She had come from Sverdlov's apartment. Her face was unrecognizable.

"Yakov Mikhailovich feels poorly, very poorly," she said. A glance at her sufficed to understand that there was no hope. We cut the session short. Vladimir Ilyich went to Sverdlov's apartment, and I left for the Commissariat to prepare to depart immediately for the front. In about fifteen minutes a phone call came from Lenin, who said in that special muted voice which meant great strain: "He is gone." "He is gone." "He is gone." For awhile each of us held the receiver in our hands and each could feel the silence at the other end. Then we hung up. There was nothing more to say. Yakov Mikhailovich was gone. Sverdlov was no longer among us.

ADOLF JOFFE

Adolf A. Joffe was born in Russia in 1883 and became a revolutionary in his youth. He met and became friends with Trotsky in Vienna in 1908, where they jointly produced a Russian paper that defended the then unpopular view that Russia was approaching a workers' *revolution. In 1917, Joffe and Trotsky belonged to a small revolutionary group that was independent of both the Bolsheviks and Mensheviks and that joined the Bolsheviks in August. After playing a leading role in the October revolution, Joffe served as chairman of the Soviet delegation at the Brest-Litovsk negotiations with the Germans in 1918. He was Soviet ambassador to Germany in 1918, to China in 1922, and to Austria in 1924. A Left Oppositionist from 1923, he committed suicide in 1927 during a period of depression worsened by Stalin's refusal to let him go abroad for medical treatment and by the news that Trotsky had been expelled from the Communist Party.*

Joffe left behind a personal letter to Trotsky whose text, as edited by Trotsky, is printed in Leon Trotsky: The Man and His Work *(1969). Stalin had other parts of the letter published in the magazine* Bolshevik *in December 1927 in an attempt to discredit the Left Opposition.*

Joffe's funeral was set for November 19, a working day in Moscow, when few workers could attend. Despite that, ten thousand turned out at the cemetery in what proved to be the last mass demonstration addressed by leaders of the Left Opposition. The translation by George Saunders of Trotsky's short speech at the funeral was first published in Intercontinental Press, *February 10, 1975.*

Comrades, Adolf Abramovich has become part of the history of the last decade above all as a diplomatic representive of the first workers' state in history. It has been said here—and in the press—that he was an outstanding diplomat. That is correct. He was a diplomat—that is, he served at the post to which he was assigned by the revolution and the workers' government. But he was a great diplomat because he was a revolutionist through and through.

By social origin, Adolf Abramovich was the product of a bourgeois environment—more precisely, of a wealthy bourgeois family. But as we know, there have been cases in history when the products of this sort of environment have made such a sharp break with their background—a break that goes to the very marrow of their bones—that from then on, there is no danger of their ever being won over to petty-bourgeois ideas. Adolf Abramovich was and remained a revolutionist to the end.

Speakers here today have referred—and rightly so—to the high level of his cultural attainments. As a diplomat he was forced to move in enemy circles, among cunning, sharp-eyed, and venomous foes. He knew this world, its customs and habits, and he assumed the ways of this world with subtlety and skill; but for him this was like putting on a uniform required by his post of duty. Adolf Abramovich never wore a uniform on his soul. It has been said here—and said correctly—that he was a stranger to routine or stereotyped attitudes on any question whatsoever. He approached every problem as a revolutionist. He held posts of responsibility but he was never a bureaucrat. Bureaucratism was alien to him. He looked at every problem from the point of view of the working class, which had raised itself from the depths of the underground to the heights of state power. He approached every problem from the point of view of the international proletariat and the international revolution. And this was the source of his strength, a strength he called on constantly to combat his own physical weakness. His strength of mind and his ability to exert its power remained with him to the very last moment, when the bullet left the dark stain that we can see here today upon his right temple.

Comrades, you might say that he withdrew from life by his own choice. And the revolution permits none of us to withdraw on our own initiative. But let no one presume to judge Adolf Abramovich. For he withdrew at a point when, in his own thinking, he had nothing left to give the revolution but his death. Then, firmly and courageously, as he had lived life, he left it.

Difficult times never frightened him. He remained on the same even keel in October 1917 when he was a member, and later chairman, of the Military Revolutionary Committee in Petrograd;

the same on the battleground outside the city as the shells from Yudenich's cannon burst all around; and the same at the diplomatic table in Brest-Litovsk, and later in so many capitals of Europe and Asia. Difficulties did not distress him. What impelled him to abandon life was the consciousness that it was impossible for him to combat those difficulties.

Comrades, let me say this—and it is a consideration I believe corresponds in full to Adolf Abramovich's last thoughts and last testament—such an action, withdrawing from life by one's own decision, has a contagious power. Let no one presume to follow the example of this old fighter in his death. No. Follow him in his life.

Those of us who were his close friends, who not only fought side by side but lived side by side with him for decades, are forced now to tear ourselves away from the vivid image of this exceptional person and friend who remains in our hearts. There was a gentle and steady glow about Adolf Abramovich that gave warmth to all around him. He was a focal point around whom others gathered—in the emigre circles, in the penal colonies, and in prison. He came, as I have already said, from a well-to-do family, but the means at his disposal in his younger years were not just his own property. They became the resources of the revolution. He helped comrades with a generous hand, not waiting to be asked—as a brother, as a true friend.

Here in this coffin we bring the mortal remains of this exceptional person, at whose side it was so easy and pleasant for us to live and fight. Let us take our leave of him in the same spirit that he lived and fought: he took his stand under the banner of Marx and Lenin; under that banner he died. And we vow to you, Adolf Abramovich, we will carry your banner through to the end!

NICHOLAS AND ALEXANDRA
ROMANOV

Nicholas Romanov, who was born in Russia in 1868, became Tsar Nicholas II in 1894. He succeeded Alexander III, whose predecessor had been assassinated by revolutionaries in 1881. Nicholas's rule coincided with a series of major events of modern Russian and world history. His regime's entry into the Russo-Japanese War (1904-05), ending in defeat for Russia, helped bring on the revolution of 1905-07, which forced him to accept the role of "constitutional monarch" and brought a largely token parliamentary assembly, the Duma, into existence. Russia's entry into World War I under Nicholas's auspices (he personally took over the post of commander in chief of the armed forces in 1915) finally led to the revolution of February 1917.

In 1894, shortly after becoming tsar, Nicholas married the former Princess Alice, of the German princely house of Hesse. Born in 1872, she became known in history by the Russified version of her name, Alexandra Fyodorovna. Although she had been brought up in London, she quickly adapted to Russian ways after becoming tsarina.

Her failure to bear a son, as patriarchal tradition required to continue the Romanov line, led her to seek the aid of mystics. When she at last bore a son, in 1904, he proved to have inherited hemophilia. The claim to miraculous powers to stop the heir-apparent's bleeding was the key to the influence over the tsarina won by Rasputin, the peasant "man of god" from Siberia. Rasputin's sway over Alexandra, who in turn decisively influenced Nicholas, became a notorious scandal as the crisis of Russian society mounted during the war.

At the height of the February revolution Nicholas abdicated in favor of his brother Michael. But instead of accepting a new Romanov, the revolution swept away the monarchy altogether. Nicholas, Alexandra, and their son and four daughters were placed under arrest when their intention to leave the country became known. They were held at the palace of Tsarskoye Selo

*near Petrograd until August 1917, when they were transferred to
Tobolsk. In May 1918 the tsar's family was moved to Yekaterin-
burg (now Sverdlovsk). The most generally accepted account is
that in July the local Soviet authorities, fearing the prisoners
would fall into the hands of the advancing White forces and
become a rallying point for restoration of the monarchy, had
them all executed. Many rumors circulated as to the survival of
some or all of the children.*

This portrait of the Romanovs, printed as Chapter IV of The
History of the Russian Revolution, *Volume I, was written in 1930,
the year after Trotsky was forcibly exiled from the Soviet Union
to Turkey. The two subsequent chapters of that history describe
in detail how the tsar and tsarina met the crisis of war and
revolution. There Trotsky points to the striking parallels between
many of the "personal" features displayed by Nicholas and
Alexandra and those found in the earlier case of Louis XVI and
Marie Antoinette, another famous dynastic pair whose reign
ended in revolution.*

*The translation by Max Eastman of this chapter from
Trotsky's history, which was entitled "The Tsar and the
Tsarina," was first published in 1932.*

This book will concern itself least of all with those unrelated
psychological researches which are now so often substituted for
social and historical analysis. Foremost in our field of vision will
stand the great, moving forces of history, which are super-
personal in character. Monarchy is one of them. But all these
forces operate through people. And monarchy is by its very
principle bound up with the personal. This in itself justifies an
interest in the personality of that monarch whom the process of
social development brought face to face with a revolution. Moreover, we hope to show in what follows, partially at least, just
where in a personality the strictly personal ends—often much
sooner than we think—and how frequently the "distinguishing
traits" of a person are merely individual scratches made by a
higher law of development.

Nicholas II inherited from his ancestors not only a giant
empire, but also a revolution. And they did not bequeath him one
quality which would have made him capable of governing an
empire or even a province or a county. To that historic flood

which was rolling its billows each one closer to the gates of his palace, the last Romanov opposed only a dumb indifference. It seemed as though between his consciousness and his epoch there stood some transparent but absolutely impenetrable medium.

People surrounding the tsar often recalled after the revolution that in the most tragic moments of his reign—at the time of the surrender of Port Arthur and the sinking of the fleet at Tsushima, and ten years later at the time of the retreat of the Russian troops from Galicia, and then two years later during the days preceding his abdication when all those around him were depressed, alarmed, shaken—Nicholas alone preserved his tranquility. He would inquire as usual how many versts he had covered in his journeys about Russia, would recall episodes of hunting expeditions in the past, anecdotes of official meetings, would interest himself generally in the little rubbish of the day's doings, while thunders roared over him and lightnings flashed. "What is this?" asked one of his attendant generals, "a gigantic, almost unbelievable self-restraint, the product of breeding, of a belief in the divine predetermination of events? Or is it inadequate consciousness?" The answer is more than half included in the question. The so-called "breeding" of the tsar, his ability to control himself in the most extraordinary circumstances, cannot be explained by a mere external training; its essence was an inner indifference, a poverty of spiritual forces, a weakness of the impulses of the will. That mask of indifference, which was called breeding in certain circles, was a natural part of Nicholas at birth.

The tsar's diary is the best of all testimony. From day to day and from year to year drags along upon its pages the depressing record of spiritual emptiness. "Walked long and killed two crows. Drank tea by daylight." Promenades on foot, rides in a boat. And then again crows, and again tea. All on the very borderline of physiology. Recollections of church ceremonies are jotted down in the same tone as a drinking party.

In the days preceding the opening of the State Duma, when the whole country was shaking with convulsions, Nicholas wrote: "April 14. Took a walk in a thin shirt and took up paddling again. Had tea in the balcony. Stana dined and took a ride with us. Read." Not a word as to the subject of his reading. Some sentimental English romance? Or a report from the Police Department? "April 15: Accepted Witte's resignation. Marie and Dmitri to dinner. Drove them home to the palace."

On the day of the decision to dissolve the Duma, when the court as well as the liberal circles were going through a paroxysm of fright, the tsar wrote in his diary: "July 7. Friday. Very busy morning. Half hour late to breakfast with the officers. . . . A storm came up and it was very muggy. We walked together. Received Goremykin. Signed a decree dissolving the Duma! Dined with Olga and Petya. Read all evening." An exclamation point after the coming dissolution of the Duma is the highest expression of his emotions. The deputies of the dispersed Duma summoned the people to refuse to pay taxes. A series of military uprisings followed: in Sveaborg, Kronstadt, on ships, in army units. The revolutionary terror against high officials was renewed on an unheard-of scale. The tsar writes: "July 9. Sunday. It has happened! The Duma was closed today. At breakfast after Mass long faces were noticeable among many. . . . The weather was fine. On our walk we met Uncle Misha who came over yesterday from Gatchina. Was quietly busy until dinner and all evening. Went paddling in a canoe." It was in a canoe he went paddling—that is told. But with what he was busy all evening is not indicated. So it was always.

And further in those same fatal days: "July 14. Got dressed and rode a bicycle to the bathing beach and bathed enjoyably in the sea." "July 15. Bathed twice. It was very hot. Only us two at dinner. A storm passed over." "July 19. Bathed in the morning. Received at the farm. Uncle Vladimir and Chagin lunched with us." An insurrection and explosions of dynamite are barely touched upon with a single phrase, "Pretty doings!"—astonishing in its imperturbable indifference, which never rose to conscious cynicism.

"At 9:30 in the morning we rode out to the Caspian regiment . . . walked for a long time. The weather was wonderful. Bathed in the sea. After tea received Lvov and Guchkov." Not a word of the fact that this unexpected reception of the two liberals was brought about by the attempt of Stolypin to include opposition leaders in his ministry. Prince Lvov, the future head of the Provisional Government, said of that reception at the time: "I expected to see the sovereign stricken with grief, but instead of that there came out to meet me a jolly, sprightly fellow in a raspberry-colored shirt." The tsar's outlook was not broader than that of a minor police official—with this difference, that the latter would have a better knowledge of reality and be less burdened with superstitions. The sole paper which Nicholas read for years, and from which he derived his ideas, was a weekly published on state revenue by Prince Meshchersky, a vile, bribed journalist of the reactionary bureaucratic clique, despised even in his own circle. The tsar kept his outlook unchanged through two wars and two revolutions. Between his consciousness and events stood always that impenetrable medium—indifference. Nicholas was called, not without foundation, a fatalist. It is only necessary to add that his fatalism was the exact opposite of an active belief in his "star." Nicholas indeed considered himself unlucky. His fatalism was only a form of passive self-defense against historic evolution, and went hand in hand with an arbitrariness, trivial in psychological motivation, but monstrous in its consequences.

"I wish it and therefore it must be—" writes Count Witte. "That motto appeared in all the activities of this weak ruler, who only through weakness did all the things which characterized his reign—a wholesale shedding of more or less innocent blood, for the most part without aim."

Nicholas is sometimes compared with his half-crazy great-great-grandfather Paul, who was strangled by a camarilla acting in agreement with his own son, Alexander "the Blessed." These two Romanovs were actually alike in their distrust of everybody due to a distrust of themselves, their touchiness as of omnipotent nobodies, their feeling of abnegation, their consciousness, as you might say, of being crowned pariahs. But Paul was incomparably more colorful; there was an element of fancy in his rantings, however irresponsible. In his descendant everything was dim; there was not one sharp trait.

Nicholas was not only unstable, but treacherous. Flatterers called him a charmer, bewitcher, because of his gentle way with the courtiers. But the tsar reserved his special caresses for just those officials whom he had decided to dismiss. Charmed beyond measure at a reception, the minister would go home and find a letter requesting his resignation. That was a kind of revenge on the tsar's part for his own nonentity.

Nicholas recoiled in hostility before everything gifted and significant. He felt at ease only among completely mediocre and brainless people, saintly fakers, holy men, to whom he did not have to look up. He had his *amour propre*—indeed it was rather keen. But it was not active, not possessed of a grain of initiative, enviously defensive. He selected his ministers on a principle of continual deterioration. Men of brain and character he summoned only in extreme situations when there was no other way out, just as we call in a surgeon to save our lives. It was so with Witte, and afterwards with Stolypin. The tsar treated both with ill-concealed hostility. As soon as the crisis had passed, he hastened to part with these counselors who were too tall for him. This selection operated so systematically that the president of the last Duma, Rodzianko, on the 7th of January 1917, with the revolution already knocking at the doors, ventured to say to the tsar: "Your Majesty, there is not one reliable or honest man left around you; all the best men have been removed or have retired. There remain only those of ill repute."

All the efforts of the liberal bourgeoisie to find a common language with the court came to nothing. The tireless and noisy Rodzianko tried to shake up the tsar with his reports, but in vain. The latter gave no answer either to argument or to impudence, but quietly made ready to dissolve the Duma. Grand Duke Dmitry, a former favorite of the tsar, and future accomplice in the murder of Rasputin, complained to his colleague, Prince Yusupov, that the tsar at headquarters was becoming every day more indifferent to everything around him. In Dmitry's opinion the tsar was being fed some kind of dope which had a benumbing action upon his spiritual faculties. "Rumors went round," writes the liberal historian Miliukov, "that this condition of mental and moral apathy was sustained in the tsar by an increased use of alcohol." This was all fancy or exaggeration. The tsar had no need of narcotics: the fatal "dope" was in his blood. Its symptoms merely seemed especially striking on the background of those great events of war and domestic crisis which led up to the revolution. Rasputin, who was a psychologist, said briefly of the tsar that he "lacked insides."

This dim, equable and "well-bred" man was cruel, not with the active cruelty of Ivan the Terrible or of Peter, in the pursuit of historic aims—what had Nicholas II in common with them?—but with the cowardly cruelty of the late born, frightened at his own doom. At the very dawn of his reign Nicholas praised the Phanagoritsy regiment as "fine fellows" for shooting down workers. He always "read with satisfaction" how they flogged with whips the bob-haired girl-students, or cracked the heads of defenseless people during Jewish pogroms. This crowned black sheep gravitated with all his soul to the very dregs of society, the Black Hundred hooligans. He not only paid them generously from the state treasury, but loved to chat with them about their exploits, and would pardon them when they accidentally got mixed up in the murder of an opposition deputy. Witte, who stood at the head of the government during the putting down of the first revolution, has written in his memoirs: "When news of the useless cruel antics of the chiefs of these detachments reached the sovereign, they met with his approval, or in any case his defense." In answer to the demand of the governor-general of the Baltic States that he stop a certain lieutenant-captain, Richter, who was "executing on his own authority and without trial nonresistant persons," the tsar wrote on the report: "Ah, what a fine fellow!" Such encouragements are innumerable. This "charmer," without will, without aim, without imagination, was more awful than all the tyrants of ancient and modern history.

The tsar was mightily under the influence of the tsarina, an influence which increased with the years and the difficulties. Together they constituted a kind of a unit—and that combination shows already to what an extent the personal, under pressure of circumstances, is supplemented by the group. But first we must speak of the tsarina herself.

Maurice Paléologue, the French ambassador at Petrograd during the war, a refined psychologist for French academicians and concierges, offers a meticulously licked portrait of the last tsarina: "Moral restlessness, a chronic sadness, infinite longing, intermittent ups and downs of strength, anguishing thoughts of the invisible other world, superstitions—are not all these traits, so clearly apparent in the personality of the empress, the character-istic traits of the Russian people?" Strange as it may seem, there is in this saccharine lie just a grain of truth. The Russian satirist Saltykov, with some justification, called the ministers and governors from among the Baltic barons "Germans with a Russian soul." It is indubitable that aliens, in no way connected with the people, developed the most pure culture of the "genuine Russian" administrator.

But why did the people repay with such open hatred a tsarina who, in the words of Paléologue, had so completely assimilated their soul? The answer is simple. In order to justify her new situation, this German woman adopted with a kind of cold fury all the traditions and nuances of Russian medievalism, the most meager and crude of all medievalisms, in that very period when the people were making mighty efforts to free themselves from it. This Hessian princess was literally possessed by the demon of autocracy. Having risen from her rural corner to the heights of Byzantine despotism, she would not for anything take a step down. In the orthodox religion she found a mysticism and a magic adapted to her new lot. She believed the more inflexibly in her vocation, the more naked became the foulness of the old regime. With a strong character and a gift for dry and hard exaltations, the tsarina supplemented the weak-willed tsar, ruling over him.

On March 17, 1916, a year before the revolution, when the tortured country was already writhing in the grip of defeat and ruin, the tsarina wrote to her husband at military headquarters: "You must not give indulgences, a responsible ministry, etc. . . . or anything *they* want. This must be your war and your peace, and the honor yours and our fatherland's, and not by any means the Duma's. They have not the right to say a single word in these matters." This was at any rate a thoroughgoing program. And it was in just this way that she always had the whip hand over the continually vacillating tsar.

After Nicholas's departure to the army in the capacity of fictitious commander in chief, the tsarina began openly to take charge of internal affairs. The ministers came to her with reports as to a regent. She entered into a conspiracy with a small camarilla against the Duma, against the ministers, against the staff-generals, against the whole world—to some extent indeed against the tsar. On December 6, 1916, the tsarina wrote to the tsar: ". . . Once you have said that you want to keep Protopopov, how does he [Premier Trepov] go against you? Bring down your fist on the table. Don't yield. Be the boss. Obey your firm little wife and our Friend. Believe in us." Again three days later: "You know you are right. Carry your head high. Command Trepov to work with him. . . . Strike your fist on the table." Those phrases sound as though they were made up, but they are taken from authentic letters. Besides, you cannot make up things like that.

On December 13 the tsarina suggests to the tsar: "Anything but this responsible ministry about which everybody has gone crazy. Everything is getting quiet and better, but people want to feel your hand. How long they have been saying to me, for whole years, the same thing: 'Russia loves to feel the whip.' That is *their* nature!" This orthodox Hessian, with a Windsor upbringing and a Byzantine crown on her head, not only "incarnates" the Russian soul, but also organically despises it. *Their* nature demands the whip—writes the Russian tsarina to the Russian tsar about the Russian people, just two months and a half before the monarchy tips over into the abyss.

In contrast to her force of character, the intellectual force of the tsarina is not higher, but rather lower than her husband's. Even more than he, she craves the society of simpletons. The close and long-lasting friendship of the tsar and tsarina with their lady-in-waiting Vyrubova gives a measure of the spiritual stature of this autocratic pair. Vyrubova has described herself as a fool, and this is not modesty. Witte, to whom one cannot deny an accurate eye, characterized her as "a most commonplace, stupid, Petersburg young lady, homely as a bubble in the biscuit dough." In the society of this person, with whom elderly officials, ambassadors, and financiers obsequiously flirted, and who had just enough brains not to forget about her own pockets, the tsar and tsarina would pass many hours, consulting her about affairs, corresponding with her and about her. She was more influential than the State Duma, and even than the ministry.

But Vyrubova herself was only an instrument of "The Friend," whose authority superseded all three. ". . . This is my *private* opinion," writes the tsarina to the tsar, "I will find out what our Friend thinks." The opinion of the "Friend" is not private, it decides. ". . . I am firm," insists the tsarina a few weeks later, "but listen to me, i.e., *this means* our Friend, and trust us in everything. . . . I suffer for you as for a gentle soft-hearted child—who needs guidance, but listens to bad counselors, while a man sent by God is telling him what he should do."

The Friend sent by God was Grigory Rasputin.

". . . The prayers and the help of our Friend—then all will be well."

"If we did not have Him, all would have been over long ago. I am absolutely convinced of that."

Throughout the whole reign of Nicholas and Alexandra, soothsayers and hysterics were imported for the court not only from all over Russia, but from other countries. Special official purveyors arose, who would gather around the momentary oracle, forming a powerful Upper Chamber attached to the monarch. There was no lack of bigoted old women with the title of countess, nor functionaries weary of doing nothing, nor of financiers who had entire ministries in their hire. With a jealous eye on the unchartered competition of mesmerists and sorcerers, the high priesthood of the Orthodox Church would hasten to pry their way into the holy of holies of the intrigue. Witte called this ruling circle, against which he himself twice stubbed his toe, "the leprous court camarilla."

The more isolated the dynasty became, and the more unsheltered the autocrat felt, the more he needed some help from the other world. Certain savages, in order to bring good weather, wave in the air a shingle on a string. The tsar and tsarina used shingles for the greatest variety of purposes. In the tsar's train there was a whole chapel full of large and small images, and all sorts of fetishes, which were brought to bear, first against the Japanese, then against the German artillery.

The level of the court circle really had not changed much from generation to generation. Under Alexander II, called the "Liberator," the grand dukes had sincerely believed in house spirits and witches. Under Alexander III it was no better, only quieter. The "leprous camarilla" had existed always, changing only its personnel and its method. Nicholas II did not create, but inherited from his ancestors, this court atmosphere of savage medievalism. But the country during these same decades had been changing, its problems growing more complex, its culture rising to a higher level. The court circle was thus left far behind.

Although the monarchy did under compulsion make concessions to the new forces, nevertheless inwardly it completely failed to become modernized. On the contrary it withdrew into itself. Its spirit of medievalism thickened under the pressure of hostility and fear, until it acquired the character of a disgusting nightmare overhanging the country.

Towards November 1905—that is, at the most critical moment of the first revolution—the tsar writes in his diary: "We got acquainted with a man of God, Grigory, from the Tobolsk province." That was Rasputin—a Siberian peasant with a bald scar on his head, the result of a beating for horse-stealing. Put forward at an appropriate moment, this "Man of God" soon found official helpers—or rather they found him—and thus was formed a new ruling circle which got a firm hold of the tsarina, and through her of the tsar.

From the winter of 1913-14 it was openly said in Petersburg society that all high appointments, posts, and contracts depended upon the Rasputin clique. The "Elder" himself gradually turned into a state institution. He was carefully guarded, and no less carefully sought after, by the competing ministers. Spies of the Police Department kept a diary of his life by hours, and did not fail to report how on a visit to his home village of Pokrovsky he got into a drunken and bloody fight with his own father on the

street. On the same day that this happened—September 9, 1915—
Rasputin sent two friendly telegrams, one to Tsarskoye Selo to
the tsarina, the other to headquarters to the tsar. In epic
language the police spies registered from day to day the revels of
the Friend. "He returned today 5 o'clock in the morning
completely drunk." "On the night of the 25-26th the actress V.
spent the night with Rasputin." "He arrived with Princess D. (the
wife of a gentleman of the bedchamber of the tsar's court) at the
Hotel Astoria." And right beside this: "Came home from
Tsarskoye Selo about 11 o'clock in the evening." "Rasputin came
home with Princess Sh— very drunk and together they went out
immediately." In the morning or evening of the following day a
trip to Tsarskoe Selo. To a sympathetic question from the spy as
to why the Elder was thoughtful, the answer came: "Can't decide
whether to convoke the Duma or not." And then again: "He came
home at 5 in the morning pretty drunk." Thus for months and
years the melody was played on three keys: "pretty drunk," "very
drunk," and "completely drunk." These communications of state
importance were brought together and countersigned by the
general of gendarmes, Gorbachev. The bloom of Rasputin's
influence lasted six years, the last years of the monarchy. "His
life in Petrograd," says Prince Yusupov, who participated to some
extent in that life, and afterward killed Rasputin, "became a
continual revel, the drunken debauch of a galley slave who had
come into an unexpected fortune." "I had at my disposition,"
wrote the president of the Duma, Rodzianko, "a whole mass of
letters from mothers whose daughters had been dishonored by
this insolent rake." Nevertheless the Petrograd metropolitan,
Pitirim, owed his position to Rasputin, as did the almost illiterate
Archbishop Varnava. The procuror of the holy synod, Sabler, was
long sustained by Rasputin; and Premier Kokovtsev was removed
at his wish, having refused to receive the "Elder." Rasputin
appointed Stürmer president of the council of ministers, Protopopov minister of the interior, the new procuror of the synod, Raev,
and many others. The ambassador of the French Republic,
Paléologue, sought an interview with Rasputin, embraced him
and cried, *"Voilá, un véritable illuminé!"* hoping in this way to
win the heart of the tsarina to the cause of France. The Jew
Simanovich, financial agent of the "Elder," himself under the eye
of the secret police as a night club gambler and usurer—
introduced into the Ministry of Justice through Rasputin the
completely dishonest creature Dobrovolsky.

"Keep by you the little list," writes the tsarina to the tsar, in regard to new appointments. "Our friend has asked that you talk all this over with Protopopov." Two days later: "Our friend says that Stürmer may remain a few days longer as President of the Council of Ministers." And again: "Protopopov venerates our friend and will be blessed."

On one of those days when the police spies were counting up the number of bottles and women, the tsarina grieved in a letter to the tsar: "They accuse Rasputin of kissing women, etc. Read the apostles; they kissed everybody as a form of greeting." This reference to the apostles would hardly convince the police spies. In another letter the tsarina goes still farther. "During vespers I thought so much about our friend," she writes, "how the Scribes and Pharisees are persecuting Christ pretending that they are so perfect . . . yes, in truth no man is a prophet in his own country."

The comparison of Rasputin and Christ was customary in that circle, and by no means accidental. The alarm of the royal couple before the menacing forces of history was too sharp to be satisfied with an impersonal God and the futile shadow of a Biblical Christ. They needed a second coming of "the Son of Man." In Rasputin the rejected and agonizing monarchy found a Christ in its own image.

"If there had been no Rasputin," said Senator Tagantsev, a man of the old regime, "it would have been necessary to invent one." There is a good deal more in these words than their author imagined. If by the word *hooliganism* we understand the extreme expression of those antisocial parasite elements at the bottom of society, we may define Rasputinism as a crowned hooliganism at its very top.

KOTE TSINTSADZE

Alipi (Kote) M. Tsintsadze, born in Georgia in 1887, joined the Bolsheviks in 1903, doing party work in several Transcaucasian cities when he was not in tsarist prisons or exile. In the period of the 1905 revolution he organized, according to his own statement, "a fighting detachment of Bolsheviks for the purpose of robbing state treasuries." His closest co-worker in this activity was the legendary Kamo.

During the civil war he was chairman of first the Georgian and then the All-Caucasus Cheka, at a time when only the most incorruptible people were chosen for such posts. He was also a member of the Georgian Communist Party's Central Committee and the Georgian Soviet's Central Executive Committee, and one of the Communists in those committees who resisted Stalin's trampling on the national rights of the Georgian republic in 1922; in that dispute Lenin was on Tsintsadze's side and against Stalin's. Tsintsadze became a Left Oppositionist in 1923, was expelled from the Communist Party in 1927, was sent into exile despite his bad health in 1928, and died in 1930 an unrepentant enemy of Stalinism. Tsintsadze's Memoirs *were printed in a Georgian periodical in 1923-24 but have not been translated into English.*

The translation of Trotsky's article, dated January 7, 1931, was first published, under the title "At the Fresh Grave of Kote Tsintsadze," in The Militant, *February 15, 1931. It has been revised here by George Saunders.*

It took quite exceptional conditions—tsarism, the underground, prison and Siberian exile, the long years of struggle against Menshevism, and especially, the experience of three revolutions—

93

to produce fighters like Kote Tsintsadze. His life was entirely bound up with the history of the revolutionary movement for more than a quarter of a century. He took part in all the stages of the proletarian insurgency—from the first propaganda circles to the barricades and seizure of power. For many years he carried on the painstaking work of the underground organizer, in which the revolutionists constantly tied threads together and the police constantly untied them. Later he stood at the head of the Transcaucasian Cheka, that is, at the very center of power, during the most heroic period of the proletarian dictatorship.

When the reaction against October had changed the composition and the character of the party apparatus and its policies, Kote Tsintsadze was one of the first to begin a struggle against these new tendencies hostile to the spirit of Bolshevism. The first conflict occurred during Lenin's illness. Stalin and Ordzhonikidze, with the help of Dzerzhinsky, had carried out their coup in Georgia, replacing the core of Old Bolsheviks with careerist functionaries of the type of Eliava, Orakhelashvili, and the like. It was precisely on this issue that Lenin prepared to launch an implacable battle against the Stalin faction and the apparatus at the Twelfth Congress of the party. On March 6, 1923, Lenin wrote to the Georgian group of Old Bolsheviks, of which Kote Tsintsadze was one of the founders: "I am following your case with all my heart. I am indignant over Ordzhonikidze's rudeness and the connivance of Stalin and Dzerzhinsky. I am preparing for you notes and a speech" [*Collected Works,* volume 45].

The subsequent course of events is sufficiently well known. The Stalin faction crushed the Lenin faction in the Caucasus. This was the initial victory for reaction in the party and opened up the second chapter of the revolution.

Tsintsadze, suffering from tuberculosis, bearing the weight of decades of revolutionary work, persecuted by the apparatus at every step, did not desert his post of struggle for a moment. In 1928 he was deported to Bakhchisaray, where the wind and dust did their disastrous work on the remnants of his lungs. Later he was transferred to Alushta, where the chill and rainy winter completed the destruction.

Some friends tried to get Kote admitted to the Gulripshi Sanatorium at Sukhum, where Tsintsadze had succeeded in saving his life several times before during especially acute sieges of his illness. Of course, Ordzhonikidze "promised"; Ordzhonikidze "promises" a great deal to everyone. But the cowardliness of his character—rudeness does not exclude cowardice—always made him a blind instrument in the hands of Stalin. While Tsintsadze was literally struggling against death, Stalin fought all attempts to save the old militant. Send him to Gulripshi on the coast of the Black Sea? And if he recovers? Connections might be established between Batum and Constantinople. No, impossible!

With the death of Tsintsadze, one of the most attractive figures of early Bolshevism has disappeared. This fighter, who more than once risked his life and knew very well how to chastise the enemy, was a man of exceptional mildness in his personal relations. A good-natured sarcasm and a sly sense of humor were combined in this tempered terrorist with a gentleness one might almost call feminine.

The serious illness from which he was not free for a moment could neither break his moral resistance nor even succeed in overcoming his good spirits and gently attentive attitude toward people.

Kote was not a theoretician. But his clear thinking, his revolutionary passion, and his immense political experience—the living experience of three revolutions—armed him better, more seriously and firmly, than does the doctrine formally digested by those of less fortitude and perseverance. Just as Shakespeare's Lear was "every inch a king," Tsintsadze was every inch a revolutionary. His character revealed itself perhaps even more strikingly during the last eight years—years of uninterrupted struggle against the advent and entrenchment of the unprincipled bureaucracy.

Tsintsadze instinctively fought against anything resembling treachery, capitulation, or disloyalty. He understood the significance of the bloc with Zinoviev and Kamenev. But morally he could not tolerate this group. His letters testify to the full force of his revulsion—there is no other word for it—against those Oppositionists who, in their eagerness to insure their formal membership in the party, betray it by renouncing their ideas.

Number 11 of the *Biulleten Oppozitsii* published a letter from Tsintsadze to Okudzhava. It is an excellent document—of tenacity, clarity of thought, and conviction. Tsintsadze, as we said, was not a theoretician, and he willingly let others formulate the tasks of the revolution, the party, and the Opposition. But any time he detected a false note, he took pen in hand, and no "authority" could prevent him from expressing his suspicions and from making his replies. His letter written on May 2 last year and published in number 12-13 of the *Biulleten* testifies best to this. This practical man and organizer safeguarded the purity of doctrine more reliably and attentively than do many theoreticians.

We often encounter the following phrases in Kote's letters: "a bad 'institution,' these waverings"; "woe to the people who can't wait"; or, "in solitude weak people easily become subject to all kinds of contagion." Tsintsadze's unshakable courage buoyed up his dwindling physical energy. He even viewed his illness as a revolutionary duel. In one of his letters several months before he died he wrote that in his battle against death he was pursuing the question: "Who will conquer?" "In the meantime, the advantage remains on my side," he added, with the optimism that never abandoned him.

In the summer of 1928, referring indirectly to himself and his illness, Kote wrote to me from Bakhchisaray: ". . . for many, many of our comrades and friends the thankless fate lies in store of ending their lives somewhere in prison or deportation. Yet in the final analysis this will be an enrichment of revolutionary history, from which a new generation will learn. The proletarian youth, when they come to know about the struggle of the Bolshevik Opposition against the opportunist wing of the party, will understand on whose side was the truth."

Tsintsadze could write these simple yet superb lines only in an intimate letter to a friend. Now that he is no longer alive, these lines may and must be published. They summarize the life and morality of a revolutionist of the highest caliber. They must be made public precisely so that the youth can learn not only from theoretical formulas but also from this personal example of revolutionary tenacity.

The Communist parties in the West have not yet brought up fighters of Tsintsadze's type. This is their besetting weakness, determined by historical reasons but nonetheless a weakness. The Left Opposition in the Western countries is not an exception in this respect and it must well take note of it.

Especially for the Opposition youth, the example of Tsintsadze can and should serve as a lesson. Tsintsadze was the living negation and condemnation of any kind of political careerism, that is, the inclination to sacrifice principles, ideas, and tasks of the cause for personal ends. This does not in the least rule out justified revolutionary ambition. No, political ambition plays a very important part in the struggle. But the revolutionary begins where personal ambition is fully and wholly subordinated to the service of a great idea, voluntarily submitting to and merging with it. Flirtation with ideas, dilettante dabbling with revolutionary formulations, changing one's views out of personal career considerations—these things Tsintsadze pitilessly condemned through his life and his death. His was the ambition of unshakable revolutionary loyalty. This is what the proletarian youth should learn from him.

CHAROLAMBOS

Little more than Trotsky writes in this essay is known about Charolambos the fisherman, who worked as Trotsky's guide when he went fishing in the waters off Prinkipo, the island where Trotsky lived during most of his exile in Turkey (1929-33). Neither his full name nor his age is known, although Jean van Heijenoort, who became a secretary of Trotsky in 1932, recalls that Charolambos was in his twenties at that time, and that he was a citizen of Turkey and a member of its Greek national minority.

This article was written on July 15, 1933, shortly after Trotsky learned that the French government had finally revoked a World War I decree barring him from France "forever," and a few days before he and Natalia Sedova sailed from Turkey to France.

The translation by Max Eastman was first published, under the title "Farewell to Prinkipo (Pages from a Diary)," in The Modern Monthly, *March 1934.*

So! Distinct and incontestable French visas have been affixed to our passports. In two days we depart from Turkey. When I arrived here with my wife and son—four and a half years ago—the light of "prosperity" was shining brightly in America. Today, those times seem prehistoric, almost legendary.

Prinkipo is an island of peace and forgetfulness. The life of the world reaches here after long delays and hushed down. But the crisis found its way here too. From year to year fewer people come from Istanbul, and those who do come have less and less money. Of what use is the superabundance of fish when there is no demand for it?

Prinkipo is a fine place to work with a pen, particularly during autumn and winter when the island becomes completely deserted and woodcocks appear in the park. Not only are there no theaters here, but no movies. Automobiles are forbidden. Are there many such places in the world? In our house we have no telephone. The braying of the donkey acts soothingly upon the nerves. One cannot forget for a minute that Prinkipo is an island, for the sea is under the window, and there is no hiding from the sea at any point on the island. Ten meters away from the stone fence we catch fish, at fifty meters—lobsters. For weeks at a time the sea is as calm as a lake.

But we are in close connection with the world outside, for we get mail. That is the climax of the day. The post brings fresh newspapers, new books, letters from friends, and letters from foes. This pile of printed and written paper holds much that is unexpected, especially from America. I find it difficult to believe that so many people exist in this world who are urgently concerned with the salvation of my soul. In the course of these years I have received such a quantity of religious literature as would suffice for the salvation not of a single person, but of a brigade of confirmed sinners. All the pertinent places in the devout books are considerately scored on the margins. However, no fewer people are interested in my soul's perdition, and they express their corresponding wishes with a laudable frankness, even though anonymously. Graphologists demand that I forward my handwriting to have my character analyzed. Astrologists request to be told the day and hour of my birth to draw my horoscope. Autograph collectors wheedle for my signature to add to those of two American presidents, three heavyweight champions, Albert Einstein, Colonel Lindbergh, and of course Charlie Chaplin. Such letters arrive almost exclusively from America. Gradually I have learned to guess from the envelope whether the request will be for a cane toward the home museum, or whether a desire will be expressed to recruit me as a Methodist preacher, or a prophecy forthcoming of eternal tortures on one of the vacant spits in hell. As the crisis sharpened, the proportion of these letters swung decidely in favor of the infernal regions.

The post brings much that is unexpected. A few days ago it brought the French visa. The skeptics—and there were such in our house too—were put to shame. We are leaving Prinkipo. Our house is already almost empty; wooden boxes stand below, and young hands are busy hammering nails. In our old and neglected villa, the floors this spring were decorated with paint of a composition so mysterious that tables, chairs, and even feet, stick lightly to the floor even now, four months later. It is strange, but it seems to me that during these years my feet have grown a little into the soil of Prinkipo as well.

I have had few ties, really, with the island itself, the circumference of which can be covered on foot in two hours. But for that reason I made more ties with the waters that wash it. During these fifty-three months, with the help of my invaluable tutor, I have become very intimate with the Sea of Marmora. His name is Charolambos, and his universe is described by a radius of approximately four kilometers around Prinkipo. But Charolambos knows his universe. To an undiscerning eye the sea seems identical throughout its whole extent. Yet the bottom of the sea enfolds an immeasurable variety of physical organisms, minerals, flora and fauna. Charolambos, alas, is illiterate, but he reads with artistry the beautiful book of the Sea of Marmora. His father and grandfather and great-grandfather, and the grandfather of his great-grandfather, were fishermen. His father still fishes even now. The old man's specialty is lobsters. In summer he catches them not with nets as other fishermen do—as his son and I do—but he hunts them. It is the most enthralling spectacle. The old man discerns the lobster's hiding place under a rock through the water at a depth of five or eight meters and more. With a very long pole tipped with iron he pushes the rock over and the exposed lobster flees. The old man gives an order to the oarsman, pursues the lobster, and with a second long pole to which is attached a small reticular bag upon a square frame, he overhauls the lobster, covers it, and pulls it out. When the sea is disturbed by a ripple, the old man sprinkles oil upon the water with his fingers and peers through the fatty mirror. In a good day he catches thirty, forty, and more lobsters. But everyone has become impoverished during these years, and the demand for lobsters is as low as for Ford's automobiles.

Fishing with nets, being professional, is considered unworthy of a free artist. A superficial and false attitude! Fishing with a net is a high art. One must know the time and place for each kind of fish. One must know how to spread the net in a semicircle, sometimes a circle, even in a spiral, depending upon the configuration of the bottom and a dozen other conditions. One must lower the net noiselessly into the water, unrolling it rapidly from a moving boat. And finally—as the last act—the fish must be driven into the net. Today this is done as it was done ten thousand and more years ago, by means of stones cast from the boat. By this barrage the fish are first driven into the circle and then into the net itself. A different quantity of stone is required for this at different times of the year and under different conditions of sea. From time to time the supply must be replenished on the shore. But in the boat there are two permanent stones on long strings. One must know how to throw them with force and immediately retrieve them from the water. The stone should fall close to the net. But woe to the fisher if it plunks into the net itself and becomes entangled! Then Charolambos chastises one with an annihilating look—and justly. Out of politeness and a sense of social discipline, Charolambos admits that I am generally not bad at casting stones. But I need only compare my work with his, and pride departs immediately. Charolambos sees the net after it is already invisible to me, and he knows where it is when it is no longer visible to him either. He feels it not only in front of him, but behind his back. His extremities are always in contact with that net through some mysterious fluids. Pulling the net up is stiff work, and Charolambos wears a wide woolen scarf tightly wound around his belly, even during the hot July days. One must row without either overpassing or lagging behind the curve of the net, and that is my job. I was not quick at learning to note the almost imperceptible motions of the hand by means of which the master directs his assistant.

Often after casting fifteen kilos of stone into the water, Charolambos pulls out the net with a lonely little fish the size of my thumb. Sometimes the entire net lives and quivers with captured fish. How explain this difference? "Deniz," replies Charolambos, shrugging his shoulders. Deniz means "sea," and this word resounds like "destiny."

Charolambos and I converse in a new language which has grown up slowly out of Turkish, Greek, Russian, and French words—all violently distorted and seldom used according to their honest connotation. We construct phrases after the manner of two- or three-year-old children. However, I firmly call out in Turkish the names of the more common operations. Chance observers have concluded from this that I command the Turkish language freely, and the papers have even announced that I translate American authors into Turkish—a slight exaggeration!

Sometimes it happens that no sooner have we got the nets lowered than we hear a sudden splash and a snort behind our backs. "Dolphin!" yells Charolambos in alarm. Danger! The dolphin bides his time until the fishermen drive the fish into the net with stones, and then he tears them out one by one, along with big chunks of the net itself by way of seasoning. "Shoot, M'sieu!" yells Charolambos. And I shoot from a revolver. A young dolphin will be scared by this and flee. But the old pirates cherish a complete contempt for that automatic popgun. Merely out of politeness they swim a little way off after the shot, and give a snort and bide their time. More than once were we compelled to pull up our empty net in a hurry and change the fishing ground.

The dolphin is not the only enemy. The little black gardener from the north shore is very expert at cleaning out other people's nets if they are left overnight without surveillance. Toward evening, he pulls out in his skiff as if to fish, but in reality to find a point of vantage whence he can well observe all those who are bringing out their nets for the night. There are people who steal nets (Charolambos and I have lost not a few during these years), but this is risky and bothersome. The net must be altered lest it be recognized; it must be tended, patched, and painted from time to time with pitch. The little gardener leaves all these wearisome cares to the owners of the nets; he contents himself with the fish and the lobsters. Charolambos and he cross glances in passing, sharper than a knife. We resort to subterfuge; pulling away some distance, we go through the pantomime of casting a net, and then, rounding the little island full of rabbits, we secretly lower our net into the water. In about one case out of three we succeed in fooling the enemy.

The chief fish here are barbonnel and rouget. The chief fisher of rouget is the old man Kochu. He knows his fish, and sometimes it seems as though the fish know him. When rouget abounds, Kochu deals a quick strategic blow to his possible rivals. Going out earlier than anybody else, he works the watery field not from one end to the other, but after the fashion of a chessboard, as a knight jumps, or in some even more fancy figure. No one knows except Kochu where the net has already passed and where it has not. Having blocked off in this manner a large section of the sea, Kochu then fills in at leisure the unutilized squares. A great art! Kochu has succeeded in learning the sea because Kochu is old. But even Kochu's father worked until last year with another old fellow, a former barber. In a decrepit skiff they laid nets for lobsters, and they themselves, corroded to the bones with sea salt, resembled two aged lobsters. Both of them are now resting in the

Prinkipo cemetery, which holds more people than the little village.

However, it should not be inferred that we restricted ourselves to nets. No, we used all the methods of fishing that promised booty. With hook and line we caught big fish weighing up to ten kilos. While I would be pulling up some invisible monster, now following me obediently and now frantically balking, Charolambos would watch me with unmoving eyes, eyes without a shadow of respect left in them. Not without reason did he fear that I would lose the precious prey. . . . At every awkward move of mine, he would growl savagely and menacingly. And when the fish finally became visible in the water, so beautiful in its transparency, Charolambos would whisper in admonition, "Buyuk, M'sieu" (a big one). To which I would reply, panting, "Buyuk, Charolambos." At the boatside we catch up the prey in a small net. And now the beautiful monster, played over by all the colors of the rainbow, shakes the boat with its last blows of resistance and despair. In our joy, we eat an orange apiece, and in a language comprehensible to no one but us, and which we ourselves only half understand, share the sensations of the adventure.

This morning the fishing was poor. The season is over, the fish have gone to deep water. Toward the end of August they will return, but then Charolambos will be fishing without me. He is now downstairs nailing up cases of books, of the utility of which he is obviously not entirely convinced. Through the open window can be seen the small steamer which brings the functionaries from Istanbul to their summer homes. Empty shelves yawn in the library. Only in the upper corner over the arch of the window does the old life go on as usual. Swallows have built a nest there, and directly above the British "blue books" have hatched a brood which has no interest in French visas.

For better or worse, the chapter called "Prinkipo" is ended.

ANATOLI LUNACHARSKY

*Anatoli V. Lunacharsky was born in Russia in 1875 and joined
a Marxist study group in Kiev as a high school student in 1892.
He became a Social Democrat in 1898 after emigration to Western
Europe, and joined the Bolsheviks in 1904. He left them in 1908
because of philosophical and tactical differences. He rejoined the
Bolsheviks in 1917, played a prominent role as agitator and
propagandist in the October revolution, and became the People's
Commissar of Education in the first Soviet government. He held
that post until 1929, and died in 1933 on his way to Spain, to
which he had been appointed Soviet ambassador.*

*This "exceptionally gifted personality," as Lenin called him,
"wrote about fifteen hundred articles on various questions of
classical and contemporary literature, painting, music and
culture," according to Soviet editor A. Lebedev. He also "wrote
series of lectures on the history of Russian and West European
literature, works on literary and aesthetical problems, papers on
the most important problems of art and politics, brilliant essays
dedicated to almost every celebrated artist the world has known."
His writings were not in official favor after his death and went
out of print until after Stalin died, when interest was revived and
republication began. A representative collection in English
compiled by Lebedev and entitled* On Literature and Art *was
published in Moscow in 1965. His 1923 book was published in
English under the title* Revolutionary Silhouettes *in 1967.*

*No biography exists in English, but an informative book about
the early years of the Soviet department of education he headed,*
The Commissariat of Enlightenment *by Sheila Fitzpatrick, was
published in 1970.*

*Trotsky's obituary was written in France and dated January 1,
1934. The translation from the Russian by George C. Myland was
first published in* Writings of Leon Trotsky (1933-34) *(1972).*

For the last decade, political events have swept us apart and placed us in different camps, so that I have been able to keep up with the fortunes of Lunacharsky only through the newspapers. But there were years when we were bound by close political ties and when our personal relations, while not exceptionally intimate, were of a very friendly character.

Lunacharsky was four or five years younger than Lenin and about as many years older than I. Though in itself not very great, this age difference nevertheless meant that we belonged to different revolutionary generations. When he entered political life as a high school student in Kiev, Lunacharsky could still be influenced by the last rumblings of the terrorist struggle of the Narodnaya Volya [People's Will] against tsarism. For my closer contemporaries, the struggle of the Narodnaya Volya was already only a legend.

From his student years on, Lunacharsky astonished people with his many-sided talent. He wrote verses, of course; he easily grasped philosophical ideas, performed excellently at student cultural soirees, was an unusually good orator, and showed no lack of colors on his literary palette. As a twenty-year-old youth he was able to deliver lectures on Nietzsche, argue about the categorical imperative, defend Marx's theory of value, and compare Sophocles and Shakespeare. His exceptional gifts were organically combined with the wasteful dilettantism of the aristocratic intelligentsia, which at one time had found its highest journalistic expression in the person of Alexander Herzen.

Lunacharsky was connected with the revolution and socialism for a period of forty years, i.e., for his whole conscious life. He passed through prisons, exile, and emigration, remaining all the while an unshakable Marxist. During these long years, thousands upon thousands of his former comrades-in-arms from the same circles of the aristocratic and bourgeois intelligentsia migrated into the camp of Ukrainian nationalism, bourgeois liberalism, or monarchist reaction. For Lunacharsky, the ideas of the revolution were not a youthful enthusiasm: they entered into his nerves and blood vessels. This is the first thing that must be said over his fresh grave.

However, it would be incorrect to represent Lunacharsky as a man of firm will and stern temper, as a fighter who was never distracted. No. His steadfastness was very—it seemed to many of us, excessively—elastic. Dilettantism possessed not only his intellect but also his character. As an orator and writer, he readily strayed from the subject. A literary image not infrequently drew him far from the development of his basic thought. As a politician, too, his glance wandered right and left. Lunacharsky was too receptive to each and every philosophical and political novelty to fail to be attracted by it and to play with it.

Undoubtedly, this dilettantish generosity of his nature weakened his inner critical sense. His speeches were most frequently improvisations and, as always in such circumstances, were free of neither prolixity nor banality. He wrote or dictated with extraordinary freedom and barely corrected his manuscripts. His intellectual concentration, his ability to censor himself, were not sufficient for him to create those works of more lasting and indisputable value for which his talent and knowledge were fully adequate.

But however Lunacharsky digressed, he returned every time to his basic thought, not only in particular articles and speeches but also in all of his political activity. His various and sometimes unexpected fluctuations had a limited scope; they never went outside the boundaries of the revolution and socialism.

As early as 1904, about a year after the split of the Russian Social Democracy into the Bolshevik and Menshevik factions, Lunacharsky, who had arrived in the emigre movement directly from penal exile within Russia, adhered to the Bolsheviks. Lenin, who just before that had broken with his teachers (Plekhanov, Axelrod, Zasulich) and his closest co-thinkers (Martov, Potresov) was very much alone in those days. He was painfully in need of a collaborator to do work in the field, something that Lenin did not like to waste his powers on—nor was it in him to do so. Lunacharsky arrived as a true gift of fate. He had hardly stepped down from the railway carriage before he threw himself into the noisy life of the Russian emigration in Switzerland, France, and all of Europe: he gave lectures, debated, polemicized in the press, led study circles, made jokes and witticisms, sang off-key, and captivated young and old with his many-sided education and his sweet reasonableness in personal relations.

A compliant softness was a not unimportant feature in this man's character. He was a stranger to petty vanity, but also to a matter of much greater concern: defending what he himself recognized as the truth, from friend as well as enemy. Throughout his life, Lunacharsky would fall under the influence of people who were not infrequently less knowledgeable and talented than he but of a firmer cast of mind. He came to Bolshevism through his older friend Bogdanov. The young scholar—scientist, doctor, philosopher, economist—Bogdanov (whose real name was Malinovsky) assured Lenin ahead of time that his younger friend Lunacharsky, on arriving abroad, would without fail follow his example and adhere to the Bolsheviks. The prediction was fully confirmed. But that same Bogdanov, after the defeat of the 1905 revolution, drew Lunacharsky away from the Bolsheviks to a small group of superintransigents that combined a sectarian "refusal to acknowledge" the victorious counterrevolution with abstract preaching of a "proletarian culture" cooked up by laboratory methods.

In the dark years of reaction (1908-12), when there was an epidemic collapse into mysticism on the part of wide circles of the intelligentsia, Lunacharsky, together with Gorky, to whom he was bound by a close friendship, paid tribute to the mystical searchings. While not breaking with Marxism, he began to represent the socialist ideal as a new form of religion and seriously occupied himself with the search for a new ritual. The sarcastic Plekhanov called him "the blessed Anatole." The nickname stuck for a long time. Lenin no less unmercifully flogged his former and future collaborator. Although it gradually softened, the enmity lasted until 1917, when Lunacharsky, not without resistance and not without strong external pressure, this time from me, again adhered to the Bolsheviks. He entered a period of tireless agitational work, which became the high point of his political life. At this time, too, there was no lack of impressionistic leaps. Thus, he almost broke with the party in the most critical moment, in November 1917, when a rumor arrived from Moscow that the Bolshevik artillery had destroyed St. Basil's Church. A connoisseur and admirer of art could not forgive such vandalism! Fortunately, Lunacharsky, as we know, was amiable and agreeable; and besides, St. Basil's Church did not suffer at all in the days of the Moscow insurrection.

In his position of People's Commissar of Education, Lunacharsky was irreplaceable in relations with the old university circles, and pedagogical circles in general, who were convinced that they could expect complete liquidation of science and art from the "ignorant usurpers." Lunacharsky, effortlessly and enthusiastically, showed this shut-in milieu that the Bolsheviks not only respected culture but were not unacquainted with it. More than one academic druid had to stare open-mouthed at this vandal, who could read half a dozen modern languages and two ancient ones and, in passing, unexpectedly displayed such a many-sided erudition as to suffice without difficulty for ten professors. To Lunacharsky belongs much of the credit for reconciling the patented, diploma-bearing intelligentsia to Soviet power. But in the actual effort of organizing the educational system, he proved to be hopelessly incapable. After the first ill-fated attempts, in which dilettantish fantasy was woven together with administrative helplessness, Lunacharsky himself ceased to pretend to practical leadership. The Central Committee provided him with assistants, who, screened by the personal authority of the people's commissar, firmly held the reins in their hands.

This gave Lunacharsky all the more leisure time to devote to art. The minister of the revolution not only appreciated and understood the theater but also was a prolific playwright. His plays disclose the variety of his knowledge and interests, the surprising ease of his insight into the history and culture of various countries and epochs, and, finally, an unusual ability to combine invention and borrowing. But no more than that. They do not bear the stamp of authentic artistic genius.

In 1923, Lunacharsky published a small volume entitled *Silhouettes,* dedicated to the characterization of the leaders of the revolution. The book appeared at a very inappropriate time: suffice it to say that Stalin's name was not even mentioned in it. By the following year *Silhouettes* had been withdrawn from circulation, and Lunacharsky himself felt he was half in disgrace. But here, too, he was not abandoned by his fortunate trait: compliancy. He quickly reconciled himself to the transformation in the personal composition of the leadership or, in any event, fully subordinated himself to the new masters of the situation. Nevertheless he remained to the end an alien figure in their ranks. Lunacharsky knew the past of the revolution and the party too well, pursued too many different interests, was, in the final analysis, too educated, not to be out of place in the bureaucratic ranks. Removed from the post of people's commissar, in which, by the way, he succeeded in fully accomplishing his historic mission, Lunacharsky remained almost without duties, right up to his assignment as ambassador to Spain. But he did not succeed in occupying his new post: death overtook him in Menton. Neither friend nor honest opponent will deny respect to his shade.

NATALIA SEDOVA

Natalia I. Sedova was born in the Ukraine in 1882 and became a radical in the late 1890s. As a student in Switzerland, she became a member of the Iskra *group. In 1902 she met Trotsky in France; they fell in love and lived together until his death. They had two sons, Leon and Sergei, both murdered by the Stalinists in the 1930s. She was active in the 1905 and 1917 revolutions, and after the founding of the Soviet republic worked for several years in the Commissariat of Education, where she was in charge of preserving museums, art treasures, and historical monuments from the ravages of revolution and civil war. After Trotsky's assassination in 1940 she lived in Mexico until 1961, when she made a visit to France, where she became ill and died in 1962.*

In the 1940s she collaborated with Victor Serge when he was writing The Life and Death of Leon Trotsky, *but declined his invitation to be listed as co-author. The publishers of the English translation (1975) disregarded her wishes in this respect.*

In 1935, Trotsky kept a diary while he and Sedova were living in France and Norway. It was a period of great isolation and insecurity for them, aggravated by the fact that they had heard of Sergei's arrest in the Soviet Union but were unable to do much to save him. In his diary, largely devoted to political reflections, Trotsky began to write down some of his feelings about Sedova. The six entries printed here, written between March and June, are taken from Trotsky's Diary in Exile, 1935, *published in 1958 in a translation by Elena Zarudnaya.*

March 23, 1935

The radio is playing the *Symphonie héroïque,* Concert Pasdeloup. I envy N. when she is listening to great music: she listens with all the pores of her soul and body. N. is not a musician, but she is something more than that: her whole nature is musical; in her sufferings as well as in her—infrequent—joys, there is always a deep melody which ennobles all her experiences. Even though she is interested in the small daily facts of politics, she does not usually combine them into one coherent picture. Yet when politics go deep down and demand a complete reaction, N. always finds in her inner music the right note. The same is true of her judgments of people, and not only personal, psychological ones, but also those she makes as a revolutionary. Philistinism, vulgarity, and cowardice can never be concealed from her, even though she is exceptionally lenient toward all minor human vices.

Sensitive people, even quite "simple" people—and children too—instinctively feel the musicality and depth of her nature. Of those who pass her by with indifference or condescension, without noticing the forces concealed in her, one can almost always say with certainty that they are superficial and trivial.

March 27, 1935

In 1903 in Paris a performance of Gorky's *The Lower Depths* was organized, the proceeds from which were to benefit *Iskra*. There was talk of giving a part to N., very likely on my initiative. I thought she would play her part well, "sincerely." But nothing came of it, and the part was given to someone else. I was surprised and distressed. Only later I understood that N. cannot "act a part" in any sphere. She always and under all conditions, all her life and in all possible surroundings—and we have changed quite a few of them—has remained true to herself, and has never allowed her surroundings to influence her inner life . . .

Today on our walk we went up a hill. N. got tired and unexpectedly sat down, all pale, on the dry leaves (the earth is still a bit damp). Even now she still walks beautifully, without fatigue, and her gait is quite youthful, like her whole figure. But for the last few months her heart has been acting up now and then. She works too much—with passion, as in everything she undertakes—and today it showed during the steep ascent up the hill. N. sat down all of a sudden—she obviously just *could not* go any further—and smiled apologetically. What a pang of pity I felt for youth, *her* youth . . . One night we ran home from the Paris

Opera to the rue Gassendi, 46, *au pas gymnastique,* holding hands. It was in 1903. Our combined age was forty-six . . . N. was probably the more indefatigable one. Once, while a whole crowd of us were walking somewhere in the outskirts of Paris, we came to a bridge. A steep cement pier sloped down from a great height. Two small boys had climbed on to the pier over the parapet of the bridge and were looking down on the passersby. Suddenly N. started climbing toward them up the steep smooth slope of the pier. I was petrified. I didn't think it was possible to climb up there. But she kept walking up with her graceful stride, on high heels, smiling to the boys. They waited for her with interest. We all stopped anxiously. N. went all the way up without looking at us, talked to the children, and came down the same way, without having made, as far as one could see, a single superfluous effort or taken a single uncertain step . . . It was spring, and the sun was shining as brightly as it did today when N. suddenly sat down in the grass . . .

"*Dagegen ist nun einmal kein Kraut gewachsen* [There's no herb growing which can cure that]," Engels wrote about old age and death. All the events and experiences of life are arranged along this inexorable arch between birth and the grave. This arch constitutes life itself. Without this arch there would be not only no old age, but also no youth. Old age is "necessary" because it has experience and wisdom. Youth, after all, is so beautiful exactly because there is old age and death.

Perhaps all these thoughts come to mind because the radio is playing Wagner's *Götterdämmerung.*

April 5, 1935

The depth and strength of a human character are defined by its moral *reserves.* People reveal themselves completely only when they are thrown out of the customary conditions of their life, for only then do they have to fall back on their reserves. N. and I have been together for almost thirty-three years (a third of a century!), and in tragic hours I am always amazed at the reserves of her character . . . Whether because our strength is declining, or for some other reason, but I should very much like to fix N.'s image on paper, at least partially.

May 16, 1935

We are not cheerful these days. N. is unwell: temperature of 38⁰ [C]—apparently a cold, but there may also be malaria mixed in with it. Every time N. is ill, I feel anew the place she fills in my life. She bears all suffering, physical as well as moral, silently, quietly, inside herself. Right now she is more upset about my health than her own. "If only you would get well," she said to me today, lying in bed, "that's the only thing I want." She rarely says such things. And she said this so simply, evenly, and quietly, and at the same time from such a depth, that my whole soul was stirred . . .

My condition is not encouraging. The attacks of illness have become more frequent, the symptoms are more acute, my resistance is obviously getting weaker. Of course, the curve may yet take a temporary turn upward. But in general I have a feeling that liquidation is approaching.

It's been about two weeks since I have written much of anything: it's too difficult. I read newspapers, French novels, Wittels's book about Freud (a bad book by an envious pupil), etc. Today I wrote a little about the interrelationship between the physiological determinism of brain processes and the "autonomy" of thought, which is subject to the laws of logic. My philosophical interests have been growing during the last few years, but alas, my knowledge is too insufficient, and too little time remains for a big and serious work . . .

I must give N. her tea . . .

June 8, 1935

Externally everything in our home remains as before. But in actual truth everything has changed. Every time I recall Seryozha, it is with a sharp pain. But N. does not "recall" him, she always carries a deep sorrow inside her. "He put his trust in us . . . ," she said to me the other day (her voice still echoes in my heart) . . . "He thought that since we left him there, it was the way things had to be." And it has turned out that we have sacrificed him. That is just what it is . . .

Now, on top of this, my health has taken a sharp turn for the worse. This too N. takes very hard. One thing after another. Meanwhile she has to do a great deal of housework. Every day I am amazed anew: where does she get so much concentrated, passionate, and at the same time restrained energy?

S.L. Kliachko, our old Vienna friend, who thought very highly of N., once said that the only voice like hers that he had heard was Eleonora Duse's. (For S.L., Duse was the highest expression of the female personality.) But Duse was a tragic actress, while N. has nothing "theatrical" about her. She cannot "act," "perform a role," "imitate." She experiences everything with the utmost completeness and gives an artistic expression to her experiences. The secret of this artistry: depth, spontaneity, and wholeness of character.

Concerning the blows that have fallen to our lot, I reminded Natasha the other day of the life of archpriest Avvakum. They were stumbling on together in Siberia, the rebellious priest and his faithful spouse. Their feet sank into the snow, and the poor exhausted woman kept falling into the snowdrifts. Avvakum relates:

"And I came up, and she, poor soul, began to reproach me, saying: 'How long, archpriest, is this suffering to be?' And I said, 'Markovna, unto our very death.' And she, with a sigh, answered: 'So be it, Petrovich, let us be getting on our way.' "

I can say one thing: never did Natasha "reproach" me, never—even in the most difficult hours; nor does she reproach me now, in the most sorrowful days of our life, when everything has conspired against us . . .

June 26, 1935

N. is fixing up our living quarters. How many times she has done this! There are no wardrobes here, and many other things are lacking. She is hammering nails in by herself, stringing cords, hanging things up and changing them around; the cords break; she sighs to herself and begins all over again. She is guided in this by two considerations: cleanliness and attractiveness. I remember with what heartfelt sympathy—almost tenderness—she told me in 1905 about a certain fellow prisoner, a common criminal, who had "understood" cleanliness and helped N. to clean up their cell. How many "furnishings" we have changed in thirty-three years of living together: a Geneva *mansarde*, flats in the working-class districts of Vienna and Paris, and the Kremlin and Arkhangelskoe, a peasant hut near Alma-Ata, a villa in Prinkipo, and much more modest villas in

France . . . N. has never been *indifferent* to her surroundings, but always *independent* of them. I easily "let down" under difficult conditions: that is, become reconciled to the dirt and disorder around me, but N.—*never*. She raises every environment to a certain level of cleanliness and orderliness, and does not allow it to fall below that level. But how much energy, inventiveness, and vital force it requires! . . .

I lie down now for days at a time. Today N. and I were arranging a chaise longue behind the barn. "Do you want it this way?" she asked me with a shade of regret. "Why?" "The view is better on the other side." Indeed, the view was incomparably better on the opposite side. Of course anyone, or almost anyone, can tell a better view from an inferior one. But N. cannot help feeling the difference with her whole being. She cannot sit down facing a fence, and suffers with pity if somebody else faces that way.

N. and I have lived a long and hard life together, but even now she does not cease to *amaze* me by the unspoiled, integral, artistic quality of her nature.

Lying on my chaise longue, I remembered how N. and I had been subjected to a sanitary inspection aboard ship when we arrived in New York in January 1917. American officials and doctors are very unceremonious, especially with passengers not in the first class—we were traveling second class. Natasha was wearing a veil. The doctor, thinking of trachoma, suspected something wrong behind the veil, quickly lifted it up and made a move with his fingers to lift up her eyelids . . . N. did not protest, said nothing, did not step back; she was just surprised. She glanced at the doctor questioningly and blushed a little. But the coarse Yankee immediately dropped his hands and stepped back apologetically: there was such an irresistible dignity of womanhood in her face, in her glance, in her whole figure . . . I remember what a feeling of pride in Natasha I had as we walked down the ramp to the New York pier.

FRIEDRICH ENGELS

Friedrich Engels, co-founder with Karl Marx of the modern revolutionary socialist movement, was born in the Rhine province of Germany in 1820. He met Marx in Cologne in 1842 and in Paris in 1844, and joined him in Brussels in 1845 to begin a political collaboration and friendship that lasted until Marx's death. Together they became members of the League of the Just, which evolved into the International Communist League, in whose name they wrote the renowned Communist Manifesto *in 1847. Engels took part, as adjutant in a volunteer corps fighting against the Prussians, in a revolutionary uprising in Baden in 1849, and after its suppression fled to England, where Marx also took asylum. For the next two decades, Engels worked in his father's textile business in Manchester, chiefly in order to support the destitute Marx while he completed his* Capital *and other theoretical works. In 1864 they played central roles in the formation of the International Workingmen's Association, the First International. In 1870 Engels left his job in Manchester and moved to London to devote himself to fulltime political and literary activity. After Marx died in 1883, Engels took over the task of completing his friend's unpublished manuscripts and continuing the immense work of counseling the growing number of national movements dedicated to socialism. In the last years before his death in 1895, he also was active in the congresses of the new Second International.*

Biographies include Friedrich Engels *by Gustav Mayer (1936) and* Frederick Engels: A Biography *(1974), which has a great deal of information even though it is written by a Moscow committee. Moscow is also publishing in English an edition of Marx's and Engels's collected works that may run into fifty volumes, but*

Engels's major books are separately available in English. The 1935 volume collecting Engels's letters to Kautsky, which Trotsky reviews here, has not yet been published in English.

Trotsky's article, dated October 15, 1935, was written in Norway. The translation by John G. Wright was first published, under the title "Engels's Letters to Kautsky," in The New International, *June 1936.*

The year 1935 marks the fortieth anniversary of the death of Friedrich Engels, one of the authors of the *Communist Manifesto.* The other author was Karl Marx. This anniversary is notable, among other things, for the fact that Karl Kautsky, having passed his eighty-first year, has finally published his correspondence with Engels.* To be sure, Kautsky's own letters have been preserved only in rare instances, but almost all of Engels's letters have come down to us. The new letters of course do not reveal a new Engels. His enormous international correspondence, as much of it as was preserved, has been published almost in its entirety; his life has been subjected to ample study. Nevertheless this latest book is a very valuable gift to those who are seriously interested in the political history of the final decades of the last century, the course of development of Marxian ideas, the destiny of the working class movement and, finally, in the personality of Engels.

During Marx's lifetime, Engels, as he himself put it, played second fiddle. But with his co-worker's last illness, and especially after the latter's death, Engels became the direct and unchallenged leader of the orchestra of world socialism for a period of twelve years. By that time Engels had long rid himself of his commercial ties; he was entirely independent so far as money was concerned, and he was able to devote his entire time to editing and publishing the literary legacy of Marx, to pursue his own scientific researches, and to engage in an enormous correspondence with the left-wing leaders of the working class movement in all countries. His correspondence with Kautsky dates from the closing period of Engels's life (1881-95).

---

* *Aus der Frühzeit des Marxismus, Engels Briefwechsel mit Kautsky,* Herausgegeben und erläutet von Karl Kautsky. Orbis-Verlag, Prague, 1935.—L.T.

Engels's personality, unique in its purposefulness and lucidity, has been subjected to diverse interpretations in the ensuing years—such is the logic of the struggle. Suffice to recall that during the last war, Ebert, Scheidemann, and others portrayed Engels as a German patriot, while the publicists of the Entente pictured him as a Pan-Germanist. On this as well as other points the letters help to strip away tendentious encrustations from Engels's personality. But their gist does not lie here. The letters are remarkable primarily because they are characteristic of the man. One can say without fear of exaggeration that every new human document pertaining to Engels reveals him to have been finer, nobler, and more fascinating than we had previously known.

The second party to the correspondence has also a claim to our interest. In the early 1880s, Kautsky came to the fore in the role of the official theoretician of the German Social Democracy, which in its own turn became the leading party in the Second International. As was the case with Engels during Marx's lifetime, so Kautsky, too, played at best second fiddle while Engels lived—and he did his playing at a great remove from the first violinist. After Engels's death, the authority of the disciple grew rapidly, reaching its zenith during the epoch of the first Russian revolution (1905).

In his commentary to the correspondence, Kautsky describes his agitation on his first visit to the homes of Marx and Engels. A quarter of a century later, many young Marxists—in particular the writer of this article—experienced the very same agitation as they climbed the stairway of the modest, tidy house in Friedenau in the suburbs of Berlin, where Kautsky lived for many years. He was then considered the outstanding and unchallenged leader in the international, at any rate, upon questions of theory. He was referred to by opponents as the "pope" of Marxism.

But Kautsky did not long maintain his high authority. Great events during the past quarter of the century dealt him crushing blows. During and after the war Kautsky personified irritable indecisiveness. What had hitherto been suspected only by a few was now fully confirmed, namely, that his Marxism was essentially academic and contemplative in character. When Kautsky writes Engels from Vienna, during a strike, in April 1889, that "my thoughts are more on the streets than at this writing table" (p. 242), these words seem utterly unexpected and almost false coming even from the pen of a young Kautsky.

Throughout his whole life, the writing table remained his field of operation. He looked upon street events as hindrances. He was a popularizer of the doctrine, an interpreter of the past, a defender of the method. Yes, this he was, but never a man of action, never a revolutionist, or an heir to the spirit of Marx and Engels.

The correspondence lays bare completely not only the radical difference between the two personalities but also something utterly unexpected, for the present generation at any rate—the antagonism that existed between Engels and Kautsky, which finally led to a break in their personal relations.

The General

Engels's insight into military matters, based not only upon his extensive special knowledge but also upon his general capacity for a synthesized appraisal of conditions and forces, enabled him to publish in the London *Pall-Mall Gazette*, during the Franco-Prussian War, remarkable military articles, ascribed by fame to one of the highest military authorities of the time (the Messrs. "Authorities," doubtless, surveyed themselves in the mirror not without considerable astonishment). In his intimate circle Engels was dubbed with the playful nickname of the "General." This name is signed to a number of his letters to Kautsky.

Engels was not an orator, or it may be that he never had the occasion to become one. Towards "orators" he displayed even a shade of disrespect, holding, not without foundation, that they incline to turn ideas into banalities. But Kautsky recalls Engels as a remarkable conversationalist, endowed with an inexhaustible memory, remarkable wit, and precision of expression. Unfortunately, Kautsky himself is a mediocre observer, and no artist at all: in his own letters Engels stands out infinitely more clearly than in the commentaries and recollections of Kautsky.

Engels's relations with people were foreign to all sentimentalism or illusions and permeated through and through with a penetrating simplicity and, therefore, were profoundly human. In his company around the evening table, where representatives of various countries and continents gathered, all contrast disappeared as if by magic between the polished radical duchess Schack and the not at all polished Russian nihilist Vera Zasulich. The rich personality of the host manifested itself in this happy capacity to lift himself and others above everything secondary and superficial, without departing in the least from either his views or even his habits.

One would seek in vain in this revolutionist for bohemian traits so prevalent among the radical intellectuals. Engels was intolerant of sloppiness and negligence both in small and big things. He loved precision of thought, precision in accounting, exactitude in expression and in print. When a German publisher attempted to alter his spelling, Engels demanded back several galleys for revision. He wrote, "I would no sooner allow anybody to foist his spelling on me than I would a wife" (p. 147). This irate and at the same time jocose sentence almost brings Engels back to life again!

In addition to his native tongue, over which his mastery was that of a virtuoso, Engels wrote freely in English, French, and Italian; he read Spanish and almost all Slavic and Scandinavian languages. His knowledge of philosophy, economics, history, physics, philology, and military science would have sufficed for a goodly dozen of ordinary and extraordinary professors. But even apart from all this he possessed his main treasure: winged thought.

In June 1884, when Bernstein and Kautsky, affecting Engels's own likes and dislikes, complained to him of the incipient pressure of all sorts of "erudite" philistines in the party, Engels said in reply, "the main thing is to concede nothing and, in addition, to remain absolutely calm" (p. 119). While the General himself did not always retain "absolute calm" in the literal sense of the term—on the contrary, he was wont on occasion to boil over magnificently—he was always able to rise quickly above temporary mishaps and restore the necessary balance between his thoughts and emotions. The elemental side of his personality was optimism combined with humor towards himself and those close to him, and irony towards his enemies. In his optimism there was not a modicum of smugness—the term itself rebounds from his image. The subsoil springs of his joy of living had their source in a happy and harmonious temperament, but the latter was permeated through and through with the knowledge that brought with it the greatest of joys: the joy of creative perception.

Engels's optimism extended equally to political questions and to personal affairs. After each and every defeat he would immediately seek out those conditions which would prepare a new upsurge, and after every blow life dealt him he was able to pull himself together and look to the future. Such he remained to his dying day. There were times when he had to remain on his back for weeks in order to get over the effects of a rupture he suffered from a fall during one of the "gentry's" riding to foxes. At times his aged eyes refused to function under artificial light, which one cannot do without even during daytime in the London fogs. But Engels never refers to his ailments except in passing, in order to explain some delay, and only in order to promise immediately thereupon that everything would shortly "proceed better," and then the work will be resumed at full speed.

One of Marx's letters has a reference to Engels's habit of playfully winking during a conversation. This helpful "winking" passes through Engels's entire correspondence. The man of duty and of profound attachments least of all resembles an ascetic. He was a lover of nature and of art in all its forms, he loved the company of clever and merry people, the presence of women, jokes, laughter, good dinners, good wine, and good tobacco. At times he was not averse to the belly-laughter of Rabelais, who readily looked for his inspiration below the navel. In general, nothing human was alien to him. Not seldom in his correspondence do we run across references to the effect that several bottles of good wine were opened in his house to celebrate the New Year, or the happy outcome of German elections, his own birthday, and sometimes events of lesser importance. Rarely do we come across the General's complaints about his having to remain prone on the sofa "instead of drinking with you . . . well, what is postponed is not yet lost" (p. 335). The writer was at the time over seventy-two years of age. Several months later, a false rumor circulated through the press that Engels was gravely ill. The seventy-three-year-old General writes, "So, anent the rapidly ebbing resistance, and the hourly expected demise, we emptied several bottles" (p. 352).

Was he, perhaps, an epicurean? The secondary "boons of life" never held sway over this man. On the other hand, he was genuinely interested in the kinship customs of savages or in the enigmas of Irish philology, but always in indissoluble connection with the future destinies of mankind. If he permitted himself to joke trivially, it was only in the company of untrivial people. Underlying his humor, irony, and joy of living one always feels an ardent moral spirit—free of all rhetoric or posturing, deeply hidden, but all the more genuine for that, and ever ready for sacrifice. The man of commerce, the possessor of a mill, a hunter's horse, and a wine cellar, was a revolutionary communist to the marrow of his bones.

Marx's Executor

Kautsky does not exaggerate in the least when he states in his commentary to the correspondence that in the entire history of the world it would be impossible to find a parallel instance of two men of such powerful temperaments and ideological independence as Marx and Engels who remained throughout their entire lives so indissolubly bound together by the evolution of their ideas, their social activity, and personal friendship. Engels was quicker on the uptake, more mobile, enterprising and many-sided; Marx, more ponderous, more stubborn, harsher to himself and to others. Himself a luminary of the first magnitude, Engels recognized Marx's intellectual authority with the same simplicity that he generally showed in establishing personal and political relationships.

The collaboration of these two friends—here is the context in which this word attains its fullest meaning!—extended so deeply as to make it impossible for anyone ever to establish the line of demarcation between their works. However, infinitely more important than the purely literary collaboration was the spiritual community that existed between them, and that was never broken. They either corresponded daily, sending epigrammatic notes, understanding each other with half-statements, or they carried on an equally epigrammatic conversation amid clouds of cigar smoke. For some four decades, in their continual struggle against official science and traditional superstitions, Marx and Engels served each other in place of public opinion.

Engels looked upon providing Marx with material assistance as a most important political obligation; and it was chiefly on this account that he bound himself to many years' drudgery in "accursed trade"—a sphere in which he functioned as successfully as he did in all others: his estate grew and together with it the well-being of Marx's family improved. After Marx died, Engels transferred to Marx's daughters all his accustomed care and solicitude. The old servant of the Marx couple, Hélène Demuth, who was an inseparable part of the family, immediately became the housekeeper of Engels's home. Towards her Engels behaved with a tender loyalty, sharing with her all his interests that were within her grasp, and after she died he complained how much he missed her advice not only in personal but in party matters. Engels willed to the daughters of Marx practically his entire estate, which amounted to 30,000 pounds, outside of the library, furniture, etc.

If in his younger years Engels withdrew into the shadows of the textile industry in Manchester in order to provide Marx with the opportunity to work on *Capital,* then, subsequently, as an old man, without complaining and, one can say with assurance, without any regrets, he put aside his own researches in order to spend years deciphering the hieroglyphic manuscripts of Marx, painstakingly checking translations, and no less painstakingly correcting his writings in almost all the European languages. No. In this "epicurean" there was an altogether uncommon stoic!

Reports about the progress of the work on Marx's literary legacy provide one of the most constant leitmotifs in the correspondence between Engels and Kautsky, as well as other co-thinkers. In a letter to Kautsky's mother (1885)—a rather well-known writer of popular novels at the time—Engels expresses his hope that old Europe will finally swing into motion again, and he adds, "I only hope that sufficient time will be left for me to conclude the third volume of *Capital,* and then, let her rip!" (p. 206). From this semijocular statement one may clearly gather the importance he attached to *Capital*; but there is also something else to be gathered, namely, that revolutionary action stood for him above any book, even *Capital.* On December 3, 1891, i.e., six years later, Engels explains to Kautsky the reasons for his protracted silence: ". . . responsible for it is the third volume, over which I am sweating again." He is busy not only deciphering the chapters in the murderous manuscript on money capital, banks, and credit, but he is also studying at the same time literature on the respective subjects. To be sure, he knows in advance that in the majority of cases he can leave the manuscript just as it came from the pen of Marx, but he wants to secure himself against editorial errors by his auxiliary researches. Added to all this there is the bottomless pit of minute technical details! Engels carries on a correspondence on whether or not a comma is needed in such and such a place, and he especially thanks Kautsky for uncovering an error in spelling in the manuscript. This is not pedantry—but conscientiousness to which nothing is unimportant that bears upon the scientific sum total of Marx's life.

Engels, however, was furthest removed from any blind adulation of the text. Checking over a digest of Marx's economic theory written by the French socialist Deville, Engels, according to his own words, often felt the temptation to delete or correct sentences here and there, which on further examination turned out to be . . . Marx's own expressions. The gist of the matter is that "in the original, thanks to what had preceded, they were clearly qualified. But in Deville's case, they were invested with an absolutely generalized, and by reason of this, incorrect meaning" (p. 95). These few words provide a classic characterization of the common abuse of the ready-made formulas of the master (*magister dixit*).

But this is not all. Engels not only deciphered, polished, transcribed, corrected, and annotated the second and third volumes of *Capital* but he maintained an eagle-eyed vigil in defense of Marx's memory against hostile attacks. The conservative Prussian socialist Rodbertus and his admirers claimed that Marx had used the scientific discovery of Rodbertus without making any reference to the latter—in other words, that Marx plagiarized Rodbertus. "A monstrous ignorance is required to make such an assertion," wrote Engels to Kautsky in 1884 (p. 140). And once again, Engels applied himself to the study of the useless Rodbertus in order fully to refute these charges.

In an equally illuminating way the letters to Kautsky reflect the episode in which the German economist Brentano accused Marx of falsely quoting Gladstone. Engels, if anyone, was acquainted with the scientific scrupulousness of Marx, whose attitude towards every idea of his opponent, no matter how absurd, was akin to the attitude of a bacteriologist towards a disease-bearing bacillus. Time after time in Engels's letters to Marx and to their mutual friends one runs across his chiding the excess of conscientiousness on Marx's part. It is not at all surprising, therefore, that he put all other work aside in order angrily to refute Brentano.

Engels cherished the idea of writing a biography of Marx. No one could have written it as he, for, of necessity, it would have been in large measure Engels's own autobiography. He writes to Kautsky: "I will get down to work at the first possible moment upon this book on which I have so long pondered with pleasure" (p. 382). Engels vows not to be sidetracked: "I am now seventy-four years old—I have to hurry." Even today one cannot reflect without sorrow on the fact that Engels did not manage to "hurry" and fulfill his project.

For the oil portrait of Marx which was in preparation in Switzerland, Engels supplied through Kautsky the following color description of his deceased friend: "A complexion as dark as it is generally possible for a South European to be, without much color on the cheeks: . . . mustaches black as soot, tinged with white, and snow-white hair on head and beard" (p. 149). This description makes clear why Marx received the nickname "the Moor" in his family and intimate circle.

The Teacher of Leaders

During the first two years Engels addressed his correspondent as "Dear Mr. Kautsky" (the term "comrade" was not then in current use); after they had drawn closer in London, he abbreviated the form of salutation to merely "Dear Kautsky"; from March 1884, Engels adopted the familiar form of address in writing to Bernstein and Kautsky, each of whom was twenty-five years younger than himself. Kautsky writes not without good reason that "from 1883 Engels looked upon Bernstein and myself as the most reliable representatives of the Marxian theory" (p. 93). The transition to the familiar form of address no doubt reflects the favorable attitude of a teacher toward his pupils. But this outward familiarity is no proof of actual intimacy: this was hindered chiefly by the fact that Kautsky and Bernstein were imbued with philistinism to a considerable measure. During their long sojourn in London, Engels helped them to acquire the Marxian method. But he could not implant in them either revolutionary will or the ability to think boldly. The pupils were and remained the children of another spirit.

Marx and Engels awakened in an epoch of storms, and they passed through the revolution of 1848 as full-fledged fighters. Kautsky and Bernstein went through their formative period during the comparatively peaceful interval between the epoch of wars and revolutions from 1848 to 1871 and the epoch that had its inception with the Russian revolution of 1905, continued through the world war of 1914, and has far from reached its conclusion even today. Through his entire long life Kautsky was able to circumnavigate those conclusions that threatened to disturb his mental and physical peace. He was not a revolutionist, and this was an insurmountable barrier that separated him from the Red General.

But even apart from this there was too great a difference between them. It is indubitable that direct personal acquaintance with Engels worked only to his advantage: his personality was richer and more attractive than anything he did and wrote. In no case can the same be said of Kautsky. His best books are far wiser than he was himself. He lost greatly from personal intercourse. It may be that this in part explains why Rosa Luxemburg, who lived side by side with Kautsky, had gauged his philistinism before Lenin did, although she was inferior to Lenin in political insight. But this relates to a much later period.

From the correspondence it becomes absolutely self-evident that there always remained an invisible barrier between the teacher and the pupil not only in the sphere of politics but also in the sphere of theory. Engels, who was generally chary of praise, sometimes referred with enthusiasm (*Ausgezeichnet*) to the writings of Franz Mehring or George Plekhanov; but his praise of Kautsky was always restrained, and one senses a shade of irritation in his criticism. Like Marx, when Kautsky first appeared in his home, Engels, too, was repelled by the omniscience and the passive self-satisfaction of the young Viennese. How readily he found answers to the most complex questions! True, Engels himself was inclined to hasty generalizations; but he, in turn, had the wings and vision of an eagle, and as years passed he more and more adopted Marx's merciless scientific conscientiousness towards himself. But Kautsky with all his capabilities was a man of the Golden Mean.

"Nine-tenths of the contemporary German authors," thus did the teacher warn his pupil, "write books about other books" (p. 139). In other words: no analysis of living reality, no progressive movement of thought. Using the occasion of Kautsky's book on questions of primitive society, Engels tried to instill in him the idea that it was possible to say something really new in this enormous and dark province only by a throughgoing and exhaustive study of the subject. And he adds quite mercilessly, "Otherwise books like *Capital* would not be so rare" (p. 85).

A year later (September 20, 1884) Engels again chides Kautsky about his "sweeping assertions in spheres in which you yourself do not feel at all certain" (p. 144). One finds this thought passing through the entire correspondence. Chiding Kautsky for having condemned "abstraction"—without abstract thinking, no thinking is generally possible—Engels gives a classic definition which shows the difference between a vivifying and a lifeless abstraction: "Marx reduces the common content in things and relations to its most universal conceptual expression; his abstraction consequently reproduces in concept form the content already lodged in things themselves. Rodbertus, on the other hand, creates for himself a more or less imperfect mental expression and measures all things by his concept, to which they must be equated" (p. 144). Nine-tenths of the errors in human thinking are embraced in this formula. Eleven years later, in his last letter to Kautsky, Engels, while giving due recognition to Kautsky's researches on the *Precursors of Socialism*, once again chides the author for his inclination toward "commonplaces wherever there is a gap in the research." "As to style, in order to remain popular, you either fall into the tone of an editorial, or assume the tone of a school teacher" (p. 388). One could not express more aptly the literary mannerisms of Kautsky!

At the same time, the intellectual magnanimity of the master toward his pupil was truly inexhaustible. He used to read the most important articles of the prolific Kautsky in their manuscript form, and each of his letters of criticism contains precious suggestions, the fruit of serious thought, and sometimes of research. Kautsky's well-known work, *Class Antagonisms in the French Revolution*, which has been translated into almost all the languages of civilized mankind, also, it appears, passed through the intellectual laboratory of Engels. His long letter on social groupings in the epoch of the great revolution of the eighteenth century—as well as on the application of the materialist method to historical events—is one of the most magnificent documents of the human mind. It is much too terse, and each of its formulas presupposes too great a store of knowledge for it to enter into general reading circulation; but this document, so long kept hidden, will forever remain not only the source of theoretical instruction but also of esthetic joy to anyone who has seriously pondered the dynamics of class relations in a revolutionary epoch, as well as the general problems involved in the materialist interpretation of events.

Kautsky's Divorce and His Conflict with Engels

Kautsky asserts—not without a purpose in the back of his mind, as we shall see—that Engels was a poor judge of men. Marx was no doubt to a larger measure a "fisher of men." He was better able to play on their strong and weak sides, and gave proof of this, for instance, by his rather difficult work in the extremely heterogeneous General Council of the First International. However, Engels's correspondence is the best possible proof that while he did not always maneuver happily in his personal relationships, this flowed from his stormy directness and not at all from his inability to understand people. Kautsky, who himself is very myopic on questions of psychology, adduces as examples Engels's stubborn defense of Aveling, the friend of Marx's daughter, a man who, with all his indubitable capacities, was a person of little worth. Cautiously, but very persistently, Kautsky strives to purvey the idea that Engels did not give evidence of psychological sensitivity in relation to Kautsky himself. This is his purpose in raising the particular question of Engels's capacity as a judge of men.

All his life Engels had a particularly tender attitude toward women, as those who were doubly oppressed. This citizen of the world with an encyclopedic education was married to a simple textile worker, an Irish girl, and after she died he lived with her sister. His tenderness to both was truly remarkable. Marx's inadequate response to the news of the death of Mary Burns, Engels's first wife, raised a little cloud in their relations, from all indications the first and last cloud throughout the forty years of their friendship. Towards Marx's daughters, Engels behaved as if they were his own children; but at a time when Marx, apparently not without the influence of his wife, attempted to intervene in the emotional life of his daughters, Engels gave him carefully to understand that such matters concern nobody except the participants themselves. Engels had particular affection for Eleanor, Marx's youngest daughter. Aveling became her friend; he was a married man who had broken with his first family. This circumstance engendered around the "illegal" couple the stifling atmosphere of genuinely British hypocrisy. Is it greatly to be marveled at that Engels came to the strong defense of Eleanor and her friend, even irrespective of his moral qualities? Eleanor fought for her love for Aveling as long as she had any strength left. Engels was not blind but he considered that the question of Aveling's personality concerned Eleanor, first and foremost. For his part, he assumed only the duty to defend her against hypocrisy and evil gossip. "Hands off!" he stubbornly told the pious hypocrites. In the end, unable to bear up under the blows of personal life, Eleanor committed suicide.

Kautsky also refers to the fact that Engels supported Aveling in politics. But this is explained by the simple fact that Eleanor, like Aveling, functioned politically under the direct guidance of Engels himself. To be sure, their activity was far from producing the desired results. But the activity of their opponent Hyndman, whom Kautsky continued to support, also resulted in shipwreck.

The cause for the failures of the initial Marxian attempts must be sought in the objective conditions of England so magnificently dissected by Engels himself. Engels's personal antagonism towards Hyndman arose in particular from the latter's stubborn persistence in refusing to mention Marx's name, justifying himself by the aversion of the English to foreign authorities. Engels, however, suspected that in Hyndman himself there was lodged "the most chauvinistic John Bull extant" (p. 140). Kautsky tries to invalidate Engels's suspicion on this score, as if Hyndman's shameful behavior during the war—not a word about this from Kautsky!—had not laid bare his rotten chauvinism to the core. How much more penetrating did Engels prove to be in this case as well!

However, the chief instance of Engels's "inability" to judge men relates to Kautsky's own personal life. In the correspondence just now published, a considerable, if not the central, place is occupied by Kautsky's divorce from his first wife. This ticklish circumstance no doubt kept Kautsky so long from making the old letters public. Today, for the first time, the entire episode is opened to the press. . . . The youthful Kautsky couple spent more than six years in London in constant and unclouded communion with Engels and his family circle. The General was literally thunderstruck by the news of the divorce proceedings between Karl and Luise Kautsky that came almost immediately after their arrival on the Continent. The closest friends willy-nilly all became the moral arbiters in this conflict. Engels immediately and unconditionally took the wife's side and did not change his position to his dying day.

In a letter of October 17, 1888, Engels writes in reply to Kautsky: "One must first of all weigh in the balance the difference between the positions of men and women under the present conditions. . . . Only in extreme cases, only after mature deliberation, only if it is absolutely clear that such a step is necessary, should a man resort to this most extreme measure, but even then, only in its most prudent and mildest form" (p. 227). Coming from the lips of Engels, who well knew that matters of the heart concern only the parties involved, these words have an unexpected moralizing ring. However, it was no accident that he addressed them to—Kautsky. We have neither the occasion nor the basis for analyzing the marital conflict, all the elements of which are not at our disposal. Kautsky himself virtually refrains from any remarks upon this family episode which has long since receded into the past. From his reserved comments, however, one must conclude that Engels came to his position under the one-sided influence of Luise. But whence this influence? During the divorce both parties remained in Austria. As in Eleanor's case, Kautsky obviously evades the gist of the matter. By his entire makeup—all other things being equal—Engels was inclined to come to the defense of the underdog. But it is obvious that in his eyes "all other things" were not equal. The very possibility of Luise's influencing him speaks in her favor. On the other hand, there were many traits in Kautsky's personality that clearly repelled Engels. This he could pass over in silence so long as their relations were confined to questions of theory and politics. But after he was drawn into the family quarrel upon the initiative of Kautsky himself, he spoke out what was in his mind without any particular leniency. A man's views and a man's morals are, as is well known, not at all identical. In Kautsky the Marxist, Engels clearly sensed a Viennese petty bourgeois, self-satisfied, egotistic, and conservative. One of the most important measuring rods of a man's personality is his attitude towards women. Engels was obviously of the opinion that in this sphere Kautsky the Marxist still required certain precepts of bourgeois humanism. Whether Engels was right or wrong, that is precisely the explanation for his conduct.

In September 1889, when the divorce had already become a fact, Kautsky, with an obvious desire to demonstrate that he was not at all so hard-hearted and egotistical, wrote carelessly to Engels about his feeling "sorry" for Luise. But it was precisely this word that brought down upon him a new outburst of indignation. The irate General thundered in reply: "In this entire affair, Luise has deported herself with such heroism and womanhood . . . that if, in general, anyone is to be pitied, it is not Luise of course" (p. 248). These merciless words—which follow upon a more conciliatory statement that "you two alone are competent to judge, and whatever you approve, we others must accept" (p. 248)—provide a perfect key to Engels's position on the question and serve well to illuminate his personality.

The divorce case dragged on for a long time, so that Kautsky found himself compelled to spend a whole year in Vienna. On his return to London (autumn 1889) he no longer received from Engels the warm welcome he had become accustomed to. Moreover, Engels, almost demonstratively, invited Luise to become the manager of his household that had been orphaned by the death of Hélène Demuth. Luise soon married for the second time and lived in Engels's house with her husband. Finally, Engels made Luise one of his heirs. The General was not only magnanimous but stubborn in his attachments.

On May 21, 1895, ten weeks prior to his death, Engels from his sickbed wrote a letter to Kautsky, extremely irritable in tone and full of splenetic reproaches, apropos of a really accidental matter. Kautsky swears categorically that these reproaches were entirely unfounded. Maybe so. But he received no answer to his attempt to dispel the old man's suspicions. On August 6, Engels passed away. Kautsky attempts to explain away the break so tragic to himself by the sickly irritability of the master. The explanation is obviously inadequate. Along with the angry reproaches, Engels's letter contains evaluations of complex historical problems, gives a favorable estimate of Kautsky's latest scholarly work, and generally testifies to a highly lucid state of mind. Besides, we know from Kautsky himself that the change in their relations occurred seven years prior to the break and immediately assumed an unequivocal character.

In January 1889, Engels still firmly intended to appoint Kautsky and Bernstein as his and Marx's literary executors. Soon, however, he renounced this idea so far as Kautsky was concerned. He asked, under an obviously artificial pretext, that Kautsky return the manuscripts already given him for deciphering and transcribing (*Theories of Surplus Value*). This took place in the same year, 1889, when there was as yet no question of sickly irritability. We can only venture a guess as to the reasons why Engels expunged Kautsky from the list of his literary executors; but they imperatively flow from all the circumstances in the case. Engels himself, as we know, viewed the publication of Marx's literary heritage as the main business of his life. There is not even a hint of such an attitude on the part of Kautsky. The **young**, prolific writer was too much preoccupied with himself to pay to Marx's manuscripts the attention Engels demanded. Perhaps the old man feared that the prolific Kautsky, consciously or unconsciously, might put several of Marx's ideas to use as his own "discoveries." This is the only explanation for the replacement of Kautsky by Bebel, who was theoretically less qualified but had the complete confidence of Engels. The latter had no such confidence in Kautsky.

While up to now we have heard from Kautsky that Engels, *in contradistinction to Marx*, was a poor psychologist, in another place in his commentaries he brackets both his masters. He writes, "They were obviously not great judges of men" (p. 44). This statement seems incredible, if we recall the wealth and the incomparable precision of personal characterizations which abound not only in Marx's letters and pamphlets but also in his *Capital*. It may be said that Marx was able to establish a man's type from individual traits in the same manner as Cuvier reconstructed an animal from a single jawbone. If Marx in 1852 was not able to see through the Hungarian-Prussian provocateur, Bangya—the only instance to which Kautsky makes reference!— it only goes to prove that Marx was neither a clairvoyant nor a witch-doctor but was liable to make mistakes in evaluating people, particularly those who turned up accidentally. By his assertion, Kautsky obviously seeks to obviate the impression of the unfavorable reference made by Marx about him after Marx's first and last meeting with him. Completely contradicting himself, Kautsky writes two pages later that "Marx had well mastered the art of handling people, showing this in the most brilliant and indubitable manner in the General Council of the International" (p. 46). A question remains: how is a man to manage people, and "brilliantly" to boot, without his being able to plumb their character? It is impossible not to conclude that Kautsky has drawn a poor balance-sheet on his relations with his teachers!

Appraisals and Prognoses

Engels's letters abound in characterizations of individuals and in succinct appraisals of events in world politics. We shall confine ourselves to a few examples. "The paradoxical literateur, Shaw, is very talented and witty as a writer but absolutely worthless as economist and politician" (p. 338). This remark made in the year 1892 preserves its full force even in our time. The well-known journalist, V. T. Stead, is characterized as "an absolutely hare-brained fellow but a brilliant horse-trader" (p. 298). Of Sidney Webb, Engels briefly remarks: "ein echter Britischer politician" (a genuinely British politician). This was the harshest term in Engels's lexicon.

In January 1889, in the heat of the Boulanger campaign in France, Engels wrote: "The election of Boulanger brings the situation in France to a breaking point. The Radicals . . . have turned themselves into flunkeys of opportunism, and thereby they have literally given nourishment to Boulangerism" (p. 231). These words are astonishing in their modernity—one need only put fascism in place of Boulangerism.

Engels lashes the theory of the "evolutionary" transformation of capitalism into socialism as the "pious and joyful 'growing over' of hoary swinishness into a socialist society." This epigrammatic formula anticipates the conclusions of a debate that, at a later time in history, was to last many years.

In the same letter Engels rips apart the speech of a Social Democratic deputy, Vollmar, "with its . . . excessive and unauthorized assurances that the Social Democrats will not remain on the sidelines if their fatherland is attacked, and will consequently help defend the annexation of Alsace-Lorraine. . . ." Engels demanded that the leading organs of the party publicly disavow Vollmar. During the Great War when the social-patriots bandied Engels's name about for whatever purpose suited them, it never entered Kautsky's mind to publish these lines. Why bother? The war caused sufficient worries without that.

On April 1, 1895, Engels protested against the use made of his preface to Marx's *Class Struggles in France* by the central organ of the party, *Vorwärts*. By means of deletions, the article is so distorted, Engels fumes, "that I am made out to be a peaceful worshipper of legality at any price." He demands that this "shameful impression" (p. 383) be removed at any price. Engels, who at that time was nearing his seventy-fifth birthday, obviously had not yet made ready to renounce the revolutionary enthusiasm of his youth!

If one is to speak at all of Engels's mistakes concerning people, one should cite as examples not Aveling, the sloven in personal matters, and not the spy Bangya, but the outstanding leaders of socialism: Victor Adler, Guesde, Bernstein, Kautsky himself, and many others. All of them, without a single exception, betrayed his expectations—to be sure, after he was already dead. But precisely this all-embracing character of the "mistake" proves that it does not involve any problems of individual psychology.

In 1884, Engels, referring to the German Social Democracy, which was scoring rapid victories, wrote that it was a party "free from all philistinism in the most philistine country in the world; free from all chauvinism in the most victory-drunk country in Europe" (p. 154). The subsequent course of events proved that Engels had visualized the future course of revolutionary development too much along the straight line. Above all he did not foresee the mighty capitalist boom which set in immediately after his death and which lasted up to the eve of the imperialist war. It was precisely in the course of these fifteen years of economic affluence that the complete opportunistic degeneration of the leading circles of the labor movement took place. This degeneration was fully revealed during the war, and, in the last analysis, it led to the infamous capitulation to National Socialism.

According to Kautsky, Engels, even back in the eighties, was of the alleged opinion that the German revolution "would first bring the bourgeois democracy to power, and the Social Democracy only later on." In contrast to which, Kautsky himself foresaw that the "impending German revolution could only be proletarian" (p. 190). The remarkable thing in connection with this old difference of opinion, which is hardly reproduced correctly, is that Kautsky fails even to raise the question of what the German revolution of 1918 really was. For in that case he would have had to say: This revolution was a proletarian revolution; it immediately placed the power in the hands of the Social Democracy; but the latter, with the assistance of Kautsky himself, returned the power to the bourgeoisie which, proving incapable of holding onto power, had to call on Hitler for help.

Historical reality is infinitely richer in possibilities and in transitional stages than the imagination of the greatest genius. The value of political prognoses is not that they coincide with every stage of reality but that they assist in discerning its genuine development. From this standpoint, Friedrich Engels has passed the bar of history.

Rosa Luxemburg, Karl Liebknecht, H.G. Wells, Karl Kautsky
(clockwise from left).

Georgi Plekhanov, Vera Zasulich, Vladimir Ilyich Lenin.

Nicholas and Alexandra Romanov with daughters.

Mikhail Glazman (above); Adolf Joffe, Yakov Sverdlov (below, left to right).

Lev Kamenev

Grigori Zinoviev

Anatoli Lunacharsky (center), with Konstantin Stanislavski (left) and George Bernard Shaw (right).

Charolambos, Leon Trotsky, and Natalia Sedova

Friedrich Engels

Natalia Sedova

Joseph Stalin

Leon Sedov

Abel Yenukidze, Nadezhda Krupskaya (above); Édouard Herriot, Maxim Gorky (below).

ÉDOUARD HERRIOT

Édouard Herriot, born in France in 1872, was the principal leader of the principal political party of his country between the two world wars, the Radical Socialists (or Radicals), which, despite its name, was a conventional bourgeois party that sought to remain in power by coalitions to its right or left. In addition to trying to keep his party in the middle of the road, Herriot represented the center group of his own party.

Herriot entered politics in 1905 by being elected mayor of Lyons, and remained in that post almost half a century, except for a brief period during World War II. Elected to the Senate in 1912 and to the Chamber of Deputies in 1919, he became premier of France the first time in 1924 at the head of a left bloc between the Radicals and the Socialist Party. This cabinet gave way to a right bloc in 1925, but Herriot came back to the premier's seat a second time in 1926, and for a third time in 1932, after the Radicals won the parliamentary elections. When France entered a state of political crisis in 1934, Herriot accepted posts in various rightist cabinets, 1934-36, that preceded the victory of the People's Front in 1936. The People's Front was a left bloc like the one he had organized in 1924, except that it included the Communist as well as the Radical and Socialist parties. Herriot at first was cool to the People's Front, but finally accepted it and became president of the Chamber of Deputies, 1936-40, in which post he collaborated with the increasingly rightward-moving premiers who led France into World War II.

He refused to go into exile with de Gaulle after Pétain took over, remaining behind as a loyal opponent of the Vichy regime. He was arrested in 1942 and later was taken to Germany as a hostage. He resigned the lifetime presidency of the Radical Socialist Party a year before his death in 1957.

Trotsky wrote this essay, dated November 7, 1935, while he was in an Oslo hospital, shortly after the People's Front was

organized but before its electoral victory. The translation by John
G. Wright was first published, under the title "Édouard Herriot:
Man of the Golden Mean," in Fourth International, *December*
1941.

Édouard Herriot, mayor of Lyons, minister without portfolio, is today the central figure in the political life of France. He occupies this position not so much by virtue of his personality as by the political function he fulfills in his party, and his party in the country. Tracing their genealogy to the Jacobins (one of their many misconceptions!), the Radicals represent the middle classes of France, i.e., the predominant mass of the population. The social crisis that broke out in France later than in other countries implies primarily a crisis of the middle classes, and consequently a crisis of their political representation: this constitutes the real basis of the crisis of parliamentary democracy. The middle classes are dissatisfied, even exasperated. At the top they are pulled toward fascism, the nether strata pull to revolution. The position of the Radicals is becoming increasingly more unstable.

But, as is well known, the fire flares most brightly just before flickering out. Today, more than ever before, the Radicals are at the focus of politics. They are being courted persistently and even importunately by the Right and the Left. The Radical leaders sit in the Laval government and affix their signatures to the draconian financial decrees. At the same time, the Radical Party as a whole participates in the "People's Front," which hurls bolts of rhetoric against the Laval government and its decrees. The conservative and semi-official *le Temps* issues daily appeals to Herriot's patriotism and his tried and tested sagacity. *L'Humanité,* the organ of the Communists—very prudent, very moderate, and very patriotic Communists—with equal directness chants hymns in praise of Herriot's democratism, his republican trustworthiness, and his friendship to the Soviet Union.

Herriot undoubtedly finds the praise of *le Temps* very soothing and cannot help frowning at the clumsy praise of *l'Humanité.* But there are two wings in his party. One ascends to the banks, the other descends to the peasantry. Édouard Herriot is compelled to "keep up a good front while playing a poor hand." But will the equivocal game long continue? Will the mayor of Lyons long remain the central political figure in France?

The oratorical art of France is so rich in classical models, ready-made formulas, and traditional associations as to make it very difficult, especially on the basis of the corrected record with half the life taken out, to distinguish oratorical individuality against the solid background of national traditions. After the death of Jaurès, the athletic and impassioned master who sought to bring ideals from the philosophic heavens down to the crime-splotched earth, Briand, the "charmer," who used to justify himself by flattering the vices and weaknesses of others, was considered the best orator in France. As for Herriot, who after the death of Briand is assigned by many the first place, he has neither the devastating pathos of Jaurès nor the wheedling persuasiveness of Briand. The orator honestly reflects the "Radical" politician, he is prosaic. His eloquence strides in slippers—indeed, substantial ones—rather than on stilts. Satisfying his higher spiritual needs in the sphere of literature and music, Herriot keeps his common sense free for politics and especially for the rostrum. If this orator has a pose, it is a pose of simplicity, not credulous, but not openly perfidious either.

Common sense, however, would prove much too vapid, were it not seasoned with sentimentality. Herriot readily invests his arguments with the semblance of a personal confession, and never forgets reminders of his own sincerity. If he resorts to irony, he so mitigates it with qualifications as to make it appear a form of good nature. Witnesses have remarked that Herriot, in case of need, can draw tears, including his own. But these are tears which, after relieving the soul, dry up opportunely. His whole style is indelibly colored with an imposing, though not very self-confident, tint of the Golden Mean. Undoubtedly, an outstanding parliamentary orator, but not a great one.

Herriot takes his position consciously and persistently upon the terrain of common sense. Not without good cause does he see—at least he saw until yesterday—the mainspring of his power in his ability to think and feel as "all" do—discounting, of course, those who think otherwise. He is the "average Frenchman," but on a larger scale, so to say, the foremost of his peers, endowed with the gift of precise exposition, with a many-sided and preeminently humanistic education, a powerful voice, and a physique that inspires confidence. These are no trifles. But, perhaps, all these are not quite enough.

The best pedagogue is not he who descends to his pupils from the heights but he who rises to new levels together with them.

Herriot's power as orator consists of such pedagogic directness of intercourse with his audience. Its secret, however, lies in the fact that Herriot lacks utterly any kind of social insight or political perspective. Together with his audience, with the resourceful aid of common sense, he strives to find a way out of difficulties, and it must often seem to his listeners as if their leader were thinking out loud for them.

No doubt, Herriot is sincerely convinced that the logic of a civilized petty bourgeois is a logic common not only to all Frenchmen but to all mankind. He reasons as though it were possible to reduce all contradictions to a common denominator by means of arguments. He sermonizes and lectures. "We are no longer schoolchildren!" Tardieu once flung at him. And the impolite truism was met with bellows of approval from the benches on the Right, where much better knowledge obtains of what is wanted. Politics would be a very simple matter indeed were it reducible to a system of logical arguments. As a matter of fact, politics consists of clashes between social and national interests. But here the prerogatives of common sense cease, as well as Herriot's persuasiveness as orator.

In the struggle to gain the confidence of the average Frenchman, Herriot is most concerned lest he be taken, because of his reputation as a leftist, for an improviser, a dilettante, or worst of all, a dreamer. Says he, "As for myself, I have very little taste for synthesis. . . .   In the face of all complications, the true method to apply is the method of analysis which articulates and which is native to Frenchmen." This philosophic tirade rang in its time like an unfriendly dig at Briand, who put instinct in place of analysis of problems. Herriot indubitably imitates Poincaré in his diligent assortment of quotations and classification of documents. But the numbered arguments of a notary, the beloved manner of Poincaré, have little in common with the school of Pascal and Descartes: that is not analysis as yet. Besides, politics, in contradistinction to exercises in seminaries, is not exhausted by analysis and synthesis; politics is the art of making great decisions. Analysis and synthesis serve only to orient the will. But it is obvious that the orator cannot supply what the politician lacks: the will to action.

Often, after appealing either to his political or his personal conscience, Herriot adds, on occasion, "Incidentally, that is one and the same thing." Is that the case? As a matter of fact, the politics of Radicalism is the politics of perpetual internal conflict;

its words diverge from its actions, the intentions from the results. The cause for this duality, however, lies not in the "personal conscience" of leaders but in the character of their social support.

Passing on one of its wings into the big bourgeoisie and descending on the other to the proletariat, petty-bourgeois Radicalism is doomed to the role of an unstable center. The very objective contradictions that it seeks to overcome are those which rip its own ranks asunder. Within the Radical Party, Herriot himself seeks to maintain as in the past the post of center. Thanks to this he becomes the fulcrum of the centrifugal forces of modern society. Afraid of sliding to the Left, he unequivocally pulls to the Right. But all the places there are already occupied by parties and politicians in whom the big bourgeoisie puts more trust than in Herriot. At the left stand the Socialists, in close collaboration with faded Communists.

A few years ago, Herriot was compelled to put aside his good nature and to engage in a violent battle with his Socialist "friends" in order to assure himself, as mayor, a small majority in the municipality of Lyons. In parliament, the Socialists gave the Radicals equivocal support with the aim of pushing them out of the villages as they had already pushed them out of the urban centers. From the right wing incessant invitations came to Herriot to join the ranks of the bourgeois "concentration" bloc. But Herriot at first tried to resist: for the aim of the "national" invitations, which are the specialty of *le Temps,* is "to encircle the Radicals and strangle them."

"I say to you, without animosity,"—Herriot used to address himself to the right sector of the Chamber, before he had allowed himself to be "encircled"—"that you are mistaken." And immediately thereupon, the orator would turn to the left wing with "And I say to you in all friendliness that you, too, are mistaken." Such is the symmetry of the Golden Mean. But it is unstable, in our epoch which abhors symmetry. Herriot had only to appear at a session of his own fraction to be once again obliged to turn his face alternately to each wing, primarily, by the way, towards the left, with the words, "You are mistaken." A politician of the middle line, he would be unable to find himself unless he veered away from the flanks.

Upon diverse occasions, not always fortuitous, Herriot is given to calling upon his opponents to admit that he and his party are not lacking, at any rate, in "virility." Again, illusions! If by virility is understood not personal courage but political resoluteness for great actions, then French Radicalism is a direct negation of virility. Here, too, the cause lies outside of isolated individuals: the characters of leaders are selected, educated, and formed in conformance with the historical cause they serve.

The social relations in France seem, especially alongside those of Germany, to be very stable. Kaleidoscopic as they are, the politics of the Third Republic have long remained a constant quantity. The cause of this stability lies in the feeble movement of her economic life and population. France hoards, accumulates, puts money in circulation, but does not change her productive base. During months and years of prosperity, she extends her golden antennae far and wide, but only in order to withdraw them the moment that alarm is felt in the world atmosphere. This wisdom is negative and defensive, and besides, it comes into an ever greater contradiction with the European hegemony of the nation. The international politics of France are above all the politics of finance capital. The average Frenchman who entrusts his vote to the Radicals, and his savings to the banks, feels helpless in the ocean of world politics, with its flood and ebb tides, cross currents and whirlpools. Here, the bankers and the industrial magnates have the decisive word. Coming into conflict with them, Radicalism loses its last vestiges of virility.

Upon assuming power in 1924, and finding himself subjected to a cruel fire from the benches of the parliamentary Right, especially on the part of heavy industry and the banks, Herriot placated them and justified himself with: "I place the interests of the nation above any theory." From the scientific standpoint, this formula is astounding in its naiveté. "Theory," i.e., the program of a party, is intended to be nothing else but a thoroughly worked-out expression of the "interests" of the nation. By counterposing theory to "interests," Herriot admitted ten years ago that the program of the Radicals, with all its moderateness, could find no place in the postwar reality.

The crisis of the franc and state finances in 1924 immediately placed the Radical administration face to face with the entire system of finance capital. The Bourse pretended to be in extreme terror of the Radicals. In reality, it was Herriot who felt mortal terror of the Bourse; that is why he pleaded with it not to take his program seriously. In the end, Herriot yielded his post to Poincaré. Together with his enemy Tardieu, Herriot spent two years in the "concentration" ministry, which he subsequently left only upon the categorical insistence of his party, against his own will, "with death in his heart." Herriot's entire constitution is such that he prefers having the authoritative representatives of big business not in the opposition but rather in his own administration. The difficulty, however, is that the Bourse's politicians prefer to have *their own* administration once more, with Herriot a hostage as in 1926-28, rather than a super-arbiter vacillating between the interests of the big bourgeoisie and the illusions of the petty bourgeoisie, as in 1924 and in 1932.

The fact that, at the critical moment, Poincaré represented the banks so authoritatively has forever established his authority in the mind of Herriot. The leader of the Radicals has subsequently allowed no opportunity to pass by without reiterating, sometimes two and three times in the same speech, his profound reverence for Poincaré. Is it possible to conceive a Jacobin who would bow respectfully before the authority of . . . a Necker? Yet Herriot continues to consider himself a Jacobin.

Appealing in December 1932 for the payment of the installment due on the American debt, Herriot stressed that he was only under compulsion to bear the consequences of somebody else's policy. When the Chamber of Deputies went on record for nonpayment, Herriot exclaimed: "Tomorrow somebody else may perhaps be able to tie the threads together. I shall assist him from without." But the task of "tying the threads together" fell upon Herriot himself. Whether in questions of foreign or domestic policy, Herriot as a short-term minister and premier invariably began by referring to the situation which he had inherited and which predetermined his course, as if someone else each time decided for him what must be done. The key to the riddle is simple: the logic of French imperialism is mightier than the sympathies of the "average Frenchman." Upon assuming power, the Radicals are compelled to defend the very same interests that are served by the National Bloc. They retain only freedom to choose the phraseology.

Herriot's final argument against those who balked at paying the installment due was: "You are ready to disrupt the concord of liberty against dictatorship for the sake of 480,000,000 francs." This does not ring at all badly in the political sound-chamber of France. But the concord between "the three great democracies" remains only a pious hope of the Radicals. The reality at that time—and it is still a reality today, though somewhat warped— was that France was allied with three reactionary dictatorships: Poland, Rumania, and Yugoslavia. The pacifist lawyer or schoolteacher is doomed to carry out policies as minister different from those his heart desires. Hence, it is quite natural that the Radical deputies feel displeased with their ministers and the Radical voters with their deputies. No less natural is it that the displeasure of both is doomed to impotence. Reducing the complex mechanics to its simplest formula, we must say that in all major questions the petty bourgeois is under the fatal necessity of bowing to the big bourgeois.

Shortly after the fall of his second ministry, Herriot disclosed to the Athenian Telegraph Agency the ultimate meaning of his politics: "What I defended in my last speeches—is the morals of Plato." In the figure of "passionately beloved" Greece, Herriot greeted the birthplace of his doctrine: "I sacrificed myself in order to remain true to my ideals." In reality, his sacrifice was not so tragic in character; pressed by the Socialists and by his own fraction, Herriot chose to be defeated honorably upon an international issue, in expectation of the inevitable time when the Chamber of Deputies cooled off from the last elections and shifted its center of gravity to the right. At first glance, it might appear paradoxical that this gospel of philosophic idealism should be addressed to the Greece of Venizelos and Tsaldaris, which hardly serves as a model in the question of paying debts. But it is impossible not to admit that Herriot's good intentions towards Wall Street did actually retain on this occasion their platonic character.

It would be a mistake to consider this excessively exalted motivation for a parliamentary defeat to be nothing more than an unsuccessful turn of phrase. No. The philosophy of absolute values enters as a necessary element into Herriot's spiritual economics. Bowing to yesterday with purely conservative humility, Herriot reconciles in the astral voids of philosophy the contradiction between his "theory" and the policies foisted upon him; this method has the added advantage of not increasing the overhead expense. Just as the cult of pure ideas did not hinder Plato himself, the "divine" broad-shouldered idealist, from trading in olive oil and dealing with slaves as beasts of burden, so the worship of eternal morals does not hinder Herriot from supporting the Versailles system. It is the merit of Platonism that it permits double-entry bookkeeping, one entry for the spirit, the other for the flesh. Were it not for fear of offending the Voltairean and the man of good morals in M. Herriot, we could say that he is motivated in the last analysis by the self-same psychological forces that impel certain Catholic ladies in high society to divide their activity between adultery and the Church. Herriot treats history in somewhat the same manner as he does philosophy; he derives moral solace from it rather than lessons for action. Doubtful as it may seem, such a method enables him to trace his genealogy from the revolutionists of the year 1793.

The Radicals believe that of the traditions of the Jacobins they have most completely assimilated their anticlericalism and patriotism. But anticlericalism has long ceased to be a militant doctrine; this business has been reduced to a peaceful division of labor between the secular republic and the Catholic Church. As for patriotism, in the case of the Jacobins it was inextricably bound up with the proclamation of a revolutionary principle and its defense against feudal Europe. Herriot's patriotism proclaims no new idea but clings closely to the patriotism of Tardieu. The shades of Robespierre and Saint-Just have been invoked in vain. Not for nothing did Poincaré himself say patronizingly of Herriot, "National reactions are peculiar to the man."

Herriot's references to the Jacobins have always had an incorporeal character. When in need of historic examples, he quotes more readily from the "great liberal" Lamartine and even Count de Broglie. In one of his parliamentary speeches Herriot quoted a banal statement of Louis XV as proof of . . . the peace-loving quality of the "French spirit"! Idealists generally treat history as a wholesale warehouse of moral tracts. Lack of discrimination in the choice of authorities to them appears to be objectivity. Least accidental, by the way, are the references to Lamartine. This peacock of a poet was not only the false historian of the Girondists but also their epigone in politics. Herriot's Radicalism has nothing in common with the Mountain; it is the same Girondism, but a Girondism that passed through the fires of 1848 and 1871, and in them burned up the remnants of its illusions.

Herriot undoubtedly would have made an ideal French mayor had he not been handicapped by world contradictions, wars and threats of war, reparations and debts, German and Italian fascism, in short, by everything that goes to make up our epoch, not to mention the crisis, unemployment, the dissatisfaction of the functionaries, the dictatorial aspirations of Tardieu, the armed detachments of Colonel de la Rocque, and the perfidious friendship of Blum.

Herriot's positive program, which he himself so easily disavows, consists of the withered principles of liberalism in a dilute solution of "socialism": private initiative and personal liberty—first and foremost; but—"within a social milieu harmonized by the state"; "the producer and the consumer must understand that there is a solidarity of interests between them"; "the peasant and the worker are—brothers." Add free education, secularization of the schools, and the program of domestic policies is well nigh exhausted. Upon this foundation rises the radiant idea of "Progress," and the image of France, torch in hand.

In the domain of foreign policy, Herriot's politics are even less definitive—if that is conceivable. "Concord between the three great democracies"; "peace is created by having faith in peace"; "from discussion is always born conciliation"; "we do not need general ideas—what we need is to study the facts." Behind such aphorisms the average Frenchman presupposes a program of action; as a matter of fact, nothing exists behind them save perplexity in the face of the complicated world situation.

It would be vain to seek for creative thought from the Radical leader whose religion is watchful caution. Briand managed splendidly without the categorical imperative, and without philosophic ideas in general; but his ready wit provided him in case of need with broad elastic formulas, if not with creative ideas. It is sufficient to recall—and today, it already sounds like a historic anecdote—that on September 15, 1929, during a diplomatic luncheon at which the representatives of twenty-seven nations were gathered, Briand proposed to initiate work for the creation of the United States of Europe. There is a gesture of which Herriot is incapable! Not that he would be averse to the idea of a United States of Europe, or, if it suits you —of the whole world. A beautiful idea! An exalted idea! But much too exalted to mix with practical politics.

The theatrical postwar diplomacy with its unending personal interviews sped by airplanes, with its discussions at Geneva barren of results but brimful of plaudits, seems to have been specially created for the purpose of diverting attention away from the knots that are being drawn ever tighter. Herriot placed the greatest political importance upon his personal meetings with former British prime minister MacDonald; it was thus that "mutual understanding" was being created and renewed. The more the exalted interlocutors refrain from drawing their thoughts to their conclusion, the oftener they refer, sighing, to parliaments and public opinion, all the more do they defer questions to the next occasion, all the more do they feel constrained within the three-dimensional confines of empirical politics. MacDonald sought solace in the Old and New Testaments; Herriot, in the secular theology of idealism.

An observant foreigner cannot fail to feel amazed at the undue expansiveness reached by the vows of love for France in the speeches of French politicians of all tendencies. Given the greatest mastery of language, it is difficult each time to find a new expression for one and the same idea; small wonder that the repetitious patriotic avowals fatigue one with their monotony. Once, Herriot found it necessary to declare that his love for France was "a profound but hidden and chaste emotion." The minutes record, "Laughter from the Right." Indeed, it is difficult to consider an emotion as hidden if its chastity is certified from a political rostrum.

These patriotic harangues, which do little honor to French taste, so refined as a rule, spring not so much from legitimate pride in the great role France has played in the history of mankind—indeed, such an emotion could be more restrained—as from alarm for the present international position of France, which is obviously not commensurate with its actual forces. Historical remembrances serve only as a source for patriotic rhetoric; the exposed nerve behind it is the unquenched and acute alarm which cannot be concealed by mutual appeals for coolness and self-control.

Herriot, of course, always stood for disarmament. But material disarmament must be preceded by moral disarmament. Besides, genuine peace can be established only upon security. And security demands a strong French army. Until a rational reduction of armaments is achieved, the people must see the guarantee of peace in the weapons of France. Anyone failing to agree with this thereby discloses his malice.

An extremely restrained orator as a rule, Herriot is unable to find words harsh enough to denounce those disbelievers who have doubts about the peaceableness of France and its government. We, on our part, do not doubt for a moment the genuineness of Herriot's pacifism. We must only add, it is the pacifism of a conqueror. If we disregard the warlike nomads, the conquerors have always inclined to pacifism, all the more decisively the greater their victory and the sacrifices paid for it. The formula of satiated pacifism is a simple one: the vanquished must reconcile themselves to their fate and not seek to hamper the victor from enjoying the fruits of victory. After every new successful campaign Napoléon wanted to be left in peace. If he had to return to the wars again, it was only because those whom he had crushed refused to reconcile themselves to the tyranny of the conqueror. Had the Little Corporal been less contemptuous of ideology, he would have had little difficulty in placing his concern for peace under the aegis of Plato.

At the Disarmament Conference—in which century was it?—Herriot announced solemnly, "We have come here to proclaim our aversion to all imperialism, whether open or masked." These words would ring more convincingly had the orator taken the pains to explain what he meant by imperialism. We shall not go into theoretical definitions, but confine ourselves merely to recalling the least disputable features of imperialism. Holding backward countries by force in the status of exploited *colonies* is the most patent, though far from the only form of imperialism. To our knowledge, Herriot has never undertaken to renounce the colonial possessions of France. France's opposition, backed by force, to the unification of a nation within the boundaries of a national state (the questions of *Anschluss,* and of the Polish Corridor); the strengthening of her own hegemony by giving military and financial support to outright antipopular governments in other countries (Poland, Rumania, Serbia)—if all this is not imperialism, then there is no such thing as imperialism in the universe.

Territorial seizures and violence cease to be seizures and violence for Herriot once they are sanctioned by the past, or better still, by international pacts. Moral and philosophical precepts are not decisive; patriotic interests are. Imperialism is everything that runs counter to the interests of France. Imperialists therefore are to be found always outside her frontiers.

The less Herriot tends toward practical concessions to the defeated enemy, all the more generous he becomes in the sphere of philosophic reparations. Thus, during the same conference he quoted Immanuel Kant as having foreseen in his plan for permanent peace . . . The League of Nations. One would indeed feel very sorry for the sage of Königsberg had he foreseen nothing better than this. But the appeal to Kant is very characteristic: the question is transplanted as usual from the realm of reality into the transcendental sphere, and besides, the reference to a German classic should stir the Germans to peaceableness. Unfortunately, the question of whether Kant, in his scheme of permanent peace, had likewise foreseen the Versailles treaty, is left unexplained.

The philosophic quotation, however, proved of no avail. Hitler entrenched himself upon the ruins of the Weimar democracy. Germany's program of arming entered as a terrible reality into the artificial regime of the Europe of Versailles. British diplomacy lifted its head, feeling itself again in its favorite role of arbitrator. Mussolini, using Hitler's rearming as a club, presented France with an ultimatum: a free hand in Africa, as a pledge of friendship. Laval agreed to the concession. However, before the Italo-Ethiopian conflict succeeded in terminating Ethiopia's independence, or, on the contrary, in extracting the tusks of Italian fascism, it dealt a cruel blow to the international position of France. A question mark was immediately placed over her continental hegemony. France's scurrying between Italy and England laid bare the international dependency of French imperialism with its far too narrow demographic and economic base. The crisis in the international position of France complicates her already profound internal crisis, tearing the ground from under the feet of Herriot's imperialist "pacifism." But maybe Moscow could provide a firmer support?

After the Bolsheviks had repulsed all attempts at intervention and had overcome their internal enemies, Herriot's interest in the Soviets became tinged with his remembrances of the epoch of Jacobin terror. During his visit, in 1922, to the Soviet republic, Herriot talked with the Bolsheviks—not as a co-thinker of course, but almost as a well-wisher, as one of the heirs of the Mountain, capable of "understanding" the Bolsheviks. He was interested in the economic and cultural measures of the revolution, but especially in the successes of the Red Army. On the Soviet calendar there still remained at that time one more very difficult year, but the Civil War had ended, and the stricken country was already on the upgrade. The army, whose numbers had been greatly reduced, cleaned and spruced itself, and appeared presentable enough, at any rate, in Moscow, to be shown to a foreign guest. As I recall, Herriot visited military schools and barracks. Politics is inconceivable without guile, so orders had been issued in advance that during Herriot's presence in the Commissariat of War the regiment on duty should march by, singing, beneath the windows of the office where the reception was to take place. I must say that the regiment, which was under the special supervision of the then commander in chief S.S.

Kamenev, a great lover of army songs, was considered a model unit. We were not mistaken in our appraisal of the "national reactions" of the democratic politician. When the window panes rattled from the initial blast of soldiers' voices, Herriot pulled his heavy body from the armchair and displayed immediately his familiarity not only with the melody but also with the words.

In the years that followed, Herriot's relations with the Soviets worsened gradually. During his years of collaboration with Poincaré he severely censured the regime that refused over so long a period to renounce the methods of dictatorship. However, in proportion as militant nationalism grew stronger in Germany, Herriot tended to become again much better disposed toward the Soviet Union. "As a democrat, and a great-grandson of the revolution which at times steeped its hands in blood, I refuse to fling curses and satire at Russia, now at work creating a new regime." Let it be known, incidentally, that he, Herriot, was as far removed from communism today as he had been from tsarism previously; but he had no doubt that the Bolshevik regime would ultimately create petty peasant proprietors. And France would be able to lean for support upon their army. This is the task to which world history is ultimately reducible.

Thus, Herriot became a cautious but persistent apostle of military friendship with the Soviet Union. It should be said bluntly that he did so without enthusiasm, rather constrained by bitter necessity. The big bourgeoisie finally allowed a Franco-Soviet agreement within a framework which would make it tolerable for England and yet not conflict with Italy's friendship. The future will demonstrate what this means in action. In any case, the mayor of Lyons does not assume the title "Friend of the USSR" without guile. To be sure, the collectivization of the peasantry has dealt a certain blow to his conservative hopes of a strong peasant; but Soviet diplomacy has instead become much wiser, more cautious, and more solid. And in the wake of Soviet diplomacy—the French Communist Party as well. At the last congress of the Radicals Herriot spoke demonstratively about his friend Litvinov ("Yes, my friend Litvinov"). This does not prevent him, however, from remaining in the ministry of Laval who, with much greater assurance and justification, speaks of "his friend Mussolini." It is not excluded that Herriot may become Laval's successor, and carry on the friendship with Mussolini on his own account. But for how long?

It is not in place here to enter into political speculation, all the more so because the question of what will happen to Herriot personally is inseparable from the question of the future of France and of Europe as a whole. However, one can state with assurance that the political extremes will continue to swallow up the center in the future as well. The Radicals were able to assure the equilibrium of the parliamentary seesaw only so long as the country preserved a relative social equilibrium. These happy days have gone beyond recall. Herriot's victory at the elections (May 1932) has served only to reveal the utter incapacity of his party in the face of the impending domestic and foreign catastrophes. The Radical leaders replaced one another only to reveal more and more clearly the pathetic helplessness of all groupings in the party. On February 6, 1934, Daladier, the extreme "left" among the Radicals, ingloriously capitulated to the street demonstration of the fascists and royalists. He, you see, did not want a civil war. In reality, he opened wide the gates for it. The language of facts is incontestable. At a slower pace than other European countries, France is heading towards great convulsions. Radicalism will be the first victim. Whatever aspect the coming epoch may assume, it will not be the epoch of the Golden Mean.

MAXIM GORKY

Maxim Gorky, born in Russia in 1868, spent his youth wandering as a tramp and common laborer. Although he had no formal education, he became one of Russia's outstanding authors of novels, plays, and short stories. He joined the Bolsheviks in 1905 and helped organize the first legal Bolshevik paper, but he turned away from them in the years of reaction following the defeat of the 1905 revolution, and he was openly hostile to the October revolution. He left the Soviet Union to live abroad in 1921, in Lenin's time, and did not return permanently until 1931, after which he defended Stalin's policies. Two years after his death in 1936, the Stalin regime charged that he and his son had been "murdered by the Trotsky-Bukharin gang."

Gorky's autobiographical trilogy (Childhood, In the World, *and* My Universities) *is available in English, along with most of his novels and plays.*

The translation of Trotsky's obituary, dated July 9, 1936, and written in Norway, was first published in International Review, *September-October 1936.*

Gorky died when there was nothing more for him to say. This makes quite bearable the decease of a great writer who has left a deep mark on the development of the Russian intelligentsia and the Russian working class during the last forty years.

Gorky started his literary career as a tramp poet. This was his best period as an artist. From the lower depths, Gorky carried to the Russian intelligentsia the spirit of daring, the romantic bravery, of people who had nothing to lose. The Russian intelligentsia was preparing to break the chains of tsarism. It needed daring. It passed on its spirit to the masses.

In the events of the revolution, however, there was no place for a real live tramp, except as a participant in robbery and pogroms.

By December 1905 the Russian proletariat and the radical intelligentsia that was bearing Gorky on its shoulders met—in opposition. Gorky did the honest thing. It was, in its way, a heroic effort. He turned his face to the proletariat. The important product of this about-face was *The Mother*. A wider vista opened to the writer, and he now dug deeper. But neither literary schooling nor political training could replace the splendid spontaneity of his first creative period. A tendency to cool reasoning made its appearance in the ambitious tramp. The artist began to resort to didacticism. During the years of reaction, Gorky shared himself out almost evenly between the working class, which had then abandoned the open political arena, and his old enemy-friend, the Russian intelligentsia, who had now taken unto themselves a new enthusiasm—religion. Together with the late Lunacharsky, Gorky paid his tribute to the vogue of mysticism. As a monument to his spiritual capitulation, we have his weak novel *Confession*.

Deeper than any other trait in the makeup of that extraordinary self-learner was his worship of culture. It seems that his first belated meeting with the lady had seared him for life. Gorky lacked the necessary schooling of thought and the historical intuition that might have enabled him to establish a convenient distance between himself and culture and would have given him the freedom necessary for a critical estimate. In his attitude toward culture there has always remained quite a bit of fetishism and idolatry.

Gorky approached the war with a feeling of concern for the cultural values of humanity. He was not so much an internationalist as a cultural cosmopolite, though one who was Russian to the marrow of his bones. He never attained a revolutionary outlook on war nor a dialectical understanding of culture. But he stood, nevertheless, heads above the patriotic intellectual fraternity of the time.

He received the revolution of 1917 almost in the manner of a director of a museum of culture. He was alarmed. He was in terror of "the savage soldiery and the workers who would not work." He rejoined the left-wing intelligentsia, who approved of a revolution but only if it was free from disorder. He met the October revolution in the role of an outright enemy, though a passive one.

It was very hard for Gorky to get used to the victory of October. Tormoil reigned in the land. The intelligentsia hungered and suffered persecution. Culture was, or appeared to be, in danger.

During those years, Gorky distinguished himself chiefly as a mediator between the Soviet power and the old intellectuals. He was their attorney in the court of the revolution. Lenin, who loved and valued Gorky, was very much afraid that the latter would fall victim to his connections and his weakness, and finally succeeded in having the writer leave the country voluntarily.

Gorky made his peace with the Soviet regime only when the "disorder" came to an end and there was evidence of an economic and cultural rise in the country. He warmly approved the great movement of the masses toward education. In gratefulness for that he even gave his blessing retroactively to the October overturn.

The last period of his life was undoubtedly the period of his decline. But even this decline was a natural part of his life's orbit. His tendency to didacticism received now its great opportunity. He became the tireless teacher of young writers, even schoolboys. He did not always teach the right thing, but he did it with sincere insistence and open generosity that more than made up for his too-inclusive friendship with the bureaucracy. Alongside these human, a little too human, traits existed and predominated the old concern about technology, science, and art. "Enlightened absolutism" gets along nicely with service to "culture." Gorky really believed that without the bureaucracy there would be no tractors, no five-year plans, and especially no printing presses and supplies of paper. He therefore forgave the bureaucracy the poor quality of the paper and even the sickening Byzantinism of the literature that was labeled "proletarian."

Most of the White emigration hated Gorky, characterizing him as a "traitor." Exactly what Gorky betrayed is not quite clear. Was he thought to be a traitor to the ideal of private property? The hatred shown to Gorky by the "former people" of the *bel étage* was a justly deserved, and highly complimentary, tribute to the great man.

The Soviet press is now piling over the writer's still warm form mountains of unrestrained praise. They call him no less than a "genius." They describe him as the "greatest genius." Gorky would have most likely frowned at this kind of praise. But the press serving bureaucratic mediocrity has its criteria. If Stalin, Kaganovich, and Mikoyan have been raised to the rank of genius in their lifetime, one naturally cannot refuse Gorky the epithet upon his death. Gorky will enter the history of Russian literature as an unquestionably clear and convincing example of great literary talent, not touched, however, by the breath of genius.

Of course, the dead writer is pictured now in Moscow as an unbending revolutionary and an "adamant Bolshevik." These are pure inventions of the bureaucracy. Gorky came to Bolshevism about 1905 or so, in the company of other democratic fellow travelers. He left together with them, without abandoning, however, personal friendly relations with the Bolsheviks. He entered the party only during the Soviet Thermidor. His enmity to the Bolsheviks during the October revolution and the civil war, as well as his support of the Thermidorian bureaucracy, shows quite clearly that Gorky was never a revolutionary. True it is, however, that he was a satellite of the revolution. Bound to it by the inexorable law of gravitation, he turned about the Russian revolution all his life. Like all satellites he had his "phases." The sun of the revolution sometimes lighted his face. Sometimes it fell on his back. But in all his phases, Gorky remained true to himself, to his peculiar, extremely rich, simple, and at the same time complicated nature. We take leave of him without a note of intimacy, without exaggerated praise, but with respect and gratitude. The great writer and great man has left his mark on a period of history. He has helped to lay out new historic paths.

GRIGORI ZINOVIEV
AND LEV KAMENEV

Grigori Y. Zinoviev and Lev B. Kamenev were both born in Russia in 1883, joined the Russian Social Democracy in 1901, and became Bolsheviks in 1903. Zinoviev was a member of the Bolshevik Central Committee, 1907-27. He was Lenin's closest associate in exile and returned with him to Russia in 1917. Kamenev went back to Russia in 1914 to serve as editor of Pravda and to guide the work of the Bolshevik faction in the Duma. He was arrested and exiled until the February revolution, after which he was elected to the Central Committee, 1917-27. On the eve of the October insurrection both men publicly opposed it. Lenin threatened to have them expelled for violating party discipline, but the matter was dropped after the success of the insurrection.

Under the Soviet regime Zinoviev became chairman of the Petrograd Soviet and Kamenev chairman of the Moscow Soviet. Zinoviev also became chairman of the Communist International, 1919-26, and Kamenev became Lenin's deputy as chairman of the Political Bureau and deputy chairman of the Council of People's Commissars, as well as editor of Lenin's Collected Works. In 1923 they, Stalin, and other members of the Political Bureau created a faction that launched a witch-hunt against "Trotskyism." In 1925 Zinoviev and Kamenev broke with Stalin after becoming alarmed by the policies and practices of the bureaucratic tendency around him. In 1926 they joined with Trotsky and the Left Opposition in an anti-Stalinist bloc called the United Opposition. This lasted until the end of 1927 when they and Trotsky were expelled from the Communist Party.

While Trotsky refused to renounce his ideas, Zinoviev and Kamenev capitulated to Stalin's demands and were reinstated in the party in 1928. In 1932 they were expelled again and exiled, and capitulated again and were allowed to return to Moscow in 1933. They were arrested in 1934 after the assassination of Kirov and were tried, convicted, and sentenced for "moral complicity" in the Kirov case. In August 1936 they and fourteen other defendants were indicted in the first of the infamous Moscow trials, on charges of plotting, under orders from Trotsky and in collaboration with the fascist powers, to kill Stalin and other government leaders and to restore capitalism in Russia. At the trial all of the defendants "confessed" these and other crimes, were found guilty, and were executed.

Trotsky got to know Zinoviev and Kamenev well only after 1917, and was never intimate with them even during the United Opposition bloc, although his sister was married to Kamenev. He broke off all relations with them when they capitulated in 1927 and considered them bitter political opponents for the rest of their lives. But he defended them against the Kirov charges, and set everything else aside to defend them as well as himself against the charges in the trial of the sixteen. Before he could do much, however, the Norwegian government, under pressure from Moscow, silenced him by denying him access to reporters and by seizing his articles and letters, and interned him until December 1936, when he and Natalia Sedova were placed on a tanker bound for Mexico, whose government had just granted them asylum.

On the voyage across the Atlantic, Trotsky continued his work, interrupted by the Norwegian government, of preparing the analysis of the Moscow trials that he would publish in the months to come: a book in France, Les crimes de Staline *(1937)* and his testimony to the Dewey Commission of Inquiry, published in The Case of Leon Trotsky *(1937). The following chapter from the French book, written on December 31, 1936, in the form of entries in his journal, continues from previous entries his examination of the possibility that Zinoviev and Kamenev might have been guilty. This leads Trotsky to a consideration of their personalities and record as capitulators and of the psychology necessary for terrorists.*

There are no biographies of Zinoviev or Kamenev. Zinoviev was a prolific writer but everything he wrote was and remains suppressed in the Soviet Union, and the only work by him in print in English is his 1923 History of the Bolshevik Party, reprinted in England in 1973. Unlike some Moscow trial victims, they have not been "rehabilitated" by the post-Stalin Soviet government.

The translation by John G. Wright was first published in Fourth International, *August 1941. It has been revised here by*

George Saunders, who also translated from the Russian the last six paragraphs which were missing from the 1941 version.

The year that is now ending will go down in history as the year of Cain.

In view of the warnings by Zinoviev and Kamenev about Stalin's secret schemes and designs, the question may be asked whether intentions of the very same kind did not arise in their minds in relation to Stalin after they found themselves cut off from all other means of combat. Both of them made no few turns and squandered no few principles in the last period of their lives. In that case why can't we grant the possibility that, despairing of the consequences of their own capitulations, they really did at a certain moment make a frantic turn toward terror? Later, as part of their final capitulation, they might have consented to meet the GPU halfway and to entangle me in their ill-starred designs, as a service to themselves and to the regime with which they once again sought to make peace.

This hypothesis has entered the minds of some of my friends. I have weighed it from all sides, without the slightest preconceptions or considerations of personal interest. And each time I came to the conclusion that it was utterly unfounded.

Zinoviev and Kamenev are two profoundly different types. Zinoviev is an agitator. Kamenev—a propagandist. Zinoviev was guided in the main by a subtle political instinct. Kamenev was given to reasoning and analyzing. Zinoviev was always inclined to fly off at a tangent. Kamenev, on the contrary, erred on the side of excessive caution. Zinoviev was entirely absorbed by politics, cultivating no other interests and appetites. In Kamenev there sat a sybarite and an esthete. Zinoviev was vindictive. Kamenev was good nature personified. I do not know what their mutual relations were in emigration. In 1917 they were brought close together for a time by their opposition to the October revolution. In the first few years after the victory, Kamenev's attitude toward Zinoviev was rather ironical. They were subsequently drawn together by their opposition to me, and later, to Stalin. Throughout the last thirteen years of their lives, they marched side by side and their names were always mentioned together.

Despite all their individual differences, and in addition to their common schooling in emigration under Lenin's guidance, they were endowed with almost an identical range of intellect and will. Kamenev's analytical capacity served to complement Zinoviev's feel for a situation; and jointly they would explore for a common decision. The more cautious Kamenev would sometimes allow Zinoviev to carry him along farther than he himself wanted to go, but in the long run they found themselves side by side along the same line of retreat. In the stature of their personalities they were peers, and they supplemented each other by their dissimilarities. Both of them were deeply and unreservedly devoted to the cause of socialism. Such is the explanation for their tragic union.

There are no compelling reasons for me to take upon myself any political or moral responsibility for Zinoviev and Kamenev. Discounting a brief interval—1926-27—they were always my bitter adversaries. Personally, I did not place much trust in them. Each of them, to be sure, was Stalin's intellectual superior. But they lacked sufficient character. Lenin had precisely this trait in mind when he wrote in his "testament" that it was "no accident" that Zinoviev and Kamenev were opponents of the insurrection in the autumn of 1917. They failed to withstand the pressure of bourgeois public opinion. When deep-going social shifts in the Soviet Union began to crystallize, combined with the formation of a privileged bureaucracy, it was "no accident" that Zinoviev and Kamenev allowed themselves to be swept away into the camp of Thermidor (1922-26).

They far excelled their then allies, including Stalin, in their theoretical understanding of the processes taking place. Herein lies the explanation for their attempt to break with the bureaucracy and to oppose it. In July 1926 at the plenum of the Central Committee, Zinoviev declared that "on the question of apparatus-bureaucratic repression Trotsky was correct as against us." Zinoviev, at that time, acknowledged that his mistake in waging a struggle against me was even "more dangerous" than his mistake in 1917! However, the pressure of the privileged stratum reached overwhelming proportions. It was "no accident" that Zinoviev and Kamenev capitulated to Stalin at the end of 1927 and carried with them those who were younger and less authoritative. Thereafter they expended no little effort in denouncing the Opposition.

But in 1930-32, when the country's entire organism was convulsed by the frightful consequences of the forced and unbridled collectivization, Zinoviev and Kamenev, like so many other capitulators, anxiously lifted their heads and began discussing in whispers among themselves the dangers of the government's new policy. They were caught reading a critical document which had originated in the ranks of the Right Opposition. For this terrible crime they were expelled from the party—no other charge was brought against them!—and, to top it off, were exiled. In 1933, Zinoviev and Kamenev not only recanted once again but prostrated themselves before Stalin. No slander was too vile for them to cast against the Opposition and especially against me personally. Their self-disarmament rendered them completely helpless before the bureaucracy, which could henceforth demand of them any confession whatever. Their subsequent fate was a result of these progressive capitulations and self-abasements.

Yes, they lacked sufficient character. These words, however, should not be taken too simplistically. The strength of any material is measured in terms of the forces operating on it and tending to destroy it. Between the beginning of the trial and my internment I had occasion to hear tranquil petty bourgeois people complain to me: "It's impossible to understand Zinoviev. He is so lacking in character!" And my reply to them was: "Have you yourselves experienced the full weight of the pressure to which he has been subjected for a number of years?" Unintelligent in the extreme are the comparisons, so widespread in intellectual circles, with the conduct in court of Danton, Robespierre, and others. Those were cases of revolutionary tribunes who came directly from the combat arena to face the knife of justice, still at the height of their powers, with their nerves almost unaffected, and— at the same time—without the slightest hope of survival after the trial.

Even more inappropriate are comparisons with Dimitrov's conduct in the Leipzig trial. To be sure, alongside of Torgler, Dimitrov made a favorable showing by his resoluteness and courage. But revolutionists in various lands and especially in tsarist Russia have shown no less firmness under incomparably more difficult conditions. Dimitrov was facing the most vicious class enemy. There was no evidence against him, nor could there have been. The state apparatus of the Nazis was still in its formative stages, and not adapted to totalitarian frame-ups. Dimitrov had the support of the gigantic apparatus of the Soviet state and the Comintern. From all the corners of the earth the sympathies of the popular masses went out to him. His friends were present at the trial. To become a "hero" one need only have had ordinary human courage.

But was this the situation of Zinoviev and Kamenev when they faced the GPU and the court? For ten years they had been enveloped by clouds of slander paid for in heavy gold. For ten years they had been suspended between life and death, first in a political sense, then in a moral sense, and lastly in a physical sense. Can one find in all past history examples of such systematic, refined, and fiendish destructive work upon the spines and nerves, upon all the elements of the human spirit? Zinoviev or Kamenev would have had more than ample character for a tranquil period. But our epoch of tremendous social and political convulsions demanded an extraordinary firmness of these men, whose abilities had secured them a leading place in the revolution. The disproportion between their abilities and their wills led to tragic results.

The history of my relations with Zinoviev and Kamenev can be traced without difficulty in documents, articles, and books. The *Biulleten Oppozitsii* (1929-36) alone sufficiently defines the abyss which decisively separated us from the day of their capitulation. Between us and them there were no ties whatever, no relations, no correspondence, nor even any attempts in this direction—there were none nor could there have been. In my letters and articles, I invariably advised the Oppositionists, in the interests of political and moral self-preservation, to break ruthlessly with the capitulators. Consequently, whatever I am able to say concerning the views and plans of Zinoviev-Kamenev for the last eight years of their lives can in no case be construed as the deposition of a witness. But I have in my possession a sufficient number of documents and facts which are easily verifiable; I am so well acquainted with the participants, their characters, their relations, and the entire background as to be able to state with absolute assurance that the accusation of terrorism against Zinoviev and Kamenev is from beginning to end a contemptible, police-manufactured frame-up, without an iota of truth in it.

The mere reading of the record of the court proceedings confronts every thoughtful person with the following enigma: Who exactly are these extraordinary defendants? Are they old and experienced politicians, struggling in the name of a definite program and capable of combining the means with the end, or are they victims of an inquisition, with their conduct determined not by their own reason or will but by the interests of the inquisitors? Are we dealing with normal people whose psychology is internally consistent and reflected in their words and actions, or with clinical cases who choose the least rational course, and who motivate their choice by the most incongruous arguments?

These questions apply above all to Zinoviev and Kamenev. Just what were their motives—motives that must have been exceedingly powerful—that guided them in their purported terror? At the first trial in January 1935, Zinoviev and Kamenev, while denying their participation in the assassination of Kirov, did acknowledge, by way of compensation, their "moral responsibility" for the terrorist tendencies, and in doing so they cited as the incentive for their oppositional activity their desire "to restore capitalism." If we had nothing else to go on but this unnatural political "confession," it would be sufficient to expose the lie of Stalinist justice. And indeed who can believe that Kamenev and Zinoviev were so fanatically set upon restoring the capitalism they had overthrown that they were ready to sacrifice their own as well as other heads to attain this goal? The confession of the defendants in January 1935 so crudely revealed the hand of Stalin behind it that the sensibilities of even the least exacting "friends of the Soviet Union" were jarred.

In the trial of the sixteen (August 1936) the "restoration of capitalism" is completely discarded. The impelling motive to terror is the naked "lust for power." The indictment rejects one version in favor of another as if it were a question of alternative solutions to a chess problem, with the interchange of solutions made in silence and without any commentaries. Following the state prosecutor, the defendants now repeat that they had no program, but simply were seized by an irresistible desire to capture the commanding heights of the state, regardless of the price. But we should like to ask: Just how could the assassination of the "leaders" have delivered power into the hands of people who had managed through a series of recantations to undermine confidence in themselves, to degrade themselves, to trample themselves into the mud, and thereby forever to deprive themselves of the possibility of playing any leading political role in the future?

If the goal of Zinoviev and Kamenev is incredible, their means are still more irrational. In the most carefully thought-out depositions of Kamenev it is underscored with special insistence that the Opposition had completely isolated itself from the masses, had lost its principles, and was thereby deprived of any hope of gaining influence in the future; and it was precisely *for this reason* that the Opposition came to the idea of terror. It is not hard to understand how advantageous such a self-characterization is to Stalin: it is his order that is being carried out—that is absolutely self-evident. But while the depositions of Kamenev are suited for the purpose of discrediting the Opposition, they are utterly unsuited for the justification of terror. It is precisely in conditions of political isolation that terrorist struggle signifies swift self-destruction for a revolutionary faction. We Russians are only too well aware of this from the example of Narodnaya Volya (1879-83), as well as from the example of the Social Revolutionaries in the period of reaction (1907-09). Zinoviev and Kamenev were not only brought up on these lessons, but they themselves commented innumerable times upon them in the party press. Could they, Old Bolsheviks, have forgotten and rejected the ABCs of the Russian revolutionary movement only because they wanted power so very much? To believe this is utterly impossible.

Let us suppose for a moment, however, that it actually occurred to Zinoviev and Kamenev to hope to gain power by a public disavowal of their past, supplemented by a campaign of anonymous terror. (Such a supposition is equivalent in fact to declaring them psychopaths!) In that case, what impulses would have driven those who carried out the terrorist actions, those who inevitably would have had to pay with their own heads for someone else's ideas? A hired killer who acts with the assurance of immunity, given in advance—that is believable. But terrorists without an ideal or a profound faith in their cause, offering themselves up for sacrifice?—that is inconceivable. In the trial of the sixteen, the Kirov assassination is portrayed as a small part of a vast plan for the extermination of the whole top layer of rulers. What is presented is *systematic* terror on an enormous scale. For the direct work of assassination, many dozens, if not hundreds, of fanatical, hardened, self-sacrificing fighters would have been necessary. Such people do not fall from the sky. They have to be picked, trained, organized. They have to be thoroughly imbued with the conviction that the only salvation lies in terror. Besides the active terrorists, reserves are needed. These can be counted on only if there are broad layers within the young generation inspired with sympathy for terrorism. Only by extensive propaganda in favor of terrorism can such moods be created, and such a propaganda effort would have an especially intense and passionate character, because the entire tradition of Russian Marxism goes against terror. This tradition would have to be broken down, and a new doctrine counterposed to it. If Zinoviev and Kamenev could not have repudiated their entire antiterrorist past without saying a word, even less could they have steered their supporters toward this Golgotha without a critical discussion, without polemics, without conflicts, without splits, and—without denunciations reaching the authorities. Such a drastic ideological rearming, involving hundreds and thousands of revolutionaries, could not have failed, in turn, to leave its traces in innumerable material ways (documents, letters, etc.). Where is all this? Where is the propaganda? Where is the terrorist literature? Where are the echoes of the internal struggles and debates? In the trial materials there is not even a hint of all this.

For Vyshinsky, as for Stalin, the defendants in general do not exist as human personalities. Thus, any question of their political psychology is also lost sight of. When one of the accused tried to invoke his "feelings," which he claimed prevented him from firing at Stalin, Vyshinsky alleged in reply that there were certain physical obstacles: "These . . . are the real reasons, the objective reasons; all the rest is psychology." "Psychology"! What annihilating contempt! The accused have no psychology; that is, they dare not have any. Their confessions are not the product of normal human motivation. The psychology of the ruling clique, through the mechanism of the inquisition, totally subordinates the psychology of the defendants to its own devices. The trial is modeled after some tragic puppet show. The accused are manipulated by strings, or rather, by the ropes around their necks. There is no room for "psychology."

Nevertheless, without the psychology of terrorism, terrorist action is inconceivable!

Let us for a moment allow the charges in all their absurdity: Driven by their "lust for power," the capitulator-leaders become terrorists. Hundreds of others are, in turn, so swept up by Zinoviev and Kamenev's "lust for power" that they, too, obligingly risk their necks. And all this—in alliance with Hitler! The criminal work, invisible to be sure to the unwary eye, reaches unheard-of proportions: the assassination of all the "leaders," universal sabotage, and espionage are organized. And this goes on for not just a day or a month, but almost five years! All under the mask of loyalty to the party! It is impossible to imagine more hard-bitten, cold-blooded, ferocious criminals.

But then what? In late July 1936 these monsters suddenly renounce their past and themselves and pathetically confess one after the other. None of them defend their ideas, aims, or methods of struggle. They vie in denouncing each other and themselves. No evidence is in the prosecutor's hands but the confessions of the accused. Yesterday's terrorists, saboteurs, and fascists now prostrate themselves to Stalin and swear their ardent love for him. What in the world are these fantastic defendants—criminals? psychopaths? a little of both? No, they are the clientele of Vyshinsky and Yagoda. This is what people look like who have gone through the laboratories of the GPU.

There is as much truth in Zinoviev and Kamenev's tales of their past criminal activity as in their protestations of love for Stalin. They died the victims of a totalitarian system that deserves nothing but condemnation!

ABEL YENUKIDZE

Abel S. Yenukidze was born in Georgia in 1877 and joined the revolutionary movement in the Caucasus in 1898. He helped to found the Social Democratic organization in Baku in 1900, and was an organizer of the party's underground printing press known as "Nina." Drafted into military service in 1916, he took part in the soldiers' rebellious actions in Petrograd during the February revolution and became a Bolshevik leader in the Soviet during the October revolution. He was elected secretary of the Central Executive Committee of the Soviets in 1918, and held that post until 1935. He was also a member of the Central Control Commission, 1924-34, and was elected to the Central Committee in 1934. In 1935 he was denounced for "political and personal dissoluteness" and expelled from the party as well as all his posts. In December 1937, a few weeks before the start of the third Moscow trial, the Soviet press announced that Yenukidze and other former high officials had been tried before a military court on charges of planning a coup to seize the Kremlin, espionage, bourgeois nationalism, and terrorism, including the murders of Kirov and Gorky; had confessed; and had been executed. It was widely believed that Yenukidze had refused to confess, which was why he did not live to occupy the dock at the third Moscow trial. Eight members of his family were said to have died in the purges. Yenukidze was "rehabilitated" nine years after Stalin's death.

Trotsky's article, written in Mexico, was dated January 8, 1938, but he must have added some things after that date because the text mentions the Bukharin-Rykov trial, which did not begin until March.

The translation was first published, under the title "Behind the Kremlin Walls," in The New International, *March 1939. It has been revised here by George Saunders.*

Even for those who are well acquainted with the protagonists and the situation, the latest events in the Kremlin are somewhat startling. I have felt this particularly clearly since the news came that Yenukidze, long the regularly reelected secretary of the Central Executive Committee of the Soviets, has been shot. Not that Yenukidze was a prominent figure. The statements in some of the papers asserting that he should be counted a "friend of Lenin" and a "member of the closed circle which ruled Russia" are inexact. Lenin had good relations with Yenukidze, but not better than with dozens of other people. Yenukidze was a second-class political figure, without personal ambitions, with a constant disposition to adapt himself to the situation; that is precisely why he seemed a candidate least indicated for execution. The calumnies of the Soviet press against Yenukidze began in a completely unexpected manner shortly after the Zinoviev-Kamenev trial. He was accused of immorality and of connections with the enemies of the people. What does "connection with enemies of the people" mean? It is very likely that Yenukidze, a good-hearted man, attempted to come to the aid of the families of executed Bolsheviks. The "immorality" signifies an inclination for personal comfort, too high a standard of living, women, etc. It is likely that there is a bit of truth in this. Nevertheless, things have gone far in the Kremlin, very far, if they have come to shooting Yenukidze. That is why it seems to me that the simple recital of the life of this man will enable a foreign reader to better understand what is happening behind the ramparts of the Kremlin.

Abel Yenukidze was a Georgian from Tiflis, like Stalin. The Biblical Abel was younger than Cain. Yenukidze, in contrast, was older than Stalin by two years. At the time of his execution he was about sixty years of age. It was in his youth that he joined the Bolsheviks, who were then a faction, along with the Mensheviks, in the still united Social Democratic Party. In the Caucasus in the first years of the century a remarkable clandestine printshop was established which played more than a slight role in preparing the way for the first revolution (1905). In the operation of this printshop the brothers Yenukidze, "Red" Abel and "Blacky" Simon, took an active part. The printshop was financed by Leonid Krasin, who was to become a prominent Soviet administrator and diplomat. In those years the talented young engineer, not without the cooperation of the young writer Maxim Gorky, knew how to obtain money for the revolution from liberal millionaires of the type of Savva Morozov. From then on

Krasin kept up friendly relations with Yenukidze: they called each other by their nicknames. It was from the lips of Krasin that I heard the Biblical name Abel for the first time.

In the hard period between the first and second revolutions, Yenukidze, like the majority of the so-called "Old Bolsheviks," wandered away from the party. I don't know if it was for a long time. Krasin succeeded in becoming a prominent industrial business man during these years. Yenukidze did not amass capital. At the beginning of the war he was sent into deportation, whence in 1916 he was called into military service along with the rest of his age-group. The revolution brought him back to Petersburg. I met him for the first time in the summer of 1917 in the soldiers' section of the Petersburg Soviet. The revolution shook and woke up many former Bolsheviks, but they nevertheless assumed a perplexed and unfriendly attitude toward Lenin's program of taking power. Yenukidze was not an exception, but he behaved more cautiously and temporized more than others. He was not an orator, yet he knew the Russian language well and in case of necessity he could give a discourse with less of an accent than most of the Georgians, including Stalin. Personally, Yenukidze produced a very agreeable impression because of the mildness of his character, the absence of personal pretensions, his tact. To this we must add an extreme bashfulness; at the slightest occasion Abel's freckle-covered face became intensely red.

What did Yenukidze do in the days of the October insurrection? I don't know. It is possible that he waited. In any case he was not on the other side of the barricades like Messrs. Troyanovsky, Maisky, Surits—now ambassadors—and hundreds of other dignitaries. After the establishment of the Soviet regime, Yenukidze immediately entered into the presidium of the Central Executive Committee and became its secretary. It is very probable that this was done on the initiative of the first president of the Central Executive Committee, Sverdlov, who in spite of his youth understood people and knew how to put everybody to work in the right place. Sverdlov himself attempted to give the presidium a certain political importance, and friction even arose because of this between him and the Council of People's Commissars, and particularly between him and the Political Bureau. After the death of Sverdlov in the beginning of 1919, a new president was elected on my initiative—M. I. Kalinin, who has maintained himself in this post—no small achievement—to the present day. Yenukidze continued during all this time to serve as secretary.

These two figures, Mikhail Ivanovich and Abel Safronovich, incarnated the supreme Soviet institution in the eyes of the population. On the surface the impression was created that Yenukidze held a good part of the power in his hands. But this was an optical illusion. The fundamental legislative and administrative work was done through the Council of People's Commissars under the leadership of Lenin. The principal problems, disagreements, and conflicts were resolved in the Political Bureau, which from the beginning played the role of a supergovernment. In the first three years, when all forces were concentrated on the civil war, by force of circumstance an enormous power was concentrated in the hands of the military authority. The presidium of the Central Executive Committee occupied a not very well defined but in any case not independent place in this system. Yet it would be unjust to deny it any importance. At that time nobody feared to complain, to criticize, to demand. These three important functions—demands, criticisms, and complaints—were addressed principally to the Central Executive Committee.

In the discussion of questions in the Political Bureau, Lenin more than once turned with amicable irony toward Kalinin: "Well, and what does the chief of state say about this subject?" It was not rapidly that Kalinin learned to recognize himself in this exalted pseudonym. Former peasant of Tver and worker of Petersburg, he conducted himself in his unexpectedly high post with sufficient modesty, and in any case, prudence. It was only little by little that the Soviet press built up his name and his authority in the eyes of the country. Indeed, the ruling circles for a long time did not take Kalinin seriously, in reality do not take him seriously even now. But the peasant masses were progressively habituated to the idea that "solicitation" must be done through the intermediation of Mikhail Ivanovich. This, moreover, was not limited to the peasants. Former tsarist admirals, senators, professors, doctors, lawyers, artists, and, not least, actresses were received by the "chief of state." All had something to request: whether in regard to their sons and daughters, or their requisitioned homes, or firewood for museums, or surgical instruments, or even an order for foreign cosmetics needed for the theater. With the peasants Kalinin found the necessary language without difficulty. In facing the bourgeois intelligentsia he was diffident during the first years. It was here that he was particularly in need of the aid of Yenukidze, better educated and more worldly wise. In addition Kalinin traveled frequently; therefore at Moscow receptions the president was replaced by the secretary. They worked together amicably. Both of them by character were opportunistic; the two always searched for the line of least resistance, and they adapted themselves well to each other.

In view of his high functions, Kalinin was placed on the Central Committee of the party and was even made a candidate member of the Political Bureau. Thanks to the breadth of his acquaintances and his conversations he brought to the meetings not a few valuable matter-of-fact observations. His proposals, it is true, were rarely accepted. But his arguments were heard not without attention and, in one way or another, taken into consideration. Yenukidze never was on the Central Committee; neither, for example, was Krasin. These "Old Bolsheviks," who in the period of reaction had broken with the party, were admitted during these years to posts in the Soviets but not to posts in the party. In addition, Yenukidze, as has been said, never had political pretensions. He trusted in the leadership of the party completely, and with both eyes closed. He was profoundly devoted to Lenin, with a nuance of adoration, and—it is necessary to say this in order to comprehend what follows—he was strongly attached to me. In the not numerous cases where Lenin and I differed, Yenukidze suffered profoundly. I can say, in passing, that there were many like him in that respect.

Without playing a political role, Yenukidze nevertheless occupied an important place, if not in the life of the country, at least in the life of the top ruling circles. The fact is that in his hands was concentrated the housekeeping of the Central Executive Committee: from the cooperative of the Kremlin, products were delivered only on requisitions signed by Yenukidze. The importance of this fact became apparent to me only later, and moreover through indirect signs. I had passed three years at the front. During this time the new mode of life in the Soviet bureaucracy had commenced to form itself little by little. It is not true that in these years they swam in luxury in the Kremlin, as the White press affirmed. They lived in fact very modestly. However, the differences and the privileges had appeared already and accumulated automatically. Through his function, Yenukidze found himself, so to speak, at the center of these processes.

Among many others, Ordzhonikidze, who was then the first figure in the Caucasus, took care that Yenukidze had in his cooperative the necessary quantity of products from the soil.

When Ordzhonikidze was transferred to Moscow, his obligations fell upon Orakhelashvili, whom everyone considered Stalin's flunkey. To the Kremlin from the president of the Council of People's Commissars of Georgia, Budu Mdivani, came wine from Kakhetia. From Abkhazia, Nestor Lakoba sent boxes of mandarins. All three—Orakhelashvili, Mdivani, and Lakoba—are now on the list of the executed. In 1919 I learned by chance that Yenukidze had wine in his warehouse and I proposed its prohibition. "This would be too severe," Lenin told me, jokingly. I tried to insist: "If the rumor reaches the front that in the Kremlin there is feasting I fear bad consequences." The third one included in this conversation was Stalin. "How can we Caucasians," he protested, "get along without wine?" "You see," rejoined Lenin, "you are not habituated to wine, but this would be an offense to the Georgians." "Nothing can be done," I replied, "if here at home the habits have reached such a degree of softening." I think that this little dialogue, conducted in joking tones, nevertheless conveys the temper of the time: a bottle of wine was considered a luxury.

In the same year, 1920, perhaps at the beginning of 1921, Kamenev, who was married to my sister, invited me by telephone to come to his house as I was then on one of my short trips to Moscow. I went to his place in the famous "White Corridor." One of the old servants of the Kremlin, with a particular gesture of deference and familiarity which at once placed me on guard, opened the door to Kamenev's apartment. At a large table several dignitaries of the Kremlin were seated with their wives. On the table stood bottles and dainties coming, of course, from Yenukidze's cooperative. From its appearance all this was at a petty-bourgeois level—at most, middle bourgeois. But the general atmosphere of comfort repelled me. Without greeting anyone, I turned back, closed the door, and started toward home. The servant this time had a slightly frightened and sober face. Our relations with Kamenev, which were very good in the first period after the insurrection, began to become more distant from that day. In justification for myself, I will say that I was not guided by some ridiculous puritanism but only by an immediate reaction: the affairs of the civil war possessed me then completely and undividedly.

With the introduction of the so-called "New Economic Policy" (NEP), the habits of the ruling layer began to change at a more rapid rate. In the bureaucracy itself a process of differentiation began. A minority continued living while in power at a level not any better than in the years of the emigration and paid no attention to this. When Yenukidze proposed some improvements to Lenin in his personal life, Lenin evaded him with the phrase: "No, the old slippers feel better." From different corners of the country people sent him all sorts of local products, with the Soviet arms still freshly emblazoned. "They have sent some gewgaw," complained Lenin; "we must forbid it! And why does the chief of state do nothing more than stare?" he asked, severely knitting his brows in the direction of Kalinin. The chief of state had already learned to twist out of the difficulty: "And why then have you gained such popularity?" Finally the "gewgaws" were sent to the children's hospital or to the museum.

My family did not change its habitual manner of living in the Cavaliers' Building in the Kremlin. Bukharin remained at bottom an old student. Zinoviev lived modestly at Leningrad. Kamenev, in contrast, adapted himself rapidly to the new ways; in him, alongside the revolutionary, there had always been a bit of the voluptuary. Lunacharsky, People's Commissar of Education, was even more rapidly caught in the stream. I am not inclined to believe that Stalin greatly changed his conditions of life after October. But at this period he scarcely entered into my field of view. Many others paid little attention to him. Only later, when he had gained first place, was I told that by way of distraction, apart from the bottle of wine, he enjoyed cutting a sheep's throat in his villa and shooting crows through the window. I am not able to ascertain the veracity of this story. In any case, in the arrangements of his personal life, Stalin depended in this period a great deal upon Yenukidze, who treated his fellow countryman not only without "adoration," but also without sympathy, principally on account of his brutality and his capriciousness; that is to say, those traits which Lenin had judged it necessary to mention in his "testament." The lower personnel of the Kremlin, who particularly appreciated Yenukidze for his simplicity, affability, and equity, displayed toward Stalin on the contrary an attitude of extreme hostility.

My wife, who administered the museums and the historic monuments of the country for nine years, remembers two episodes in which Yenukidze and Stalin manifested very characteristic traits. In the Kremlin, as well as in Moscow, and throughout the country, an incessant struggle was carried on for lodgings. Stalin wanted to change his, which were very noisy, for some more peaceful. The agent of the Cheka, Belenki, recommended some reception rooms in the Palace of the Kremlin. My wife opposed this: the Palace was being preserved as a museum. Lenin wrote a long letter of remonstrance to my wife: the museum furniture could be removed from several of the rooms of the Palace; special measures could be taken for the maintenance of the chambers; Stalin needs an apartment where he can sleep peacefully; in his present apartment we should place young comrades who can sleep even under the bombardment of cannon, etc. But the guardian of the museums would not yield to his arguments. Yenukidze placed himself at her side. Lenin named a commission to look into the matter. The commission concluded that the Palace was not suitable for living purposes. Finally the affable and accommodating Serebriakov yielded his apartment to Stalin. Stalin shot him seventeen years later.

We lived in the Kremlin jammed together in an extremely crowded manner. The majority worked outside the walls of the Kremlin. Meetings ended at all hours of the day and of the night, and the racket of automobiles kept us from sleeping. Finally, through the intermediation of the presidium of the Central Executive Committee, that is to say, Yenukidze, a rule was established: after eleven o'clock in the evening automobiles must stop under the arches where the living apartments began; from there all worthy dignitaries must proceed on foot. Everyone had to countersign the memo announcing this rule. But one automobile continued to disturb the peace. Awakened at three o'clock one morning, I waited at the window for the return of the automobile and questioned the chauffeur. "Don't you know the rule?" "I know, Comrade Trotsky," responded the chauffeur, "but what could I do? When we came to the arches Comrade Stalin ordered: 'Drive on!'" The intervention of Yenukidze was necessary to compel Stalin to respect the sleep of others. Stalin, we think, did not pardon his fellow countryman this petty affront.

A very abrupt change in the conditions of life of the bureaucracy appeared after Lenin's last illness and the commencement of the campaign against "Trotskyism." In all large-scale political struggles one can, in the final score, discover the question of the beefsteak. To the perspective of "permanent revolution" the bureaucracy opposed the perspective of personal well-being and comfort. Inside and outside the ramparts of the Kremlin a series of secret banquets were held. Their political aim was to rally the ranks of the "Old Guard" against me. It was during this epoch (1924) that Stalin, Dzerzhinsky, and Kamenev chatted intimately over a bottle of wine in a villa at Zubalov. To the question of what each liked best in life, Stalin, slightly exhilarated, responded with unaccustomed frankness: "To choose your victim, to prepare everything, to revenge yourself pitilessly, and then to go to sleep." This conversation was repeated more than once by Kamenev, after he had broken with Stalin. Kamenev expected the worst from his old ally, but despite all he did not foresee the terrible vengeance Stalin had reserved for him after long preparation. As to whether Stalin slept well the night after the execution of Kamenev, Zinoviev, and others, I do not know.

The arrangements for the banquets of the "Old Guard" fell for the most part on Yenukidze's shoulders. They no longer limited themselves to the modest wine of Kakhetia. It was during this period that, properly speaking, the "immorality" began which was imputed as a crime to Yenukidze thirteen years later. Abel himself was perhaps never invited to the intimate banquets where the knots of the plot were tied and reinforced. In truth he himself did not seek invitations to them, although, generally speaking, he did not shrink from attending banquets. The struggle which was opened against me went against his grain, and he displayed it in all the ways he could.

Yenukidze lived in the same Cavaliers' Building as we. A bachelor of long standing, he occupied a little apartment, where in former times some second-class functionary had his lodging. We met frequently in the corridor. He passed, weighed down, aging, guilty-faced. My wife, me, our boys he greeted with a redoubled affability in contrast to the others. But politically Yenukidze followed the line of least resistance. He aligned himself with Kalinin. And the "chief of state" began to comprehend that the strength was now not in the masses, but in the bureaucracy, and that the bureaucracy was against the "permanent revolution," for the banquets, for the "happy life," for Stalin. Kalinin himself by this time had succeeded in becoming another man. Not that he greatly added to his knowledge or deepened his political conceptions; but he had acquired the routine of the "statesman," elaborated the particular style of the astute simpleton; he had ceased to lose countenance before the professors, the artists, and above all, the actresses. Knowing little of the behind-the-scenes life in the Kremlin, I did not learn of Kalinin's new manner of life until much later and, moreover, from a source completely unexpected. In one of the humorous Soviet reviews, there appeared in 1925, as I remember it, a cartoon displaying—difficult to believe!—the chief of state in a very compromising situation. The resemblance left no room for doubt. Besides, in the text, very risqué in style, Kalinin was named by the initials, "M. I." I could not believe my eyes. "What is this?" I asked several people close to me, among them Serebriakov. "That is Stalin giving a last warning to Kalinin." "But for what reason?" "Surely not because he wishes to oversee his morality. It must be something in which Kalinin is offering opposition." In reality, Kalinin, who knew recent events too well, did not wish for a long time to recognize Stalin as chief. In other words, he feared tying his future to him. "This horse," he said in a closed circle, "will some day drag our coach into the ditch." It was only little by little, murmuring and resisting, that he turned himself against me, then against Zinoviev, and finally with yet more resistance against Rykov, Bukharin, and Tomsky, with whom he had been tied in the closest way through his moderate tendencies. Yenukidze followed the same evolution behind Kalinin, only more in the shadow, and certainly with more profound internal torments.

Because of his whole character, Yenukidze could not escape being found in the camp of Thermidor. But he was not a careerist and still less a scoundrel. It was difficult for him to detach himself from old traditions and yet more difficult to turn against the people whom he had been accustomed to respect. In critical moments, Yenukidze not only did not manifest any aggressive enthusiasm, but on the contrary, he complained, grumbled, resisted. Stalin knew this too well and more than once gave Yenukidze warnings. I knew this, so to speak, first hand. Although ten years ago the system of denunciation had already poisoned not only political life but also personal relations, still many cases of reciprocal confidence were yet maintained. Yenukidze was a friend of Serebriakov, in his time a prominent militant of the Left Opposition, and quite often opened up his heart to him. "And what more does he [Stalin] want?" complained Yenukidze. "I do all that he demands of me, but that is not enough for him. Into the bargain he wants me to take him for a genius." It is possible that Stalin had already placed Yenukidze on the list of those upon whom he should revenge himself. But since the list proved to be very long, Abel had to wait many years for his turn.

In the spring of 1925 my wife and I lived in the Caucasus at Sukhum, under the protection of Nestor Lakoba, widely known head of the republic of Abkhasia. He was (of all we must say: *was*) a very short man and, moreover, almost deaf. Despite the special sound amplifier which he carried in his pocket, it was not easy to speak with him. But Nestor knew his Abkhasia and Abkhasia knew Nestor, hero of the civil war, man of great courage, of great firmness, and of great practical sense. Mikhail Lakoba, younger brother of Nestor, was home minister of the small republic and at the same time my faithful bodyguard during my stay at Abkhasia. Mikhail was (also: *was*) a young Abkhasian, modest and jovial, one of those in whom there is no artifice. I never engaged in political conversations with the brothers. Only once did Nestor say to me: "I do not see in *him* anything of note: neither intelligence, nor talent." I understood that he spoke of Stalin, but I did not pursue the conversation.

That spring the regular session of the Central Executive Committee did not sit at Moscow, but at Tiflis in the country of Stalin and of Yenukidze. Confused rumors of the struggle between Stalin and the two other members of the triumvirate were bruited about. From Tiflis an airplane left unexpectedly with a member of the Central Executive Committee, Miasnikov, the assistant head of the GPU, Mogilevsky, and a third passenger, in order to see me at Sukhum. In the ranks of the bureaucracy the possibility of an alliance between Stalin and Trotsky was strongly whispered. In fact, in preparing himself for the break-up of the triumvirate, Stalin wished only to frighten Zinoviev and Kamenev, who easily fell into panic. However, from a careless cigarette or from some other cause, the diplomatic airplane burst into flames in the air and the three passengers perished with the pilot. A day or two later another airplane came from Tiflis bringing two members of the Central Executive Committee to Sukhum, my friends, the Soviet ambassador to France, Rakovsky, and the People's Commissar of the Postal Service, Smirnov. The Opposition at this time already suffered from persecution. "Who gave you the airplane at Tiflis?" I asked with astonishment. "Yenukidze!" "How dared he do that?" "Apparently not without the authorities knowing about it." My guests told me that Yenukidze was radiant, expecting a prompt compromise with the Opposition. However, neither Rakovsky nor Smirnov came on a political mission. Stalin, without tying himself in any way, was attempting only to spread illusions among the "Trotskyists," and panic among the Zinovievists. However, Yenukidze, with Nestor Lakoba, hoped sincerely for a change of course and they raised their heads. Stalin never pardoned them. Smirnov was shot during the Zinoviev trial. Nestor Lakoba was shot without trial, evidently in view of his refusal to confess "openheartedly." Mikhail Lakoba was shot on the verdict of a tribunal before which he had given fantastic accusatory depositions against his brother, already executed. What has happened to Rakovsky since his arrest is something that still remains unknown.

In order to tie Yenukidze more strongly, Stalin introduced him into the Central Control Commission which was named to keep an eye on party morality. Did Stalin foresee that Yenukidze himself would be accused of violating this morality? Such contradictions in any case have never stopped him. It is sufficient to say that the Old Bolshevik Rudzutak, arrested upon the same accusations, was for a number of years president of the Central Control Commission, that is to say, something like a high priest over the morals of the party and the Soviets.

Through the system of communicating channels, I knew in the last years of my Soviet life that Stalin had a particular archive in which he collected documents, circumstantial evidence, libelous rumors against all the high Soviet functionaries without exception. In 1929 at the moment of open rupture with the members of the right wing in the Political Bureau (Bukharin, Rykov, and Tomsky), Stalin succeeded in maintaining Kalinin and Voroshilov at his side only through the threat of defamatory revelations. That is, at least, what my friends wrote to me in Constantinople.

In November 1927, the Central Control Commission, with the participation of numerous representatives of the control commissions in Moscow, examined the question of the expulsions of Zinoviev, of Kamenev, and of me from the party.

The verdict was determined in advance. At the presidium sat Yenukidze. We did not spare our judges. The members of the commission were ill at ease under the accusations. Poor Abel was overcome. Then into the scene entered Sakharov, one of the most hardened Stalinists, a true gangster type, ready to do all the sordid work. Sakharov's speech was filled with vulgar insults. I demanded that he be stopped. But the members of the presidium, who knew too well who dictated that speech, dared not do anything. I declared that I would have nothing to do with such an assembly and quit the room. After some time Zinoviev and Kamenev, whom some members of the commission had tried to detain, joined me. A few minutes later in my apartment Yenukidze telephoned, begging me to return to the session. "How do you suffer this scum in the supreme institution of the party?" "Lev Davidovich," Abel implored me, "what importance has Sakharov?" "More importance than you, in any case," I replied, "since he accomplishes what is ordered of him, and you, you wail." Yenukidze stammered something indistinct, through which one could see that he hoped for a miracle. But I did not hope for a miracle. "You will not even dare to censure Sakharov?" Yenukidze became silent. "Will you not within five minutes vote for my expulsion?" A heavy sigh came as answer. It was my last discussion with Abel. Some weeks later I was already in deportation in Central Asia, a year later in exile in Turkey. Yenukidze continued to remain secretary of the Central Executive Committee. It must be confessed that I began to forget Yenukidze. But Stalin remembered him.

Yenukidze was removed several months after the assassination of Kirov, soon after the first [1935] Zinoviev-Kamenev trial when prison terms of "only" ten and five years respectively were meted out to them as allegedly "morally" responsible for the terrorist act. There can be no doubt about the fact that Yenukidze, together with dozens of other Bolsheviks, tried to protest against the unfolding slaughter of Lenin's Old Guard. What form did the protest take? Oh, far from a plot. Yenukidze argued with Kalinin, telephoned members of the Politburo, perhaps even Stalin himself. That was sufficient. As the secretary of the Central Executive Committee, Yenukidze was completely intolerable at the moment when Stalin placed his stake on the gigantic judicial frame-up.

But Yenukidze was still too important a figure, enjoyed too many comradeships, and too little resembled a conspirator or a spy (these terms at that time still preserved a shadow of meaning in the Kremlin vocabulary) for him simply to be shot without formality. Stalin decided to act in installments. The CEC of the Transcaucasian Federation—upon the secret order of Stalin—petitioned the Kremlin to "release" Yenukidze from his obligations as secretary of the CEC of the USSR in order that it might be possible to elect him as president of the highest Soviet organ of Transcaucasia. This petition was granted at the beginning of March 1935. But Yenukidze had hardly succeeded in arriving in Tiflis before newspapers carried news about his appointment . . . as the chief of the Caucasian health resorts. This appointment, bearing the character of mockery—completely in the style of Stalin—boded nothing good. Did Yenukidze actually manage the health resorts for the next two and a half years? Most probably he was simply under the surveillance of the GPU in the Caucasus.

But Yenukidze did not capitulate. The second Zinoviev-Kamenev trial (August 1936), which ended with the execution of all the defendants, embittered old Abel. The rumor that Yenukidze wrote the quasi-apocryphal "Letter of an Old Bolshevik" which appeared abroad is sheer nonsense. No, Yenukidze was incapable of taking such a step. But Abel was indignant, he grumbled, perhaps cursed. That was very dangerous. Yenukidze knew too much. It became necessary to act resolutely. Yenukidze was arrested. The original accusation bore an obscure character: a licentious way of living, nepotism, and so forth. Stalin worked in installments.

But Yenukidze did not capitulate even then. He refused to make any kind of "confession" which would have allowed him to be included in the list of defendants of the Bukharin-Rykov trial. A defendant without voluntary confessions is not a defendant. Yenukidze was shot without trial—as a "betrayer and enemy of the people." Lenin, who was able to foresee much. did not foresee such an end for Abel.

The fate of Yenukidze is the more instructive in that he himself was a man without striking traits, more a type than a personality. He fell victim to his belonging to the "Old Bolsheviks." In the life of his generation there had been a heroic period: the clandestine printshops, the skirmishes with the tsarist police, the arrests, the deportations. The year 1905 was, fundamentally, the high point in the orbit of the "Old Bolsheviks," who in their ideas did not go much further than the democratic republic. To the October revolution these people, already worn out by life and fatigue, adapted themselves in their majority reluctantly. On the other hand with more assurance they began to find places in the Soviet apparatus. After the military victory against the enemies it seemed to them that now they had before them an existence peaceful and without care.

But history deceived Abel Yenukidze. The principal difficulties were before him. In order to assure to the millions of big and little functionaries their beefsteak, their bottle of wine, and other good things, a totalitarian regime happened to be necessary. It is doubtful that Yenukidze—not at all a theoretician—deduced that the autocracy of Stalin follows from the thirst of the bureaucracy for comfort. He was simply one of the instruments of Stalin in the consolidation of the new privileged caste. The "immorality" which was imputed to him as a crime constituted in reality an organic element of the official politics. It was not because of this that Yenukidze perished, but because he could not go all the way. For a long time he suffered, submitted, and adapted himself. But he arrived at a limit beyond which he found himself unable to step. Yenukidze did not plot or prepare terrorist acts. He simply lifted his graying head with dread and despair. He recalled perhaps the old prediction of Kalinin: Stalin will drag us all into the ditch. He probably recalled the warning of Lenin: Stalin is disloyal and abuses power. Yenukidze tried to stop the hand which was leveled at the heads of the Old Bolsheviks. This was sufficient. The chief of the GPU received the order to arrest Yenukidze. But even Henry Yagoda, cynic and careerist, who had prepared the Zinoviev trial, drew back from this mission. Yagoda was then replaced by the unknown Yezhov who was tied by nothing to the past. Without difficulty Yezhov placed under the Mauser all those whom Stalin pointed his finger at. Yenukidze discovered himself to be one of these. With him the old generation of Bolsheviks disappeared from the scene—he, at least, without self-humiliation.

LEON SEDOV

Leon Sedov, the son of Natalia Sedova and Trotsky, was born in Russia in 1906, when his father was in prison facing a life sentence for having led the first Soviet in the 1905 revolution. As Trotsky's obituary article here demonstrates in detail, Sedov's entire short life was marked by the tides of revolution and counterrevolution. When Trotsky wrote this article in Mexico on February 20, 1938, there were grounds for suspecting that Sedov's death in a Paris hospital was neither natural nor accidental. Subsequent investigations, analyzed by Trotsky in two letters of protest to the French magistrate in charge of the inquiry and reprinted in Writings of Leon Trotsky (1937-38) *(1976), removed all doubt that Sedov had been murdered by agents of Stalin's secret police. In 1956, a Stalinist provocateur who had posed as Sedov's comrade and friend testified in a United States court that he had reported to the GPU as soon as Sedov had entered the hospital under an incognito.*

No biography of Sedov has been published, although Isaac Deutscher's biography of Trotsky, The Prophet Outcast *(1963), discusses Sedov's activities and his relations with his father. Sedov's major work,* The Red Book on the Moscow Trial *(1936), issued in French and Russian, has not yet been published in English.*

The following article was first published, under the title Leon Sedov—Son, Friend, Fighter, *as a pamphlet by the Young People's Socialist League (Fourth Internationalists) (1938). Its subtitle was "Dedicated to the Proletarian Youth."*

As I write these lines, with Leon Sedov's mother by my side, telegrams of condolence keep coming from different countries. And for us each telegram evokes the same appalling question:

"Can it really be that our friends in France, Holland, England, the United States, Canada, South Africa, and here in Mexico accept it as definitely established that Sedov is no more?" Each telegram is a new token of his death, but we are unable to believe it as yet. And this, not only because he was our son, truthful, devoted, loving, but above all because he had, as no one else on earth, become part of our life, entwined in all its roots, our co-thinker, our co-worker, our guard, our counselor, our friend.

Of that older generation whose ranks we joined at the end of the last century on the road to revolution, all, without exception, have been swept from the scene. That which tsarist hard-labor prisons and harsh exiles, the hardships of emigration, the civil war, and disease had failed to accomplish has in recent years been achieved by Stalin, the worst scourge of the revolution. Following the destruction of the older generation, the best section of the next, that is, the generation which awakened in 1917 and which received its training in the twenty-four armies of the revolutionary front, was likewise destroyed. Also crushed underfoot and completely obliterated was the best part of the youth, Leon's contemporaries. He himself survived only by a miracle, owing to the fact that he accompanied us into exile and then to Turkey. During the years of our last emigration we made many new friends, some of whom have entered intimately into our lives, becoming, as it were, members of our family. But we met all of them for the first time in these last few years when we had already neared old age. Leon was the only one who knew us when we were young; he became part of our lives from the very first moment of his self-awakening. While young in years, he still seemed our contemporary. Together with us, he went through our second emigration: Vienna, Zurich, Paris, Barcelona, New York, Amherst (concentration camp in Canada), and finally Petrograd.

While but a child—he was going on twelve—he had, in his own way, consciously made the transition from the February revolution to that of October. His boyhood passed under high pressure. He added a year to his age so that he might more quickly join the Young Communist League, seething at that time with all the passion of awakened youth. The young bakers, among whom he carried on propaganda, would award him a fresh loaf of white bread which he happily brought home under his arm, protruding from the torn sleeve of his jacket. Those were fiery and cold, great and hungry years. Of his own volition Leon left the Kremlin for a proletarian student dormitory, in order not to be any different from the others. He would not ride with us in an automobile, refusing to make use of this privilege of the bureaucrats. But he did participate ardently in all Red Saturdays and other "labor mobilizations," cleaning snow from the Moscow streets, "liquidating" illiteracy, unloading bread and firewood from freight cars, and later, as a polytechnic student, repairing locomotives. If he did not get to the war front, it was only because even adding two or as much as three years to his age could not have helped him; for he was not yet fifteen when the civil war ended. However, he did accompany me several times to the front, absorbing its stark impressions, and firmly understanding why this bloody struggle was being waged.

The latest press reports speak of Leon Sedov's life in Paris under "the most modest conditions"—much more modest, let me add, than those of a skilled worker. Even in Moscow, during those years when his father and mother held high posts, he lived not better but worse than for the past few years in Paris. Was this perhaps the rule among the young of the bureaucracy? By no means. Even then he was an exception. In this child, growing to boyhood and adolescence, a sense of duty and achievement awakened early.

In 1923 Leon threw himself headlong into the work of the Opposition. It would be entirely wrong to see in this nothing more than parental influence. After all, when he left a comfortable apartment in the Kremlin for his hungry, cold, and dingy dormitory, he did so against our will, even though we did not resist this move on his part. His political orientation was determined by the same instinct which impelled him to choose crowded streetcars rather than Kremlin limousines. The platform of the Opposition simply gave political expression to traits inherent in his nature. Leon broke uncompromisingly with those of his student friends who were violently torn from "Trotskyism" by their bureaucratic fathers and found a way to his baker friends. Thus, at seventeen he began the life of a fully conscious revolutionist. He quickly grasped the art of conspiratorial work, illegal meetings, and the secret issuing and distribution of Opposition documents. The Young Communist League rapidly developed its own cadres of Opposition leaders.

Leon had exceptional mathematical ability. He never tired of assisting many worker-students who had not gone through grammar school. He engaged in this work with all his energy;

encouraging, leading, chiding the lazy ones—the youthful teacher saw in this work a service to his class. His own studies in the Superior Technical Academy progressed very favorably. But they took up only a part of his working day. Most of his time, strength, and spirit were devoted to the cause of the revolution.

In the winter of 1927, when the police operation to smash the Opposition began, Leon had passed his twenty-second year. By that time a child was born to him and he would proudly bring his son to the Kremlin to show him to us. Without a moment's hesitation, however, Leon decided to tear himself away from his school and his young family in order to share our fate in Central Asia. In this he acted not only as a son but above all as a co-thinker. It was essential, whatever the cost, to guarantee our connection with Moscow. His work in Alma-Ata, during that year, was truly peerless. We called him our minister of foreign affairs, minister of police, and minister of communications. And in fulfilling all these functions he had to rely on an illegal apparatus. Commissioned by the Moscow Opposition center, Comrade X, very devoted and reliable, acquired a carriage and three horses and worked as an independent coachman between Alma-Ata and the city of Frunze (Pishpek), at that time the terminus of the railroad. It was his task to convey the secret Moscow mail to us every two weeks and to carry our letters and manuscripts back to Frunze, where a Moscow messenger awaited him. Sometimes special couriers also arrived from Moscow. To meet with them was no simple matter. We were lodged in a house surrounded on all sides by the institutions of the GPU and the quarters of its agents. Outside connections were handled entirely by Leon. He would leave the house late on a rainy night or when the snow fell heavily, or, evading the vigilance of the spies, he would hide himself during the day in the library to meet the courier in a public bath, or among the thick weeds on the outskirts of the town, or in the oriental market place where the Kirghiz crowded with their horses, donkeys, and wares. Each time he returned excited and happy, with a conquering gleam in his eyes and the precious booty under his clothing. And so for a year's time he eluded all enemies. What is more, he maintained the most "correct," almost "friendly," relations with these enemies who were "comrades" of yesterday, displaying uncommon tact and restraint, carefully guarding us from outside disturbances.

The ideological life of the Opposition seethed like a cauldron at the time. It was the year of the Sixth World Congress of the Communist International. The Moscow packets arrived with scores of letters, articles, theses, from comrades known and unknown. During the first few months, before the sharp change in the conduct of the GPU, we even received a great many letters by the official mail services from different places of exile. It was necessary to sift this diversified material carefully. And it was in this work that I had the occasion to realize, not without surprise, how this little boy had imperceptibly grown up, how well he could judge people—he knew a great many more Oppositionists than I did—how reliable was his revolutionary instinct, which enabled him, without any hesitation, to distinguish the genuine from the false, the substance from the veneer. The eyes of his mother, who knew our son best, glowed with pride during our conversations.

Between April and October we received approximately 1,000 political letters and documents and about 700 telegrams. In this same period we sent out 550 telegrams and not fewer than 800 political letters, including a number of substantial works, such as the *Criticism of the Draft Program of the Communist International* and others. Without my son I could not have accomplished even one-half of the work.

So intimate a collaboration did not, however, mean that no disputes or occasionally even very sharp clashes arose between us. Neither at that time, nor later in emigration—and this must be said candidly—were my relations with Leon by any means of an even and placid character. To his categorical judgments, which were often disrespectful to some of the "old men" of the Opposition, I not only counterposed equally categoric corrections and reservations, but I also displayed toward him the pedantic and exacting attitude which I had acquired in practical questions. Because of these traits, which are perhaps useful and even indispensible for work on a large scale but quite insufferable in personal relationships, people closest to me often had a very hard time. And inasmuch as the closest to me of all the youth was my son, he usually had the hardest time of all. To a superficial eye it might even have seemed that our relationship was permeated with severity and aloofness. But beneath the surface there glowed a deep mutual attachment based on something immeasurably greater than bonds of blood—a solidarity of views and appraisals, of sympathies and antipathies, of joys and sorrows experienced together, of great hopes we had in common. And this mutual attachment blazed up from time to time so warmly as to reward us three hundredfold for the petty friction in daily work.

Thus four thousand kilometers from Moscow, two hundred and fifty kilometers from the nearest railway, we spent a difficult and never-to-be-forgotten year which remains in our memory under the sign Leon, or rather Levik or Levusyatka as we called him.

In January 1929, the Political Bureau decided to deport me "beyond the borders of the USSR"—to Turkey, as it turned out. Members of the family were granted the right to accompany me. Again without any hesitation Leon decided to accompany us into exile, tearing himself forever from the wife and child he dearly loved.

A new chapter, with its first pages almost blank, opened in our life. Connections, acquaintances, and friendships had to be built anew. And once again our son became all things for us: our go-between in relations with the outside world, our guard, collaborator, and secretary as in Alma-Ata, but on an incomparably broader scale. Foreign languages, with which he had been more familiar in his childhood than he was with Russian, had been almost completely forgotten in the tumult of the revolutionary years. It became necessary to learn them all over again. Our joint literary work began. My archives and library were wholly in Leon's hands. He had a thorough knowledge of the works of Marx, Engels, and Lenin, was very well acquainted with my books and manuscripts, with the history of the party and the revolution, and the history of the Thermidorian falsification. In the chaos of the Alma-Ata public library he had already studied the files of *Pravda* for the Soviet years and gathered the necessary quotations and references with unfailing resourcefulness. Lacking this precious material and without Leon's subsequent researches in archives and libraries, first in Turkey, later in Berlin, and finally in Paris, not one of my works during the past ten years would have been possible. This applies especially to *The History of the Russian Revolution*. Vast in point of quantity, his collaboration was by no means of a "technical" nature. His independent selection of facts, quotations, characterizations, frequently determined the method of my presentation as well as the conclusions. *The Revolution Betrayed* contains not a few pages which I wrote on the basis of several lines from my son's letters and the quotations which he sent from Soviet newspapers inaccessible to me. He supplied me with even more material for the biography of Lenin. Such collaboration was made possible only because our ideological solidarity had penetrated our very flesh and blood. My son's name should rightfully be placed next to mine on almost all my books written since 1928.

In Moscow, Leon had lacked a year and a half to complete his engineering course. His mother and I insisted that while abroad he return to his abandoned science. In Prinkipo a new group of young co-workers from different countries had meanwhile been successfully formed, in intimate collaboration with my son. Leon consented to leave only because of the weighty argument that in Germany he would be able to render invaluable services to the International Left Opposition. Resuming his scientific studies in Berlin (he had to start from the beginning), Leon simultaneously threw himself headlong into revolutionary activity. In the International Secretariat he soon became the representative of the Russian section. His letters for that period to his mother and myself show how quickly he acclimated himself to the political atmosphere of Germany and Western Europe, how well he judged people and gauged the differences and countless conflicts of that early period of our movement. His revolutionary instinct, already enriched by serious experience, enabled him in almost all cases to find the right road independently. How many times were we gladdened when upon opening a letter just arrived, we discovered in it the very ideas and conclusions which I had just recommended to his attention. And how deeply and quietly happy he was over such coincidences of our ideas! The collection of Leon's letters will undoubtedly constitute one of the most valuable sources for the study of the inner prehistory of the Fourth International.

But the Russian question continued to occupy the center of his attention. While still in Prinkipo he became the actual editor of the *Biulleten Oppozitsii* from its inception (the middle of 1929), and took complete charge of this work upon his arrival in Berlin (the beginning of 1931), where the *Biulleten* was immediately transferred from Paris. The last letter we received from Leon, written on February 4, 1938, twelve days before his death, begins with the following words: "I am sending you page proofs of the *Biulleten,* for the next ship will not leave for some time, while the *Biulleten* will come off the press only tomorrow morning." The appearance of each issue was a minor event in his life, a minor event which demanded great exertions; making up the issue, polishing the raw material, writing articles, meticulous proofreading, prompt correspondence with friends and collaborators, and, not the least, gathering funds. But how proud he was over each "successful" number!

During the first years of emigration he engaged in a vast correspondence with Oppositionists in the USSR. But by 1932 the GPU destroyed virtually all our connections. It became necessary to seek fresh information through devious channels. Leon was always on the lookout, avidly searching for connecting threads with Russia, hunting up returning tourists, Soviet students assigned abroad, or sympathetic functionaries in the foreign representations. To avoid compromising his informant, he chased for hours through the streets of Berlin and later of Paris to evade the GPU spies who trailed him. In all these years there was not a single instance of anyone suffering as a consequence of indiscretion, carelessness, or imprudence on his part.

In the files of the GPU he was referred to by the nickname of "synok" or "Little Son." According to the late Ignace Reiss, in the Lubyanka [Prison] they said on more than one occasion: "The Little Son does his work cleverly. The Old Man wouldn't find it so easy without him." This was the actual truth. Without him it would not have been easy. Without him it will be hard. It was just for this reason that agents of the GPU, worming their way even into the organizations of the Opposition, surrounded Leon with a thick web of surveillance, intrigues, and plots. In the Moscow trials his name invariably figured next to mine. Moscow was seeking an opportunity to get rid of him at all costs!

After Hitler assumed power, the *Biulleten Oppozitsii* was immediately banned. Leon remained in Germany for several weeks, carrying on illegal work, hiding from the Gestapo in different apartments. His mother and I sounded the alarm, insisting on his immediate departure from Germany. In the spring of 1933 Leon finally decided to leave the country which he had learned to know and to love, and moved to Paris, where the *Biulleten* followed him. Here Leon again resumed his studies. He had to pass an examination for the French intermediate school and then for the third time to begin with the first term in the Faculty of Physics and Mathematics at the Sorbonne. In Paris he lived under very difficult conditions, in constant want, occupying himself with scientific studies at the university at off moments; but thanks to his exceptional ability he completed his studies, i.e., obtained his diploma.

His main efforts in Paris, even to a greater extent than in Berlin, were devoted to the revolution and the literary collaboration with me. During recent years Leon himself began to write more systematically for the press of the Fourth International. Isolated indications, especially the notes on his reminiscences for my autobiography, made me suspect while still in Prinkipo that he had literary gifts. But he was loaded down with all sorts of other work, and inasmuch as we held our ideas and subject matter in common, he left the literary work to me. As I recall, in Turkey he wrote only one major article: "Stalin and the Red Army—or How History Is Written," under the pseudonym of N. Markin, a sailor-revolutionist to whom in his childhood he was bound by a friendship deepened by profound admiration. This article was included in my book *The Stalin School of Falsification*. Subsequently his articles began to appear more and more frequently in the pages of the *Biulleten* and in other publications of the Fourth International, written each time under the pressure of necessity. Leon wrote only when he had something to say and when he knew that no one else could say it better. During the period of our life in Norway I received requests from various places for an analysis of the Stakhanovist movement, which to some extent caught our organizations by surprise. When it became clear that my prolonged illness would prevent me from fulfilling this task, Leon sent me a draft of an article by him on Stakhanovism, with a very modest accompanying letter. The work appeared to me excellent both in its serious and thorough analysis and in the terseness and clarity of its presentation. I remember how pleased Leon was by my warm praise! This article was published in several languages and immediately provided a correct point of view upon this "socialist" piecework under the whip of the bureaucracy. Scores of subsequent articles have not added anything essential to this analysis.

Leon's chief literary work was his *Red Book on the Moscow Trial*, devoted to the trial of the sixteen (Zinoviev, Kamenev, Smirnov, et al). It was published in French, Russian, and German. At that time my wife and I were captives in Norway, bound hand and foot, targets of the most monstrous slander. There are certain forms of paralysis in which people see, hear, and understand everything but are unable to move a finger to ward off mortal danger. It was to such political paralysis that the Norwegian "socialist" government subjected us. What a priceless gift to us, under these conditions, was Leon's book, the first crushing reply to the Kremlin falsifiers. The first few pages, I recall, seemed to me pale. That was because they only restated a political appraisal which had already been made of the general condition of the USSR. But from the moment the author undertook an independent analysis of the trial, I became completely engrossed. Each succeeding chapter seemed to me better than the last. "Good boy, Levusyatka!" my wife and I said. "We have a defender!" How his eyes must have glowed with pleasure as he read our warm praise! Several newspapers, in particular the central organ of the Danish Social Democracy, said with assurance that I apparently had, despite the strict conditions of internment, found the means of participating in the work which appeared under Sedov's name. "One feels the pen of Trotsky. . . ." All this is—fiction. In the book there is not a line of my own. Many comrades who were inclined to regard Sedov merely as "Trotsky's son"—just as Karl Liebknecht was long regarded only as the son of Wilhelm Liebknecht—were able to convince themselves, if only from this little book, that he was not only an independent but an outstanding figure.

Leon wrote as he did everything else, that is, conscientiously, studying, reflecting, checking. The vanity of authorship was alien to him. Agitational declamation had no lures for him. At the same time every line he wrote glows with a living flame, whose source was his unfeigned revolutionary temperament.

This temperament was formed and hardened by events of a personal and family life indissolubly linked to the great political events of our epoch. In 1905, his mother sat in a Petersburg jail expecting a child. A gust of liberalism set her free in the autumn. In February of the next year, the boy was born. By that time I was already confined in prison. I was able to see my son for the first time only thirteen months later, when I escaped from Siberia. His earliest impressions bore the breath of the first Russian revolution, whose defeat drove us into Austria. The war, which drove us into Switzerland, hammered into the consciousness of the eight-year-old boy. The next big lesson for him was my deportation from France. On board ship he conversed, in sign language, about the revolution with a Catalan stoker. The revolution signified for him all possible boons, above all a return to Russia. En route from America, near Halifax, the eleven-year-old Levik struck a British officer with his fist. He knew whom to hit; not the sailors who carried me off the ship, but the officer who issued the orders. In Canada, during my incarceration in the concentration camp, Leon learned how to conceal letters not read by the police and how to place them unobserved in the mail box. In Petrograd he found himself immediately plunged into the atmosphere of Bolshevik-baiting. In the bourgeois school where he happened to be enrolled at the beginning, sons of liberals and Social Revolutionaries beat him up because he was Trotsky's son. Once he came to the Woodworkers' Trade Union, where his mother worked, with his hand all bloody. He had had a political discussion in school with Kerensky's son. In the streets he joined all the Bolshevik demonstrations, took refuge behind gates from the armed forces of the then People's Front (the coalition of Cadets, SRs, and Mensheviks). After the July days, grown pale and thin, he came to visit me in the jail of Kerensky-Tsereteli. In the home of a colonel they knew, at the dinner table, Leon and Sergei threw themselves, knives in hand, at an officer who had declared that the Bolsheviks were agents of the kaiser. They made approximately the same reply to the engineer Serebrovksy, now a member of the Stalinist Central Committee, when he tried to assure them that Lenin was—a German spy. Levik learned early to grind his young teeth when reading slanders in the newspapers. He passed the October days in the company of the sailor Markin who, in leisure moments, instructed him in the cellar in the art of shooting.

Thus the future fighter took shape. For him, the revolution was not an abstraction. Oh, no! It seeped into his very pores. Hence derived his serious attitude toward revolutionary duty, beginning with the Red Saturdays and tutoring of the backward ones. That is why he later joined so ardently in the struggle against the bureaucracy. In the autumn of 1927 Leon made an "Opposition-al" tour to the Urals in the company of Mrachkovsky and Beloborodov. On their return, both of them spoke with genuine enthusiasm about Leon's conduct during the sharp and hopeless struggle, his intransigent speeches at the meetings of the youth, his physical fearlessness in the face of the hooligan detachments of the bureaucracy, his moral courage which enabled him to face defeat with his young head held high. When he returned from the Urals, having matured in those six weeks, I was already expelled from the party. It was necessary to prepare for exile. He was not given to imprudence, nor did he make a show of courage. He was wise, cautious, and calculating. But he knew that danger constitutes an element in revolution as well as war. Whenever the need arose, and it frequently did, he knew how to face danger. His life in France, where the GPU has friends on every floor of the governmental edifice, was an almost unbroken chain of dangers. Professional killers dogged his steps. They lived in apartments next to his. They stole his letters, and archives and listened in on his phone conversations. When, after an illness, he spent two weeks on the shores of the Mediterranean—his only vacation for a period of years—the agents of the GPU took quarters in the same pension. When he arranged to go to Mulhouse for a conference with a Swiss lawyer in connection with a legal action against the slanders of the Stalinist press, a whole gang of GPU agents was waiting for him at the station. They were the same ones who later murdered Ignace Reiss. Leon escaped certain death only because he fell ill on the eve of his departure, suffered from a high fever, and could not leave Paris. All these facts have been established by the judicial authorities of France and Switzerland. And how many secrets still remain unrevealed? His closest friends wrote us three months ago that he was subject to a danger too direct in Paris and insisted on his going to Mexico. Leon replied: The danger is undeniable, but Paris today is too important a battle post; to leave it now would be a crime. Nothing remained except to bow to this argument.

When in the autumn of last year a number of foreign Soviet agents began to break with the Kremlin and the GPU, Leon naturally was to be found in the center of these events. Certain friends protested against his consorting with "untested" new allies: there might possibly be a provocation. Leon replied that there was undoubtedly an element of risk but that it was impossible to develop this important movement if we stood aside. This time as well we had to accept Leon as nature and the political situation made him. As a genuine revolutionist he placed value on life only to the extent that it served the struggle of the proletariat for liberation.

On February 16, the Mexican evening papers carried a brief dispatch on the death of Leon Sedov following a surgical operation. Absorbed in urgent work, I did not see these papers. Diego Rivera on his own initiative checked this dispatch by radio and came to me with the terrible news. An hour later I told Natalia of the death of our son—in the same month of February in which thirty-two years ago she brought to me in jail the news of his birth. Thus ended for us the day of February 16, the blackest day in our personal lives.

We had expected many things, almost anything, but not this. For only recently Leon had written us concerning his intention to secure a job as a worker in a factory. At the same time he expressed the hope of writing the history of the Russian Opposition for a scientific institute. He was full of plans. Only two days prior to the news of his death we received a letter from him dated February 4, brimming with courage and vitality. Here it is before me. "We are making preparations," he wrote, "for the trial in Switzerland where the situation is very favorable as regards both so-called 'public opinion' and the authorities." And he went on to list a number of favorable facts and symptoms. "*En somme, nous marquons des points*" [All in all, we're making progress]. The letter breathes with assurance concerning the future. Whence then this malignant disease and lightning death? In twelve days? For us, the question is shrouded in deep mystery. Will it ever be cleared up? The first and natural supposition is that he was poisoned. It presented no serious difficulty for the agents of Stalin to gain access to Leon, his clothing, his food. Are judicial experts, even if untrammeled by "diplomatic" considerations, capable of arriving at a definitive conclusion on this point? In connection with chemical warfare the art of poisoning has nowadays attained an extraordinary development. To be sure the secrets of this art are inaccessible to common mortals. But the poisoners of the GPU have access to everything. It is entirely feasible to conceive of a poison which cannot be detected after death, even with the most careful analysis. And who will guarantee such care?

Or did they kill him without resorting to the aid of chemistry? This young and profoundly sensitive and tender being had had far too much to bear. The long years of the campaign of lies against his father and the best of the older comrades, whom Leon from his childhood had become accustomed to revere and love, had already deeply shaken his moral organism. The long series of capitulations by members of the Opposition dealt him blows that were no less heavy. Then followed in Berlin the suicide of Zina, my older daughter, whom Stalin had perfidiously, out of the sheerest vindictiveness, torn from her children, her family, her own milieu. Leon found himself with his older sister's corpse and her six-year-old boy on his hands. He decided to try to reach his younger brother Sergei in Moscow by phone. Either because the GPU was momentarily disconcerted by Zina's suicide or because it hoped to listen in to some secrets, a phone connection, contrary to all expectations, was made, and Leon was able to transmit the tragic news to Moscow by his own voice. Such was the last conversation between our two boys, doomed brothers, over the still-warm body of their sister.

Leon's letters to us in Prinkipo were terse, meager, and restrained when they described his ordeal. He spared us far too much. But in every line one could feel an unbearable moral strain.

Material difficulties and privations Leon bore lightly, jokingly, like a true proletarian; but of course they too left their mark. Infinitely more harrowing were the effects of subsequent moral tortures. The Moscow trial of the sixteen, the monstrous nature of the accusations, the nightmarish testimony of the defendants, among them Smirnov and Mrachkovsky, whom Leon so intimately knew and loved; the unexpected internment of his father and mother in Norway, the period of four months without any news; the theft of the archives; the mysterious removal of my wife and myself to Mexico; the second Moscow trial and its even more delirious accusations and confessions; the disappearance of his brother Sergei, accused of "poisoning workers"; the shooting of countless people who had either been close friends or remained friends to the end; the persecutions and the attempts of the GPU in France, the murder of Reiss in Switzerland, the lies, the baseness, the perfidy, the frame-ups—no, "Stalinism" was for Leon not an abstract political concept but an endless series of moral blows and spiritual wounds. Whether the Moscow masters resorted to chemistry, or whether everything they had previously done proved sufficient, the conclusion remains one and the same: *it was they who killed him.* The day of his death they marked on the Thermidorian calendar as a major celebration.

Before they killed him they did everything in their power to slander and blacken our son in the eyes of contemporaries and of posterity. Cain-Dzhugashvili [Stalin] and his henchmen tried to depict Leon as an agent of fascism, a secret partisan of capitalist restoration in the USSR, the organizer of railway wrecks and murders of workers. The efforts of the scoundrels are in vain. Tons of Thermidorian filth rebound from his young figure, leaving not a stain on him. Leon was a thoroughly clean, honest, pure human being. He could before any working-class gathering tell the story of his life—alas, so brief—day by day, as I have briefly told it here. He had nothing to be ashamed of or to hide. Moral nobility was the basic warp of his character. He unwaveringly served the cause of the oppressed, because he remained true to himself. From the hands of nature and history he emerged a man of *heroic* mold. The great awe-inspiring events which hover over us will need such people. Had Leon lived to participate in these events he would have shown his true stature. But he did not live. Our Leon, boy, son, heroic fighter, is no more!

His mother—who was closer to him than any other person in the world—and I are living through these terrible hours recalling his image, feature by feature, unable to believe that he is no more and weeping because it is impossible not to believe. How can we accustom ourselves to the idea that upon this earth there no longer exists the warm, human entity bound to us by such indissoluble threads of common memories, mutual understanding, and tender attachment? No one knew us and no one knows us, our strong and our weak sides, so well as he did. He was part of both of us, our young part. By hundreds of channels our thoughts and feelings daily reached out to him in Paris. Together with our boy has died everything that still remained young within us.

Goodbye, Leon, goodbye, dear and incomparable friend. Your mother and I never thought, never expected that destiny would impose on us this terrible task of writing your obituary. We lived in firm conviction that long after we were gone you would be the continuator of our common cause. But we were not able to protect you. Goodbye, Leon! We bequeath your irreproachable memory to the younger generation of the workers of the world. You will rightly live in the hearts of all those who work, suffer, and struggle for a better world. Revolutionary youth of all countries! Accept from us the memory of our Leon, adopt him as your son— he is worthy of it—and let him henceforth participate invisibly in your battles, since destiny has denied him the happiness of participating in your final victory.

NADEZHDA KRUPSKAYA

Nadezhda K. Krupskaya was born in Russia in 1869 and joined the first Marxist group in St. Petersburg in 1891. There she met Lenin in 1894, and with him helped organize the St. Petersburg League for the Emancipation of the Working Class in 1895. They were married in Siberian exile in 1898. When Iskra *was started in Western Europe, she served as its secretary and maintained contact with illegal groups in Russia. She also was secretary of a number of Bolshevik periodicals, and for a time a secretary of the Central Committee. After the Soviets came to power she did most of her work in the Commissariat of Education, and among groups concerned with homeless children and youth organizations. She was briefly a member of the Central Control Commission and the Central Committee after Lenin's death. Close to Zinoviev politically, she belonged for a short time to the United Opposition, but withdrew in 1926 out of fear that its activities would lead to a party split. She died in 1939.*

A biography, Bride of the Revolution: Krupskaya and Lenin *by Robert H. McNeal was published in 1972. An English version of her* Memories of Lenin, *Volume I, 1894-1907, published in 1930, is still in print.*

The translation of Trotsky's obituary, dated March 4, 1939, was first published in The New International, *April 1939.*

In addition to being Lenin's wife—which, by the way, was not accidental—Krupskaya was an outstanding personality in her devotion to the cause, her energy, and her purity of character. She was unquestionably a woman of intelligence. It is not astonishing, however, that while remaining side by side with Lenin, her political thinking did not receive an independent development. On far too many occasions, she had had the opportunity to convince herself of his correctness, and she became accustomed to trust her great companion and leader. After Lenin's death Krupskaya's life took an extremely tragic turn. It was as if she were paying for the happiness that had fallen to her lot.

Lenin's illness and death—and this again was not accidental—coincided with the breaking point of the revolution, and the beginning of Thermidor. Krupskaya became confused. Her revolutionary instinct came into conflict with her spirit of discipline. She made an attempt to oppose the Stalinist clique, and in 1926 found herself for a brief interval in the ranks of the Opposition. Frightened by the prospect of split, she broke away. Having lost confidence in herself, she completely lost her bearings, and the ruling clique did everything in its power to break her morally. On the surface she was treated with respect, or rather with semihonors. But within the apparatus itself she was systematically discredited, besmirched, and subjected to indignities, while in the ranks of the Young Communists the most absurd and gross scandal was being spread about her.

Stalin always lived in fear of a protest on her part. She knew far too much. She knew the history of the party. She knew the place that Stalin occupied in this history. All of the latter-day historiography which assigned Stalin a place alongside of Lenin could not but appear revolting and insulting to her. Stalin feared Krupskaya just as he feared Gorky. Krupskaya was surrounded by an iron ring of the GPU. Her old friends disappeared one by one; those who delayed in dying were murdered either openly or secretly. Every step she took was supervised. Her articles appeared in the press only after interminable, insufferable, and degrading negotiations between the censors and the author. She was forced to adopt emendations in her text, either to exalt Stalin or to rehabilitate the GPU. It is obvious that a whole number of the vilest insertions of this type were made against Krupskaya's will, and even without her knowledge. What recourse was there for the unfortunate, crushed woman? Completely isolated, a heavy stone weighing upon her heart, uncertain what to do, in the toils of sickness, she dragged on her burdensome existence.

To all appearances, Stalin has lost the inclination to stage sensational trials, which have already succeeded in exposing him before the whole world as the dirtiest, most criminal, and most repulsive figure in history. Nevertheless, it is by no means excluded that some sort of new trial will be staged, wherein new defendants will relate how Kremlin physicians under the leadership of Yagoda and Beria took measures to expedite Krupskaya's demise. . . . But with or without the aid of physicians, the regime that Stalin had created for her undoubtedly cut short her life.

Nothing can be further from our mind than to blame Nadezhda Konstantinovna for not having been resolute enough to break openly with the bureaucracy. Political minds far more independent than hers vacillated, tried to play hide-and-seek with history—and perished. Krupskaya was to the highest degree endowed with a feeling of responsibility. Personally she was courageous enough. What she lacked was mental courage. With profound sorrow we bid farewell to the loyal companion of Lenin, to an irreproachable revolutionist and one of the most tragic figures in revolutionary history.

JOSEPH STALIN

Joseph Stalin was born in Russian-dominated Georgia in 1879, which was also the year of Trotsky's birth. He became a Social Democrat in 1898 and a Bolshevik in 1904. He was coopted to the Bolshevik Central Committee in 1912 and elected to it for the first time in 1917. He advocated a conciliatory attitude to the Provisional Government in 1917 before Lenin reoriented the Bolsheviks toward winning power. He was elected Commissar of Nationalities in the first Soviet government, and general secretary of the Communist Party in 1922. Less than a year later Lenin called for his removal from the general secretary post because Stalin was using it to bureaucratize the party and state apparatuses. After Lenin's death in 1924, Stalin gradually eliminated his major opponents, starting with Trotsky, until he became virtual dictator in the 1930s.

The 1939 Stalin-Hitler pact, signed a month before Trotsky's essay, was followed by Hitler's invasion of the Soviet Union in 1941. During the war, when Stalin served as head of the government and commander in chief as well as general secretary, he collaborated closely with the democratic capitalist powers; one concession he gave them was the dissolution of the Communist International in 1943. The Soviet Union won the war, but at a tremendous loss of life, part of which is attributed to Stalin's mismanagement. The former Commissar of Nationalities also presided over the abrogation of national independence in Eastern Europe. The "cold war" period was accompanied by the resumption of public purges in the Soviet Union and their extension into Eastern Europe, and Stalin had just organized a new anti-Semitic purge when he died in 1953. Three years later, his successors repudiated the Stalin "cult of personality" and some of the excesses committed during his reign, and promised a

*return to Lenin's norms. But they retained the basic bureaucratic
structure they had inherited from Stalin, confining themselves to
minor reforms and a limited downgrading of Stalin's authority.
Stalin remains an idol today only to the Maoists, following their
split with the Moscow bureaucracy.*

*There are several biographies of Stalin in English, including
the one by Trotsky that he had not completed when he was killed.
Thirteen volumes of Stalin's works were translated into English
in Moscow, but the series was suspended after 1956.* Marxism and
the National Question *and several other pamphlets are also
available.*

*The translation of Trotsky's essay, dated September 22, 1939,
was first published in* Life *magazine, October 2, 1939, where it
had the title "Joseph Stalin: Hitler's New Friend Is Sized Up by
an Old Foe." Three anecdotes in this article (on Stalin's love of
wine, on his desire for special rooms in the Kremlin, and driving
on the Kremlin grounds after hours), amounting to fifty-four lines
in* Life, *are omitted here because they were previously recounted
in the article on Yenukidze.*

In 1913 I sat in the Vienna apartment of a fellow exile, before
the samovar. We drank fragrant Russian tea and we meditated,
naturally, on the overthrow of tsarism. Suddenly, without a
preceding knock, the door opened and in it appeared a person
unknown to me—of average height and rather thin, with a sallow
face on which could be seen pockmarks.

The new arrival held in his hand an empty glass. Uttering a
gutteral sound which could, had one wished, have been taken for
a greeting, he approached the samovar. He silently filled his
glass with tea and, as silently, left. I looked questioningly at my
friend, who said: "That was the Caucasian, Dzhugashvili, my
fellow countryman. He recently entered the Central Committee of
the Bolsheviks and is evidently beginning to play an important
role."

The unexpected entrance and disappearance, the a priori
enmity of manner, the inarticulate greeting, and, most important-
ly, the morose concentration of the stranger made a confused but
unusual impression on me. Have later events thrown a shadow
back on our first meeting? No, because otherwise I would have
forgotten the meeting before these later events took place. Two

months or so later, I read in the Bolshevik magazine *Prosvesh-chenie* an article on the national question with the signature, strange to me then, of J. Stalin. The article attracted attention mainly because, through the banal monotonous text, there flashed occasionally original ideas and brilliant formulas. Years afterwards I learned that the article had been inspired by Lenin and that in the manuscript of the apprentice there could be seen the hand of the master. At the time, however, I did not even connect "J. Stalin" with the mysterious Georgian who had poured tea into his glass in Vienna in such a discourteous way and who was to become, within four years, the chief of the Commissariat of Nationalities in the first Soviet government.

When I arrived in revolutionary Petrograd from a Canadian concentration camp on May 5, 1917, the leaders of all the parties of the revolution were already gathered in the capital. I immediately encountered Lenin, Kamenev, Zinoviev, Luna-charsky, all of whom I had known long before, and got to know young Sverdlov, who was to become the first president of the Soviet republic.

I did not see Stalin. Nobody mentioned him. He spoke at no public meetings at all in those days when life consisted principally of public meetings. In *Pravda*, guided by Lenin, articles appeared over the signature of Stalin. I glanced through them casually but still did not inquire about the identity of the author, evidently deciding for myself that he was one of those colorless hacks who could be found on any editorial staff.

When Stalin became a member of the government, not only the popular masses but even the outer circles of the party itself knew nothing about him. He was a member of the staff of the Bolshevik Party and because of this he had a share of power. But even among colleagues in his own commissariat, Stalin had small influence, and in all important questions, he found himself in the minority. There was still, at the time, no possibility of giving commands, and Stalin did not possess the capacity of convincing his young adversaries by debate.

When Stalin failed to get what he wanted and when his patience was exhausted by the resulting frustration, his procedure was simple. He vanished from the meeting. One of his co-workers, Pestkovsky, gave an inimitable account of the behavior of the commissar. Stalin would say, "I will be back in a minute," depart from the conference room and hide himself in some obscure cranny of the Smolny or, later, of the Kremlin.

Pestkovsky said, "It was impossible to find him. At first we used to wait for him. Later on, we merely dispersed."

Sometimes, on such occasions, the faithful Pestkovsky would stay on to wait for his superior and hear, from Lenin's room, the bell calling Stalin. "I would explain that Stalin had disappeared," Pestkovsky recalled, "but sometimes Lenin would insist on seeing him immediately. Then my task became difficult. I began a long walk through the endless corridors of the Smolny, or the Kremlin. Eventually I would find him in the most unpredictable places. Once I discovered him in the apartment of the sailor Vorontsov. He was lying on the sofa in the kitchen, smoking his pipe."

This story gives us the first key to Stalin's character, in which the chief trait is the contradiction between his extreme will to power and his insufficient intellectual equipment. While puffing his pipe on the sofa in the sailor's kitchen, he doubtless pondered upon the distressing effects of debate, upon the intolerability of disagreement, and how fine it would be to dispense with all such nonsense.

Joseph, or Soso, Dzhugashvili, fourth child of the shoemaker Vissarion Dzhugashvili, was born in the small town of Gori, near the city of Tiflis in the Caucasus, on December 21, 1879. His mother, who at the time of the birth of her fourth child was only twenty years old, worked at baking bread, washing linen, and making dresses for her more well-to-do neighbors. His father, a man of savage nature and unrestrained habits, spent most of his modest income on drink.

One of Joseph's schoolmates tells how Vissarion, by his brutal relations with his wife and his cruel blows to his son, "drove from Soso's heart love of God and people and caused him to hate his own father." The position of the Georgian woman, as a slave in the family, was imprinted upon Joseph for all his life. He later accepted the program that demanded complete equal rights for women but in his personal relations he always remained the son of his father, regarding woman as a lower being, predestined for necessary but limited functions.

Vissarion Dzhugashvili wanted to make a shoemaker of his son. Soso's mother was more ambitious and dreamed of a priest's career for him, much as Hitler's mother dreamed of making a pastor out of Adolf. When he was eleven, Joseph entered an ecclesiastical school. Here the Georgian boy made his first acquaintance with the Russian language which remained for him, forever after, a tongue drilled into him by the teacher's rod and thus alien to him. The majority of his classmates were children of priests, officials, or petty Georgian nobles. The shoemaker's son felt himself inferior in the midst of this backwoods aristocracy and learned early to grit his teeth with hate hidden in his heart.

The candidate for the priesthood discarded religion while still at school. "You know, they deceive us," he said to one of his schoolmates. "God does not really exist." The boys and girls of prerevolutionary Russia generally broke with their religion at an early age, often in childhood. The urge to do so was in the air, but the phrase "they deceive us" carries the mark of the future Stalin.

From his primary ecclesiastical school the young atheist went to the seminary in Tiflis. Here he spent five wretched years. In its regimen the seminary was something between a monastery and a prison. The lack of food was compensated for by an overabundance of church services. The curriculum consisted principally of punishments. The chief lesson learned by most of the pupils was how to hide their rebellious ideas behind a pious exterior. The Tiflis seminary produced many Caucasian revolutionists. It is not surprising that in this atmosphere Soso joined the group of future conspirators. His first political ideas were clearly embellished by his native Georgian romanticism. Soso appropriated the name Koba after the hero of a celebrated patriotic Georgian novel. Koba became Soso's revolutionary pseudonym, and his close comrades called him by it until very recent times. Now most of those who knew him well enough to use it have been shot.

In the higher seminary, the young Dzhugashvili felt his poverty even more sharply than he had in the ecclesiastical school. "He didn't have any money," relates one of his fellow students, "whereas all the rest of us got packages and spending money from our parents." Even more boundless also became Joseph's dreams for his future. He would show them. Already his comrades noticed in Joseph a tendency to find only the bad qualities in other people and to show an attitude of mistrust toward unselfish motives. He knew how to play upon the weaknesses of some adversaries and how to play others off against each other. Whoever attempted to oppose him, or even to explain to him what he did not understand, brought upon himself a "pitiless hostility," according to one of his schoolmates of that period. Koba, already, wanted to command.

By this time having begun to absorb the teachings of Darwin and Marx, and having completely lost his taste for the theological science, Joseph began to get lower marks in his divinity classrooms and found himself, before the end of the term, forced to abandon his studies in July 1899. Whether his departure was requested or merely suggested by the authorities remains disputed. At this time Joseph was twenty years old, and, judged by Caucasian standards, an adult. He considered himself a revolutionist and a Marxist.

We find him thereafter writing proclamations in Georgian and bad Russian. He works in an illegal printing shop, explains to workers' circles the mystery of surplus value, and participates in local committee meetings. His revolutionary road is marked by secret passages from one Caucasian town to another, by imprisonments, by deportations and escapes, by a new short period of illegal work, and a new arrest. The police characterize him in their reports as "discharged from an ecclesiastical seminary, leaving without papers, without determined occupation, and without living quarters." A boyhood friend remembers him at this time as gloomy, dirty, and disheveled, explaining that "his means did not allow him to dress well but, as a matter of fact, he had no interest in keeping his clothes clean and in order." The destiny of Koba is so far that of any ordinary provincial revolutionist of the tsarist epoch. One thing, however, distinguishes him sharply from his equals. This is the fact that at all stages of his road he is accompanied by rumors of intraparty intrigues, broken discipline, double-dealing, calumnies, and even denunciations of his comrades to the police. Many of these rumors are undoubtedly false. But about no other revolutionist are such tales even told.

After the split between the Bolsheviks and the Mensheviks in 1903, Koba waits cautiously for a year and a half before finally joining the Bolsheviks. Even then, however, he remains obscure. Outside of Russia there exists a revolutionary center with Lenin at its head. All young revolutionists of any prominence are in touch with this center, make trips abroad, and correspond with Lenin. In all this correspondence, the name of Koba is not mentioned once. He feels himself a provincial, proceeds cautiously, and regards his fellows with sadness and envy.

The revolution of 1905 passed by Stalin without noting him. He spent this year in Tiflis, where the Mensheviks were in control. On the 17th of October, when the tsar published the constitutional manifesto, Koba was seen gesticulating on a street lamp. But that day everyone was climbing street lamps, to address the crowds below. No orator, sure of himself only in conspiratorial offices, Koba felt lost in full view of the masses.

The reaction after 1905 brought a sharp decline in the movement of the masses and a temporary increase of terroristic acts. In the Caucacus, where the traditions of romantic brigandage and bloody vengeance were still alive, the terroristic struggle found audacious agents. They killed governors, policemen, and traitors. With bombs and guns in their hands, they seized government money for revolutionary purposes. The name of Koba is closely associated with this chapter of activity but so far his precise part in it has never been established. His political adversaries have evidently exaggerated it, relating how he personally threw the first bomb from a roof in the public square in Tiflis in order to seize government money. In the memoirs of the direct participants in the celebrated holdup of Tiflis, the name of Stalin is not mentioned once. That does not signify, however, that he took no part in terroristic activity. But he worked behind the scenes, selected people, gave them authorizations from the party, and then stepped away at the right moment.

In 1912, having at last demonstrated during the years of reaction his firmness and his fidelity to the party, Koba graduated from the provincial to the national arena. The conference of the party did not agree, it is true, to put Koba on the Central Committee, but Lenin, who had by this time noticed him favorably, succeeded in persuading the Central Committee to select him as a "co-optive" member. At that time, the Georgian adopted his Russian pseudonym, Stalin ("Steely").

Koba's choice of a new name signified not so much a personal as a party predilection. As early as 1903, future Bolsheviks had been called "hard" and future Mensheviks "soft." Plekhanov, the Menshevik leader, had called his opponents "diehards." Lenin had taken this qualification as praise. One of the then young Bolsheviks adopted the pseudonym Kamenev ("Stoney") for precisely the same reason for which Dzhugashvili began to call himself Stalin. The difference was, however, that in the case of Kamenev there was nothing stonelike, while the pseudonym of Stalin described his character.

In March 1913, Stalin was arrested in St. Petersburg and deported to Siberia, under the Arctic Circle, in the little village of Kureika. Stalin was, for his fellow exiles, a difficult neighbor.

One of these remembered afterwards, "he occupied himself with hunting and fishing. He was living in almost complete solitude." The hunting was without a gun; Stalin preferred to use traps.

In 1916, Joseph Dzhugashvili was called up for military service. Because of the partial paralysis of his left arm which, like the two connected toes on one of his feet, is an infirmity dating from his birth, he did not enter the army. Of the eight years which he spent in exile the most astonishing fact is perhaps that he did not succeed in learning a foreign language. In the Baku prison he attempted indeed to study German but rejected this hopeless enterprise and turned instead to Esperanto, consoling himself with the belief that it was the language of the future. In the domain of knowledge, particularly linguistic, the not very lively intellect of Stalin sought the path of least resistance. It is noteworthy that in the four years he spent in solitude, the years of the world war and a great crisis in world socialism, Stalin wrote not one line which was published afterwards.

Stalin returned from exile in 1917 after the overthrow of the monarchy. Together with Kamenev, he pushed out of the leadership of the party a group of young comrades, among them Molotov, present president of the Council of the People's Commissars, as too left, and oriented himself toward sustaining Kerensky's Provisional Government. But three weeks later Lenin arrived from abroad, set Stalin aside, and oriented the party toward the conquest of power. It is difficult to follow Stalin's activity during the months of the revolution. More important and capable people occupied the center of the stage and thrust him aside. He had neither theoretical imagination, nor historical perspicacity, nor the gift to grasp future events. In a complicated situation he always prefers to wait. A new idea must create its bureaucracy before Stalin can have any confidence in it.

Revolution, which has its laws and tempos, simply passes by Stalin, the cautious temporizer. It was so in 1905. It was repeated in 1917. And further, every new revolution—in Germany, in China, in Spain—caught him invariably unawares and engendered in him a feeling of dull discontent towards the revolutionary mass, which cannot be commanded by bureaucratic machinery.

Superficial psychologists like Emil Ludwig represent Stalin as a perfectly poised being, as something like a genuine child of nature. In reality, he consists entirely of contradictions. The most significant of these is the discrepancy between his ambitious will and his resources of intellect and talent. What characterized Lenin was the harmony of his psychic forces: theoretical mind, practical sagacity, strong will, endurance. All this was tied up in one active whole. Without effort he mobilized in any suitable moment different parts of his spirit. The strength of Stalin's will is not inferior perhaps to that of Lenin's, but his intellectual capacities, as compared to Lenin's, measure only 10 or 20 percent. Again, in the sphere of intellect there is a new discrepancy in Stalin: extreme development of practical sagacity and cunning at the expense of the ability to generalize and of the creative imagination. The hate for the powerful of this world was always his main driving force as a revolutionary, rather than the sympathy for the oppressed which warmed and ennobled the human image of Lenin who, however, also knew how to hate.

In the period of the October revolution, Stalin, more than anybody else, perceived his career as a series of failures. There was always somebody who publicly corrected him, overshadowed him, and pushed him into the background. Like an internal ulcer, his ambition gave him no peace and poisoned his relations with eminent persons, beginning with Lenin. In the Politburo he almost always remained silent and morose. Only among primitive people without moral prejudices did he become smoother and friendlier. In prison he associated more easily with common criminals than with the political prisoners.

Hardness represents an organic quality in Stalin. But in the course of the years he forged a considerable weapon out of this quality. On ingenuous people hardness often produces the impression of sincerity. "This man does not think slyly, he says openly everything he thinks." At the same time, he is hypersensitive, easily offended, and capricious. Feeling himself pushed aside, he turns his back, hides in a corner and smokes his pipe, is morosely silent, and dreams of revenge.

In the struggle Stalin never refutes criticism, but immediately turns it against his adversary, giving it a merciless character. The more monstrous the accusation, the better. Stalin's policy, says a critic, violates the interest of the people. Stalin answers: "My adversaries are agents of fascism." Before Hitler, Stalin had adopted the belief that the people will believe any lie so long as it is big enough. This theory, upon which the Moscow trials were based, might well be immortalized in psychology textbooks as the "Stalin Reflex."

I never was in Stalin's apartment. But the French writer Henri

Barbusse, who shortly before his death wrote two biographies—
one of Jesus Christ and one of Joseph Stalin—gave a minute
description of the small quarters on the second floor of the
Kremlin, where the dictator had his modest apartment. Babusse's
description of the menage is complemented by that of Stalin's
former secretary, Bazhanov, who fled abroad in 1928. The door of
the apartment is guarded at all times by a sentry. In a little
antechamber hang the master's military greatcoat and cap. The
three bedrooms and the living room are simply furnished. Stalin's
older son slept on a divan.

For a long time it was customary for lunch and dinner to be
delivered from the Kremlin's special kitchen. But in the last few
years, because of fear of poisoning, the Stalins have begun to
prepare their food at home. If the master is not in a good mood—
and this is often the case—everybody remains silent at the table.
"With his family," Bazhanov relates, "he conducts himself like a
despot. For whole days he observes a haughty silence at home
without answering the questions of his wife or son." After lunch,
the family chief sits in an armchair near the window and smokes
him pipe. The Kremlin inside telephone rings.

"Koba, Molotov is calling you," his wife says.

"Tell him I am asleep," Stalin answers in the presence of his
secretary, in order to demonstrate his scorn for Molotov.

Besides his Kremlin apartment, Stalin has a villa in Gorki, the
country house in which Lenin once lived and out of which Stalin
drove his widow. In one of the rooms there is a motion-picture
screen; in another, a valuable instrument which has the function
of satisfying the musical wants of the master—a pianola. They
tell how delighted Stalin was when, as a child, he was shown for
the first time this marvel of marvels. He has another pianola in
his Kremlin apartment for he cannot live without art. He spends
his hours of relaxation enjoying the melodies of *Aïda*. In music as
in politics he wants a docile machine. And the Soviet composers
accept as law every preference of the dictator who has two
pianolas.

In 1903, when Stalin was twenty-four, he married a young,
simple Georgian girl. The marriage, according to a boyhood
friend, was happy because the wife had been "raised in the holy
tradition which obligated the woman to serve." While her
husband was taking part in secret meetings, the young bride
passed nights in ardent prayer for his safety. Koba's tolerance of
her religious beliefs came only from the fact that he did not seek

in her a friend capable of sharing his ideas. The young woman died in 1907 of tuberculosis, and they buried her according to the Orthodox rites. She left a little boy named Yasha who, until he was ten, remained in the care of his mother's parents in Tiflis. Later he was taken to the Kremlin. We often found him in our son's room, for he preferred our apartment to his father's.

In my papers I find the following note from my wife: "Yasha as a boy of twelve years had a soft, tanned face, and black, glistening eyes. He resembled, I was told, his tubercular dead mother. In bearing and manner he was very graceful. To Seryozha [Trotsky's son] who was his friend, he told how his father treated him brutally, beat him for smoking. 'But it is not with blows that he will break me,' he said. 'You know,' Seryozha related to me, 'Yasha spent all last night in the corridor with the sentry. Stalin had driven him out of the apartment because he smelled of tobacco.' Once I surprised Yasha in the boy's room with a cigarette in his hand. He smiled with embarrassment. 'Go on, go on,' I said to him soothingly. 'My papa is crazy,' he replied in a tense voice. 'He smokes. But he will not allow me to do it.' "

Today Yasha is separated on not too friendly terms from his father, and lives in a faraway province as an obscure engineer. It is impossible not to relate here another episode, told me by Bukharin in 1924 when, although drawing closer to Stalin, he was still on friendly terms with me.

"I have just come from seeing Koba," he said. "Do you know how he spends his time? He takes his year-old boy from bed, fills his own mouth with smoke from his pipe, and blows it into the baby's face."

"What nonsense," I interrupted.

"By God, it's the truth," Bukharin replied with that impulsiveness which characterized him. "By God, it's the pure truth. 'It will make him stronger,' Koba roars." Bukharin mimicked Stalin's Georgian pronunciation.

"That's barbaric," I said.

"You don't know Koba. He is like that—a little peculiar."

The soft Bukharin was obviously awed by the primitiveness of Stalin. It was, however, easy to agree that the father's behavior was "peculiar." While he tempered the younger boy with smoke, he forbade the older one its use with the help of pedagogical methods employed in earlier times on him by the shoemaker Vissarion.

For his second wife, Stalin married Nadezhda Alliluyeva, a

daughter of a Russian father and a Georgian mother. Nadezhda was born in 1902. After the revolution she had worked in Lenin's secretariat, and during the civil war at the Tsaritsyn front, where Stalin was active. At the time of her marriage she was seventeen and Stalin was forty. She was very reserved and very attractive. Even after having two children, she studied at an industrial college. When a campaign of slander was started against me by Stalin, Alliluyeva, when she met my wife, was doubly attentive. She felt herself, apparently, closer to the persecuted than to the persecutor.

On November 9, 1932, Alliluyeva died suddenly. On the causes of this sudden death, the Soviet papers remained strangely silent. But in Moscow they whispered that she had committed suicide. One evening, at Voroshilov's house, they asserted, she had allowed herself to make some critical remarks, in the presence of Soviet might, on the peasant policy which doomed the villages to starvation. Stalin had answered her in a raucous voice with the crudest insult in the Russian language. The Kremlin servants noticed Alliluyeva's excited manner when she returned home. Sometime later a shot was heard from her room. Stalin received many expressions of condolence and passed on to the business of the day.

In a drama written in 1931 by the popular Russian writer Afinogenov, it is said that if one observes a hundred citizens, he will see that eighty of them act under the influence of fear. In the years of the bloody purges, fear also seized a great part of the remaining 20 percent. The mainspring of the policy of Stalin himself is now his fear of the fear which he has engendered.

Stalin personally is not a coward, but his policy reflects the fear of the privileged parvenus for their own future. Stalin never had any confidence in the masses; now he fears them. His alliance with Hitler, which astonished almost everybody, flowed inevitably from fear of the war. It was possible to foresee this alliance, but diplomats should have changed their glasses in time. This alliance was foreseen, particularly by the author of these lines. But Messrs. Diplomats, as simple mortals, prefer probable predictions to true predictions. However, in our insane epoch the true predictions are most often the improbable predictions. An alliance with France, with England, with the United States would be, of course, advantageous to the USSR in case of war. But the Kremlin wanted above all to avoid war. Stalin knows that if the USSR in alliance with the democracies should emerge from the war victorious, the Russian people would along the way with all certainty debilitate and reject the present oligarchy. The problem for the Kremlin is not to find allies for victory, but to avoid war. It is possible to attain that only by friendship with Berlin and Tokyo. This has been Stalin's goal since the victory of the Nazis.

It is also impossible to close one's eyes to the fact that not Chamberlain but Hitler overawed Stalin. In the Führer, Stalin finds not only what is in himself but also what he lacks. Hitler, for better or worse, was the initiator of a great movement. His ideas, however miserable they may be, succeeded in unifying millions of people. So arose a party which armed its leader with power never before seen in the world. At the present time Hitler— a combination of initiative, of perfidy, and of political epilepsy— prepares no less and no more than to rebuild our planet in his likeness and image.

The personality of Stalin and his career are different. It is not Stalin who created the machine. The machine created Stalin. But a machine, like a pianola, cannot replace human creative power. Bureaucracy as bureaucracy is impregnated through and through with the spirit of mediocrity. Stalin is the most outstanding mediocrity of the Soviet bureaucracy. His strength lies in the fact that he expresses the instinct of self-preservation of the ruling caste more firmly, more decisively, and more pitilessly than anyone else. But that is also his weakness. He sees clearly for a short distance, but on a historical scale he is blind. A shrewd tactician, he is not a strategist. This is demonstrated by his attitude in 1905, during the last war, and in 1917. Stalin carried in himself the consciousness of his mediocrity. Hence, his need for flattery. Hence, his envy of Hitler and a secret deference to him.

According to the account of the former chief of the Soviet espionage in Europe, Krivitsky, an enormous impression was made upon Stalin by Hitler's purge of June 1934 in the ranks of his own party. "There is a chief," the sluggish Kremlin dictator said to himself. Since that time he has without doubt imitated Hitler. The bloody purges in the USSR, the farce of "the most democratic constitution in the world," and finally the present invasion of Poland were all inspired in Stalin by the German genius with the mustache of Charlie Chaplin.

The international advocates of the Kremlin—sometimes also its adversaries—attempt to establish an analogy between the Stalin-

Hitler alliance and the Brest-Litovsk peace of 1918. This analogy is a mockery. The negotiations in Brest-Litovsk were carried on openly before all mankind. The Soviet state in those days had not a single battalion capable of fighting. Germany was attacking Russia, seizing Soviet provinces and military supplies. The Moscow government had no choice but to sign the peace, which we ourselves openly called a capitulation of disarmed revolution before a powerful robber.

And now? The present pact was concluded with the existence of a Soviet army of many millions of soldiers. The treaty's immediate task was to facilitate Hitler's crushing of Poland. Finally, the intervention of the Red Army, under cover of the "liberation" of eight million Ukrainians and White Russians, leads to the national enslavement of twenty-three million Poles. Thus, the two cases are direct opposites. The Kremlin attempts above all, with its occupation of the Western Ukraine and Western White Russia, to give to the population of the USSR a patriotic atonement for the hated alliance with Hitler.

But Stalin also has his personal motive for the invasion of Poland, as almost always, a motive of vengeance. In 1920 Tukhachevsky, the future marshal, led the Red troops against Warsaw. The future Marshal Yegorov advanced toward Lemberg [Lwów]. With Yegorov was Stalin. When it became clear that Tukhachevsky was menaced on the Vistula by a counterattack, the Moscow command ordered Yegorov to turn north in the direction of Lublin, in order to help Tukhachevsky. But Stalin feared that Tukhachevsky, after having taken Warsaw, would "seize" Lemberg, thus depriving him of this achievement. Hidden behind the authority of Stalin, Yegorov did not fulfill the order of the general staff. Only four days later, when the critical situation of Tukhachevsky became acute, did the armies of Yegorov turn north toward Lublin. But it was already too late. The catastrophe was at hand. In the high councils of the party and of the army, all knew that the person responsible for the crushing of Tukhachevsky was Stalin. The present invasion of Poland and the seizure of Lemberg is thus for Stalin a revenge for the grandiose failure of 1920.

The superiority of the strategist Hitler over the tactician Stalin is evident. By the Polish campaign Hitler ties Stalin to his chariot, deprives him of any freedom of maneuver, discredits him, and in passing kills the Comintern. Nobody will say that Hitler has become a Communist. Everybody says that Stalin has become an agent of fascism. But even at the cost of a humiliating and traitorous alliance, Stalin didn't retain his principle of peace.

No civilized nation will be able to escape this cyclone, however strict and wise may be the laws of neutrality. Less than any other nation can the Soviet Union escape it. In each new stage Hitler will present to Moscow greater and greater demands. Today he gives to his Kremlin friend for temporary safekeeping the "Greater Ukraine." Tomorrow he will raise the question of who is to be master of the Ukraine. Both Stalin and Hitler have little respect for treaties. How long will a treaty between them endure? The "sanctity" of international obligations will definitely dissolve in the clouds of poison gas. "Every man for himself" will become the slogan of the governments of the nations and of the classes.

The Moscow oligarchy, in any case, will not survive the war, by which it is so thoroughly frightened. The fall of Stalin will not serve Hitler, however, who is proceeding with the infallibility of a somnambulist to the brink of the precipice. Hitler will not succeed in rebuilding the planet, even with the help of Stalin. Other people will rebuild it.

GLOSSARY

Additional information is provided below about people, groups, events, periodicals, and concepts referred to in Trotsky's texts. Russians are not identified by country here; all others are. The following abbreviations are used in this glossary:

B = Bolshevik
Cadet = Constitutional Democrat
CP = Communist Party
M = Menshevik
October = revolution of October 1917
RSDLP = Russian Social Democratic Labor Party
SP = Socialist Party, Social Democratic Party
SR = Social Revolutionary
Whites = Russian counterrevolutionary forces
WW = World War

Adler, Victor (1852-1918)—founder and leader of Austrian SP.

Afinogenov, Aleksandr N. (1904-41)—Soviet playwright; art director of "Proletkult" theater, 1926-29.

Alexandra Romanov (tsarina)—see pages 81-92.

Alexinsky, Grigori A. (1879-   )—broke with Bolsheviks in 1909; supported monarchy in World War I; became anti-Soviet propagandist in France.

Alliluyeva, Nadezhda S. (1901-32)—CP; married Stalin in 1919; suicide.

Anschluss (union or annexation of Austria with Germany)—demand of German Nazis, achieved through occupation of Austria in 1938.

Aveling, Edward (1851-98)—British writer; member of Social Democratic Federation and Socialist League; husband of Eleanor Marx.

Avksentiev, Nikolai D. (1878-1943)—SR minister in Provisional Government; chairman of Peasant Soviet; active with White forces in civil war, anti-Soviet emigre.

Avvakum, Petrovich (c. 1621-82)—dissident priest, burned at stake for opposing church reforms of Patriarch Nikon.

Axelrod, Pavel B. (1850-1928)—a founder of Emancipation of Labor Group; M, opponent of October.

Balfour, Arthur (1848-1930)—British Conservative prime minister, 1902-05; cabinet minister, MP, author of 1917 promise to Jews of "national home" in Palestine.

Bangya, Janosh (1817-68)—officer in Hungarian revolutionary army, exposed as police agent.

Barbusse, Henri (1873-1935)—pacifist novelist; joined French CP in 1923, headed CP peace and democracy fronts.

Bebel, August (1840-1913)—a founder and central leader of German SP; formally rejected revisionism of Bernstein but tolerated growth of opportunist forces that took over party after his death.

Belinsky, Vissarion G. (1811-48)—radical critic and philosopher.

Beloborodov, Aleksandr G. (1891-1938)—B; elected to Central Committee in 1918; Commissar of Interior in 1923; expelled as Oppositionist in 1927; capitulated in 1929; executed after third Moscow trial.

Beria, Lavrenti P. (1899-1953)—Stalinist; head of secret police, 1938-53; executed after Stalin's death.

Bernstein, Eduard (1850-1932)—German SP; principal advocate of revision of Marxism from revolutionary to reformist theory and practice.

Biulleten Oppozitsii (Bulletin of the Opposition)—Russian language magazine edited by Trotsky and Sedov, published 1929-41 in France, Germany, Switzerland, and U.S.

Black Hundreds—Russian hoodlums and lynch mobs organized with tsarist approval and complicity to attack radicals and carry through pogroms against Jews.

Blum, Léon (1872-1950)—French SP leader between two world wars; premier, first People's Front, 1936-37; provisional president, 1946.

Bogdanov, Aleksander A. (1873-1928)—RSDLP, B from 1904 to 1909; after October, founder of artistic tendency "Proletkult" and director of medical institute.

Bolsheviks—revolutionary tendency led by Lenin, first as faction of RSDLP, then as independent party; forerunner of Communist Party of Soviet Union.

Boulangerism—after would-be man on horseback, Georges Boulanger (1837-91), French general and politician accused of conspiring to overthrow government in order to get revenge on Germany for loss of Franco-Prussian War.

Brentano, Ludwig (1844-1931)—German political economist, professor, pacifist.

Breshko-Breshkovskaya, Yekaterina K. (1844-1934)—SR leader; opposed October; anti-soviet in exile.

Brest-Litovsk—town on Russian-Polish border where Germany and Soviet Union signed peace treaty early in 1918. Part of CP leadership ("Left Communists") bitterly opposed treaty, which was very unfavorable to Soviet Union, but Lenin's position prevailed. German revolution in November enabled Soviet Union to recover much of territory lost by treaty.

Briand, Aristide (1862-1932)—expelled from French SP in 1906 for taking part in capitalist government; became premier five different times, including WWI coalition.

Bukharin, Nikolai I. (1888-1938)—B in 1906; editor of *Pravda*, 1917-29; head of Comintern, 1926-29; leader of Right Opposition to Stalin, 1928-29; capitulated and was given minor posts; executed after third Moscow trial.

Bund (League of Jewish Workers in Poland, Lithuania and Russia)—part of RSDLP until 1903 congress, where it split away when denied jurisdiction over Jewish workers; pro-M, opposed to October.

Burns, Mary (d. 1863)—Irish factory worker in Manchester; companion of Engels, 1845 to her death.

Cadets—see Constitutional Democrats.

Cain-Dzhugashvili—epithet Trotsky applied to Joseph Stalin; Dzhugashvili was Stalin's last name by birth.

Central Executive Committee—highest body of Soviets between congresses.

Central Committee—highest body of CP between congresses.

Central Control Commission—investigative and disciplinary body of CP.

centrists—Marxist term for those who vacillate between reform and revolution.

Charolambos—see pages 98-103.

Cheka—first Soviet secret police body, set up in 1917; reorganized and renamed GPU in 1922

Chernyshevsky, Nikolai G. (1828-89)—critic; revolutionary democrat and socialist; author of famous novel, *What Is To Be Done?*

Comintern—see Communist International.

Communist International (Comintern, Third International)— revolutionary successor to Second International, set up under Lenin in 1919 and dissolved by Stalin in 1943.

Constitutional Democrats (Cadets)—liberal capitalist party favoring constitutional monarchy or republic for Russia; opposed October.

Cuvier, Georges (1769-1832)—French zoologist.

Daladier, Edouard (1884-1970)—Radical Socialist premier of France, 1933, 1934, and 1938-40, when he signed Munich pact with Hitler.

Danton, Georges-Jacques (1759-94)—president of French Jacobin Club; minister of justice; guillotined after defeat by Robespierre.

Demuth, Hélène (d. 1890)—housekeeper of Marx family, then of Engels.

Descartes, René (1596-1650)—French scientist and philosopher.

Deutsch, Lev G. (1855-1941)—a founder of Emancipation of Labor; M, patriot in World War I.

Dimitrov, Georgi (1882-1949)—Bulgarian CP, tried and acquitted in German Reichstag fire trial, 1933; became Soviet citizen and executive secretary of Comintern, 1934-43; premier of Bulgaria, 1946-49.

Duma (council)—quasi-parliamentary body with little power of its own, convened before October when it suited tsarist interests.

Duse, Eleonora (1858-1924)—Italian actress.

Dzerzhinsky, Felix E. (1877-1926)—Polish revolutionary, elected to RSDLP central committee in 1906; after October, chairman of special commission to fight counterrevolution and sabotage (Cheka); supporter of Stalin.

Dzhugashvili, Vissarion (d. 1890)—father of Joseph Stalin.

Dzhugashvili, Yakov J.—son of Stalin and Yekaterina Svanidze, his first wife; reportedly died in Nazi concentration camp, 1943.

Ebert, Friedrich (1871-1925)—right-wing German SP; chancellor after fall of monarchy, 1918; president of Weimar republic, 1919-25.

1848 revolutions and counterrevolution—struggles for and against bourgeois democratic rights, national independence, and constitutional reforms throughout Europe.

Eliava, Shalva Z. (1855-1937)—Georgian supporter of Stalin in 1920s, purged in 1930s.

Emancipation of Labor Group—first Russian Marxist organization, founded in Geneva in 1883 by Plekhanov and others; dissolved at Second Congress of RSDLP in 1903.

Engels, Friedrich—see pages 126-44.

Fabian Society—British anti-Marxist group founded in 1884 to promote socialism through gradual reform of capitalism.

February revolution—spontaneous 1917 uprising that overthrew tsarism and brought Provisional Government to power for eight months.

First International (International Workingmen's Association)—first experience with an international workers' organization, founded in 1864 and dissolved in 1876. Its leading body, General Council, included Marx and Engels.

Fourth International (World Party of Socialist Revolution)— revolutionary successor to Third International, organized in 1938 under Trotsky's leadership.

Franco-Prussian War of 1870-71—France was defeated and lost eastern provinces, its monarchy fell, and workers seized Paris; Prussian victory helped unify Germany under Bismarck's rule.

Galicia, retreat from—German-Austrian rout of Russian troops in summer of 1915 was a major turning point in WWI; by end of year Germans had occupied all of Poland.

Girondists—moderate tendency in Great French Revolution.

Gladstone, William (1809-98)—Liberal prime minister of Britain four times.

Glazman, Mikhail S.—see pages 64-68.

Gorky, Maxim—see pages 160-63.

GPU—name of Soviet secret police in 1922, later called MVD, KGB, etc.

Guesde, Jules (1845-1922)—founder of French SP, opponent of reformism until WWI, when he joined war cabinet.

Haase, Hugo (1863-1919)—centrist in German SP; leader of Independent Social Democratic Party; member of coalition government after WWI; assassinated.

Herriot, Édouard—see pages 145-59.

Herzen, Alexander I. (1812-70)—liberal and socialist critic and editor.

Hitler, Adolf (1889-1945)—Der Führer of German National Socialist (Nazi) Party; suicide.

Hohenzollern—ruling family of Germany from 1871 to 1918 revolution, when Wilhelm II abdicated.

l'Humanité (Humanity)—daily paper of French SP, taken over by CP in 1920.

Hyndman, Henry M. (1842-1922)—British reformist and leader of Social Democratic Federation; supporter of government in WWI.

International Secretariat—top administrative body of Fourth International and its predecessors.

Iskra (Spark)—Illegal Russian paper published in exile by Lenin and Plekhanov, 1900-03.

Italo-Ethiopian War—launched by Italian fascists in 1935, it was initially successful, driving Haile Selassie out of Ethiopia; status quo was restored by Italian defeat in WWII.

Izvestia (News)—daily paper of Russian Soviets before October, of Soviet government after.

Jacobins—revolutionary party in French revolution, smashed by reactionary backlash in month of Thermidor 1794.

Jaurès, Jean (1859-1914)—French SP deputy, reformist, pacifist; assassinated.

Joffe, Adolf A.—see pages 78-80.

July days of 1917 in Petrograd (St. Petersburg)—spontaneous semi-insurrectional demonstrations by workers, followed by severe repression against Bolsheviks. **"July days" of 1918 in Moscow**—unsuccessful Left SR insurrection against Soviet government. **German "July days"** (in January 1919)—insurrectional strikes, severe repression against Spartacists (newly reorganized as CP).

Kaganovich, Lazar M. (1893-   )—Stalin lieutenant on Central Control Commission carrying out purges in 1930s; removed from all posts by Khrushchev in 1957.

Kalinin, Mikhail I. (1875-1946)—B, replaced Sverdlov as head of state in 1919; helped expel Left Opposition, 1927; leaned to Right Opposition, 1928-29, but went along with Stalin in expelling it.

Kamenev, Lev B.—see pages 164-73.

Kamenev, Sergei S. (1881-1936)—former tsarist colonel who became Red Army commander in civil war.

Kant, Immanuel (1724-1804)—German philosopher.

Kautsky, Karl—see pages 28-33.

Kautsky, Luise—Austrian SP; Engels's secretary, 1890; delegate to Brussels and Zurich congresses of Second International.

Kautsky, Minna (1836-1912)—German author of social novels; mother of Karl Kautsky.

Kazan campaign (September 1918)—first great Red Army victory, a turning point in civil war.

Kerensky, Alexander F. (1881-1970)—member of SR group who became president of Provisional Government.

Kirov, Sergei M. (1886-1934)—Stalinist head of Leningrad party organization, assassinated in GPU plot to smear Trotsky.

Krasin, Leonid B. (1870-1926)— B; Commissar of Foreign Trade; Soviet ambassador to France and Britain.

Krivitsky, Walter (1889-1941)—chief of Soviet military intelligence in Western Europe when he defected in Paris in 1937, revealing many secrets about GPU operations; possible suicide.

Krupskaya, Nadezhda K.—see pages 204-206.

Lamartine, Alphonse de (1790-1869)—French poet, liberal head of Provisional Government in 1848.

Lassalle, Ferdinand (1825-64)—founder of General Association of German Workers, which merged with Marxists to form SP.

Laval, Pierre (1883-1945)—French premier three times, twice as Radical Socialist before WWII, once as Petainist during war, for which he was executed after war.

League of Nations—international body created by allied victors after WWI, allegedly to prevent war; succeeded by United Nations after WWII.

Left Opposition (Bolshevik-Leninists)—faction led by Trotsky to reform Comintern and affiliated parties by restoring Leninist norms of workers' democracy and revolutionary internationalism, 1923-33; thereafter its members worked to replace Comintern by Fourth International.

Left SRs—see Social Revolutionaries.

Leipzig trial—see Reichstag fire trial.

Lenin, Vladimir Ilyich—see pages 48-54.

Lenin's testament—his appraisal, made in 1922-23, just before his last illness, of other Soviet leaders' strengths and weaknesses; called for Stalin's removal as general secretary; was suppressed in USSR until after Stalin's death.

Lieber, Mikhail I. (1880-1937)—leader of Jewish Bund and right-wing M; minor economic post in 1920s; executed in purges.

Liebknecht, Karl—see pages 14-27.

Liebknecht, Wilhelm (1826-1900)—cofounder and leader of German SP and Second International; father of Karl Liebknecht.

Ludwig, Emil (1881-1948)—German journalist and biographer.

Lunacharsky, Anatoli V.—see pages 104-108.

Luxemburg, Rosa—see pages 14-27.

Lvov, Georgi Y. (prince) (1861-1925)—Cadet, head of first Provisional Government; helped organize White armies.

MacDonald, Ramsay (1866-1937)—prime minister of first two British Labour governments, 1924, 1929-31; then bolted Labour Party to form "national" government with Conservatives, 1931-35.

Maisky, Ivan M. (1884-1975)—right-wing M and minister in Siberian White government during civil war; became Soviet diplomat in 1920s, ambassador to Britain, 1932-43.

Markin, Nikolai G. (1893-1918)—B sailor and friend of Trotsky family.

Martov, L. (1873-1923)—coeditor of *Iskra*; leading M; opponent of October.

Martynov, Aleksandr S. (1865-1935)—M until 1923, when he joined CP.

Marx, Eleanor (1855-98)—socialist activist in Britain; Marx's youngest daughter.

Marx, Karl (1818-83)—founder, with Engels, of scientific socialism and leader of First International.

Mdivani, Budu M. (1877-1937)—anti-Stalinist, head of Soviet Georgia; shot in purges.

Mehring, Franz (1846-1919)—German literary critic, historian, biographer of Marx; cofounder of Spartacus League and CP.

Mensheviks—centrist tendency led by Martov, first as faction of RSDLP, then as independent party, affiliated to Second International.

Mikhailovsky, Nikolai K. (1842-1904)—radical journalist and sociologist, anti-Marxist.

Mikoyan, Anastas I. (1895-   )—Armenian Stalinist; specialized in foreign and domestic trade; supported Khrushchev in 1950s before retiring.

Millerandism—after first French socialist to enter cabinet of a capitalist government (1899), Alexandre Millerand (1859-1943); expelled for this from SP; president of France, 1920-24.

Miliukov, Paul N. (1859-1943)—Cadet leader, minister for foreign affairs in first Provisional Government.

Molotov, Viacheslav M. (1890-   )—Stalinist, chairman of Council of People's Commissars, 1930-41; foreign minister, 1939-49; removed by Khrushchev in 1957.

Mrachkovsky, Sergei V. (1883-1936)—famous Red Army commander in civil war; expelled as Oppositionist in 1927; capitulated in 1929; executed after first Moscow trial.

Muraviev, Mikhail A. (1880-1918)—former tsarist officer, joined SRs and fought Whites in civil war; supported Left SR insurrection in 1918; suicide.

Mussolini, Benito (1883-1945)—*Il Duce* of Italian fascism, in power from 1922; executed by partisans.

Narodniks—populists, major tendency of Russian revolutionary movement in nineteenth century.

Narodnaya Volya (People's Will)—one of groups into which chief Narodnik organization split in 1879.

Nashe Slovo (Our Word)—daily Russian paper of Trotsky and other antiwar elements in Paris during first years of WWI.

National Bloc—right-wing coalition that governed France during most of 1920s.

National Socialism—German fascist (Nazi) party and ideology.

Necker, Jacques (1732-1804)—French financier and politician, minister of finance before revolution.

NEP—see New Economic Policy.

New Economic Policy (NEP)—adopted in 1921; allowed limited growth of free trade inside Soviet Union and foreign concessions alongside nationalized and state-controlled sections of economy; stimulated growth of wealthy peasants and commercial bourgeoisie; lasted until end of 1920s.

1905 revolution—first workers' struggle to overthrow tsarism, notable for first appearance of soviets.

Nicholas II (tsar)—see pages 81-92.

November 9, 1918, revolution—German uprising that overthrew monarchy and ended WWI; workers organized councils (soviets) but were unable to take power and democratic-capitalist Weimar republic was result.

October revolution—1917 insurrection that overthrew Provisional Government and established Soviet government.

Okudzhava, M.—Left Oppositionist, exiled in 1928.

Old Bolsheviks—those who joined party before 1917; Old Guard of party.

Orakhelashvili, Ivan (Mamiya) D. (d. 1937)—secretary, Georgian Central Committee in 1920s; Marx-Engels-Lenin Institute official in 1930s; executed as spy and traitor with Yenukidze.

Ordzhonididze, Grigori K. (1886-1937)—an organizer of Stalin's faction, later in charge of heavy industry; probably murdered.

Ozvobozhdenie (Liberation)—periodical of Russian liberals who later organized Cadet Party.

Paléologue, Maurice (1859-1944)—French ambassador to Bulgaria, 1907-12, to Russia, 1914-17.

Paris Commune—first example of workers' government, in power for seventy-two days in 1871, before being crushed brutally.

Parvus, A.L. (1869-1924)—Russian Marxist who emigrated to Germany, active in SP left wing; pro-M; a leader of St. Petersburg Soviet in 1905; on return to Germany became wealthy and supporter of German war government.

People's Front—name used in mid-1930s to designate policy of coalition between workers' and capitalist parties, favored by both Comintern and Second International; such coalitions were elected to office in Spain and France in 1936.

permanent revolution—Trotsky's theory of dynamics of struggle in underdeveloped countries and their relation to international fight for socialism.

Pestkovsky, Stanislas S. (1882-1937)—Polish B, Stalin's first assistant in Commissariat of Nationalities; later Soviet ambassador to Mexico.

Plekhanov, Georgi V.—see pages 34-40.

Poincaré, Raymond (1860-1934)—Conservative premier of France three times; president of France, 1913-20.

Poland, present invasion of—refers to German invasion from west, September 1, 1939, and Soviet invasion from east, September 19.

Polish Corridor—strip of land taken from Germany and assigned to

Poland by Versailles Treaty, demanded by Hitler to connect main part of Germany with East Prussia.

Politburo—see Political Bureau.

Political Bureau—subcommittee of Central Committee of CPSU; in Stalin's time it became superior to CC.

Port Arthur—its surrender to Japanese in January 1905 and destruction of Russian fleet at Tsushima in May led to end of Russo-Japanese War in September.

Potresov, Aleksander N. (1869-1934)—cofounder of *Iskra;* right-wing M after 1905, patriot in WWI, anti-Soviet exile.

Pravda (Truth)—Bolshevik paper started in 1912, became daily in 1917.

Prosveshchenie (Enlightenment)—legal Bolshevik magazine published in St. Petersburg, 1911-14.

Protopopov, Aleksandr D. (1866-1918)—leader of monarchist Octobrist Party, last minister of interior under Nicholas II.

Provisional Government—name of cabinets coalescing capitalist parties with Mensheviks and SRs in 1917.

purges—name used for destruction of all internal opposition or dissension by Hitler and Stalin in 1930s.

Rabocheye Delo (Workers' Cause)—paper published by one of Social Democratic tendencies opposed to working class political action ("Economists"), 1899-1902.

Radical Socialist Party (or Radical Party)—major French capitalist party between WWI and WWII.

Reichstag fire trial—where Communists were tried, in 1933 in Leipzig, for having set fire to German parliament, and were acquitted.

Reiss, Ignace (d. 1937)—Soviet secret police officer who broke with Stalinism and joined Fourth Internationalists; assassinated by GPU in Switzerland.

revisionists—tendency led by Bernstein in German SP at end of nineteenth century to transform Marxism from revolutionary to reformist theory and practice. By 1914 it had conquered most of Second International.

Right Opposition—right-wing faction of CPSU led by Bukharin, Rykov, and Tomsky against Stalin's ultraleftism in 1928-29; defeated, its leaders recanted and were tolerated until Moscow trials, when they were liquidated.

Rivera, Diego (1886-1957)—Mexican painter and Trotsky's host in Mexico; broke with Fourth International in 1939.

Robespierre, Maximilien (1758-94)—French revolutionary, Jacobin leader, overthrown by Thermidorian backlash.

Rocque, Casimir de la (1886-1946)—French fascist leader in 1930s.

Rodbertus, Johann Karl (1805-75)—German economist, "socialist of the chair," theoretician of Prussian-Junker "state socialism."

Rodzianko, Mikhail V. (1859-1924)—leader of Octobrist Party, president of Third and Fourth Dumas, 1911-17; supported Whites in civil war.

Romanov, Nicholas and Alexandra—see pages 81-92.

Rothstein, Theodore (1871-1953)—joined RSDLP, 1901; emigrated from Russia to Britain, 1890; active in labor movement and founding of British CP, 1920; returned to Russia, 1921; active in diplomatic service until 1930.

RSDLP—see Russian Social Democratic Labor Party.

Rutzutak, Yan E. (1887-1938)—Stalinist, Commissar for Communications, 1924-30; arrested and disappeared in purges; rehabilitated in 1956.

Russian Social Democratic Labor Party—affiliate of Second International, suppressed after First Congress in 1898, reorganized at Second Congress in 1903 where Bolshevik-Menshevik split occurred.

Rykov, Aleksei I. (1881-1938)—B, Commissar of Interior, 1917; Lenin's successor as chairman of Council of People's Commissars, 1924-30; leader of Right Opposition, recanted in 1929, restored to minor posts; executed after third Moscow trial.

Saint Just, Louis de (1767-94)—member of French Committee of Public Safety; arrested and executed with Robespierre.

Scheidemann, Philipp (1865-1939)—right-wing SP; helped put down German 1918 revolution; Reichstag deputy, 1898-1933, then went into exile.

Second International (Labor and Socialist International)—revolutionary successor to First International, founded in 1889; united revolutionaries and reformists until WWI, then collapsed. Reestablished in 1919.

Sedov, Leon—see pages 189-203.

Sedov, Sergei (Seryozha) L. (1908-37?)—younger son of Sedova and Trotsky, non-political but arrested and executed for refusing to denounce father.

Sedova, Natalia I.—see pages 120-25.

Serebriakov, Leonid P. (1890-1937)—B, a secretary of Central Committee, 1919-20; Commissar of Communications after civil war; expelled as Oppositionist, 1927; capitulated, 1929; executed after second Moscow trial.

Shaw, George Bernard (1856-1950)—Anglo-Irish playwright and satirist; cofounder of Fabian Society.

Smirnov, Ivan N. (1881-1936)—Red Army leader in Siberia during civil war; Commissar of Communications, 1923-27; expelled as Oppositionist, 1927; capitulated, 1929; executed after first Moscow trial.

Snowden, Ethel (1881-1951)—member of British Independent Labour Party and general do-gooder.

Social Revolutionaries—members of party that succeeded old populist movement at start of century and had wide peasant support. Most SRs supported Provisional Government and opposed October. **Left SRs** split away in 1917, formed bloc with Bolsheviks, and held posts in Soviet government until 1918, when they tried to overthrow it.

Sombart, Werner (1863-1941)—German economist noted for efforts to refute Marx's labor theory of value.

soviets—councils of workers, peasants, soldiers, which supported Provisional Government when they were led by Mensheviks and SRs, and overthrew it when they elected Bolsheviks to leadership.

Spartacus League—began in 1916 as continuator of prewar left wing of German SP, became left wing of centrist Independent Social Democratic Party in 1917, changed name to CP at end of 1918.

SRs—see Social Revolutionaries.

Stakhanovism—speedup and piecework system introduced into Soviet industry in 1935, named after "model" miner said to have increased output by 1600 percent.

Stalin, Joseph—see pages 207-21.

Stalin, Yakov (Yasha) J.—see Dzhugashvili, Yakov J.

Stalin-Hitler pact—nonaggression alliance signed in August 1939 that freed Hitler's hands to open WWII; it lasted until June 1941, when Nazis invaded USSR.

Stolypin, Pyotr A. (1862-1911)—tsarist minister who combined mass repression with agricultural reform after 1905 revolution; assassinated.

Struve, Pyotr B. (1877-1944)—liberal economist, leader of "legal Marxists" seeking to introduce western capitalist development in Russia; supported Cadets after 1905, joined White forces after 1917.

Surits, Yakov (1881-1952)—Stalin's ambassador to Germany and France in 1930s.

Sverdlov, Yakov M.—see pages 69-77.

Tardieu, André (1876-1945)—conservative French premier, 1929-30, 1932; founder of rightist Republican Center.

le Temps (Times)—Paris daily reflecting government views between two world wars.

Thermidor—Trotsky's analogous term (taken from 1794 shift to right in Great French Revolution) to designate Stalin bureaucracy's seizure of power within framework of nationalized property relations.

Third International—see Communist International.

Third Republic—parliamentary system that prevailed in France, 1871-1940, preceded by the dictatorship of Louis Napoleon and succeeded by the dictatorship of Pétain.

Tomsky, Mikhail P. (1880-1936)—chairman, Soviet trade union federation, 1922-29; leader of Right Opposition, capitulated, restored to lesser posts; suicide during first Moscow trial.

Torgler, Ernst (1893-1963)—German CP; acquitted in Reichstag trial; expelled from CP while in Nazi concentration camp; joined West German SP after WWII.

"triumvirate"—name given to Stalin, Zinoviev, Kamenev, 1923-25, when their faction sought to discredit "Trotskyism" as un-Leninist.

Troyanovsky, Aleksandr A. (1882-1955)—M leader, opposed to October; became prominent diplomat under Stalin; ambassador to U.S., 1934-39.

Tsaldars, Panages (1886-1936)—leader of Greek Popular Party; premier, 1933-35; ousted by coup.

Tsereteli, Iraklii (1882-1959)—M minister in Provisional Government.

Tsintsadze, Kote—see pages 93-97.
Tukhachevsky, Mikhail N. (1893-1937)—famous Red Army commander in civil war; named marshal in 1935; executed after secret trial for treason in 1937; "rehabilitated" in 1956.

Venizelos, Eleutherios (1864-1936)—Greek premier five times; led unsuccessful military revolt against Tsaldares regime.
Versailles—town in France, where allied victors of WWI imposed their terms and conditions on the defeated powers; peace treaty and postwar system, both named after site of conference, were opposed by communists and led to emergence of Hitler and to WWII twenty years later.
Volkova, Zinaida L. (1900-33)—Trotsky's older daughter by first marriage; suicide in Germany.
Vollmar, Georg Heinrich (1850-1922)—German SP editor, Reichstag deputy; early ideologist of reformism and "socialism in one country."
Voroshilov, Kliment Y. (1881-1969)—Stalinist, Commissar of Defense, 1925-40; president of Soviet Union, 1953-60.
Vorwärts (Forward)—daily paper of German SP, 1891-1933.
Vyshinsky, Andrei Y. (1883-1954)—M until 1920, Stalinist in 1920s; prosecuting attorney in Moscow trials; Soviet foreign minister, 1949-53.

Webb, Sidney (1859-1947)—a founder of Fabian Society and British Labour Party; chief British theoretician of gradualism; was made a lord in 1929; colonial secretary, 1930-31; later apologist for Stalinism.
Weimar—small town in Germany where democratic-capitalist Weimar republic began its short life, 1919-33.
Wells, H.G.—see pages 55-63.
Whites, White Guards—counterrevolutionary forces in Russian civil war, 1918-21.
Wilhelm II (1859-1941)—kaiser of Germany, 1888-1918.
Wilson, Woodrow (1865-1924)—Democratic president of U.S., 1913-21.
Witte, Sergei Y. (1849-1915)—tsarist minister; promised constitutional reform during 1905 revolution, was dismissed in 1906 after revolution was crushed.

Yagoda, Genrikh G. (1891-1938)—Stalinist and head of GPU who organized first Moscow trials; was himself executed after third trial.
Yegorov, Aleksandr I. (1886-1941)—appointed Red Army marshal in 1935, purged in 1938.
Yenukidze, Abel S.—see pages 174-88.
Yezhov, Nikolai I. (d. 1940)—Stalinist who replaced Yagoda as head of GPU in 1936; disappeared in 1939, after third Moscow trial.
Yudenich, Nikolai N. (1862-1933)—tsarist general who led two White assaults on Petrograd in 1919.

Zaria (Dawn)—magazine published by *Iskra* group.
Zasulich, Vera I.—see pages 41-47.
Zinoviev, Grigori Y.—see pages 164-73.

INDEX

Adler, Victor, 132, 222
Afinogenov, Aleksandr N., 218, 222
Alexinsky, Grigori A., 35, 222
Alliluyeva, Nadezhda S., 217-18, 222
Anschluss, 156, 222
Aveling, Edward, 127, 222
Avksentiev, Nikolai D., 35, 222
Avvakum, Petrovich, 113, 222
Axelrod, Pavel B., 39, 42, 222

Balfour, Arthur, 57, 222
Bangya, Janosh, 131, 222
Barbusse, Henri, 219-20, 222
Bebel, August, 17, 26, 31, 32, 223
Belinsky, Vissarion, 37, 223
Beloborodov, Aleksandr G., 199, 223
Beria, Lavrenti P., 206, 223
Bernstein, Eduard, 28, 31, 119, 132, 223
Biulleten Oppositsii, 95, 169, 195-96, 223
Black Hundreds, 20, 22, 86, 223
Blum, Léon, 153, 223
Bogdanov, Aleksander A., 107, 223
Bolsheviks, 34, 48, 223
Boulanger, Georges, 131, 223
Brentano, Ludwig, 38, 123, 223
Breshko-Breshkovskaya, Yekaterina K., 35, 223
Brest-Litovsk, treaty of, 20, 80, 220, 223
Briand, Aristide, 147, 154, 223
Bukharin, Nikolai I., 174, 180, 185, 217, 223

Bund, 39, 223-24
Burns, Mary, 127, 224

Capital, 122-23
Centrism, 28-29, 224
Charolambos, 98-103
Chernyshevsky, Nikolai G., 37, 224
Communist International (Comintern), 48, 207, 224
Constitutional Democrats (Cadets, Russia), 224, 227
Cuvier, Georges, 131, 224

Daladier, Édouard, 159, 224
Danton, Georges-Jacques, 168, 224
Demuth, Hélène, 121, 130
Descartes, René, 148, 224
Deutsch, Lev G., 39, 224
Dimitrov, Georgi, 168, 224
Duma, 81, 84, 224
Duse, Eleonora, 113, 224
Dzerzhinsky, Felix E., 94, 182, 224
Dzhugashvili, Vissarion, 210, 224
Dzhugashvili, Yakov, 217, 224-25

Eastman, Max, 12n, 64
Ebert, Friedrich, 14, 16, 19, 20, 225
Eliava, Shalva Z., 94, 225
Emancipation of Labor Group (Russia), 39, 41, 225
Engels, Friedrich, 115-33
Erfurt program, 28

Fabian Society (England), 55, 56, 61, 225
Farrell, James T., 7n

First International, 115, 225
Foot, Michael, 5n
Fourth International, 5, 11, 225
Franco-Prussian War (1870-71), 118, 225
Fromm, Erich, 10n

Galicia, retreat from (1915), 83, 225
Girondists (France), 153, 225
Gladstone, William, 123, 225
Glazman, Mikhail, 64-68
Gorky, Maxim, 160-63, 174, 175
GPU (Soviet secret police), 166, 192, 196, 200-201, 205, 225
Guesde, Jules, 132, 225

Haase, Hugo, 19, 225
Herriot, Édouard, 145-59
Herzen, Alexander I., 37, 105, 225
Hitler, Adolf, 157, 210, 219, 220-21, 225
Humanité, L', 146, 226
Hyndman, Henry M., 127-28, 226

Independent Social Democratic Party (USPD, Germany), 29
International Communist League, 115
International Workingmen's Association 115
Iskra, 34, 42, 204, 226
Izvestia, 71, 226

Jacobins, (France), 146, 157, 226
Jaurès, Jean, 37, 46, 147, 226
Joffe, Adolf, 78-80
July days, 20, 22, 73, 226

Kaganovich, Lazar M., 162, 226
Kalinin, Mikhail I., 176-78, 182-83, 185, 226
Kamenev, Lev B., 164-73, 179, 180, 182, 214
Kamenev, Sergei S., 157-58, 226
Kant, Immanuel, 156, 226
Kautsky, Karl, 28-33, 115-33
Kautsky, Luise, 128-30, 226
Kautsky, Minna, 31-32, 226
Kerensky, Alexander F., 20, 22, 226

Kirov, Sergei M., 164, 174, 227
Krasin, Leonid B., 175, 176, 227
Krivitsky, Walter, 219, 227
Krupskaya, Nadezhda K., 41, 204-206

Lakoba, Mikhail, 184, 185
Lakoba, Nestor, 179, 184
Lamartine, Alphonse de, 153, 227
Lassalle, Ferdinand, 18, 227
Laval, Pierre, 146, 158, 227
League of Nations, 156, 227
League of the Just, 115
Left Opposition, 64, 78, 93, 164, 191-99, 227
Leipzig trial, 168, 230
Lenin, Vladimir Ilyich, 20, 69, 73; interview of, with H.G. Wells, 55-63; and *Iskra,* 41-46; as a speaker, 48-54; testament of, 188, 227
Lieber, Mikhail I., 39, 227
Liebknecht, Karl, 14-27
Liebknecht, Wilhelm, 198, 227
Litvinov, Maxim, 158
Ludwig, Emil, 6n, 214, 227
Lunacharsky, Anatoli, 104-108, 180
Luxemburg, Rosa, 14-27, 125
Lvov, Georgi Y., 84, 227

MacDonald, Ramsay, 62, 154-55, 227
Maisky, Ivan M., 176, 227
Markin, Nikolai G., 197, 199, 228
Martov, L., 34, 42, 43, 228
Martynov, Aleksandr S., 39, 228
Marx, Eleanor, 127, 228
Marx, Karl, 115, 123-24, 125, 130, 228; relationship of, to Engels, 116, 121
Mdivani, Budu M., 179, 228
Mehring, Franz, 125, 228
Mensheviks, 34, 48, 228
Mikhailovsky, Nikolai K., 36, 228
Mikoyan, Anastas I., 162, 228
Millerandism, 31, 228
Molotov, Vyacheslav M., 214, 228
Morozov, Savva, 175
Moscow trials, 165, 169-73, 197, 202, 219

Mrachkovsky, Sergei V., 199, 202, 228

Muraviev, Mikhail A., 74, 228

Mussolini, Benito, 157, 228

Narodnaya Volya (People's Will), 105, 171, 228

Narodniks, 34, 41, 228

Nashe Slovo, 29, 228

National Bloc (France), 151, 228

Necker, Jacques, 151, 228

Neue Zeit, 28

New Economic Policy (NEP, Russia), 180, 229

Nicholas II, 81-92

Okudzhava, M., 95, 229

Old Bolsheviks, 176, 178, 187, 229

Orakhelashvili, Ivan D., 94, 179, 229

Ordzhonikidze, Grigori K., 94, 179, 229

Ozvobozhdenie, 16, 229

Paléologue, Maurice, 87, 229

Parvus, A.L., 31, 229

Pascal, Blaise, 148

People's Front, 145, 229

Pestkovsky, Stanislas S., 209, 210, 229

Plekhanov, Georgi, 34-40, 42, 43, 125, 213

Poincaré, Raymond, 148, 150, 151, 229

Poland, 1939 invasion of, 219, 220, 229

Polish Corridor, 156, 229-30

Port Arthur (China), 83, 230

Potresov, Aleksander N., 42, 230

Pravda, 209, 230

Prosveshchenie, 209, 230

Protopopov, Aleksandr D., 88, 230

Provisional Government (1917, Russia), 22, 84, 199, 214, 230

Psychoanalysis, 5-8

Purges, 207, 219, 230

Rabocheye Delo, 39, 230

Radical Socialist Party (Radicals, France), 131, 145, 146, 230

Rakovsky, Christian G., 184, 185

Rasputin, Grigory, 81, 86, 89-92

Reichstag fire trial (1933, Germany), 168, 230

Reiss, Ignace, 200, 230

Revisionists, 28, 230

Right Opposition, 168, 230

Rivera, Diego, 200, 230

Robespierre, Maximilien, 153, 168, 230

Rocque, Casimir de la, 153, 230

Rodbertus, Johann Karl, 123, 125, 230

Rodzianko, Mikhail V., 86, 230

Romanov, Nicholas and Alexandra, 81-92

Rothstein, Theodore, 58, 231

Russian Social Democratic Labor Party (RSDLP), 34, 48, 231

Russo-Japanese War (1904-05), 81

Rudzutak, Yan E., 185, 231

Rykov, Aleksei I., 174, 185, 231

Saint-Just, Louis de, 153, 231

Scheidemann, Philipp, 16, 19, 20, 231

Second International, 14, 28, 29-30, 115, 231

Sedov, Leon, 189-203

Sedov, Sergei, 201, 202, 231

Sedova, Natalia I., 109-114

Serebriakov, Leonid P., 183, 231

Serge, Victor, 109

Shaw, George Bernard, 8n, 131, 231

Smirnov, Ivan N., 184, 185, 202, 231

Snowden, Ethel, 60, 231

Social Democratic Party (SPD, Germany), 14, 15, 16, 18

Social Revolutionaries (SRs, Russia), 73, 74, 171, 231

Sombart, Werner, 38, 231

Soviets, 70, 232

Spartacus League (Germany), 14, 28, 232

Stakhanovism, 197, 232

Stalin, Joseph, 162, 185, 207-21; Kremlin life of, 179-182; persecution of Left Oppositionists by, 64, 78, 94, 95

Stalin-Hitler pact (1939), 207, 220, 232
Stalin-Zinoviev-Kamenev faction (triumvirate), 64, 69, 95, 184, 232
Stasova, E.D., 77
Stead, V.T., 131
Stolypin, Pyotr A., 25, 84, 232
Struve, Pyotr B., 46, 232
Surits, Yakov, 176, 232
Sverdlov, Yakov M., 69-77, 176

Tardieu, André, 153, 232
Temps, Le, 146, 232
Thermidor, 163, 167, 183, 205, 232
Third International, 48, 207, 224
Third Republic (France), 150, 232
Tomsky, Mikhail P., 185, 232
Torgler, Ernst, 168, 232
Trepov, F.F., 41, 45, 88
Triumvirate, 64, 69, 95, 184, 232
Trotsky, Leon, 15, 35, 49, 164, 194; as a writer, 5-13; expulsion of, from CP, 184-86; Kremlin days of, 179, 181; last exile of, 82, 98, 109, 194
Troyanovsky, Aleksandr A., 176, 232
Tsaldaris, Panages, 152, 232
Tsereteli, Iraklii, 20, 232
Tsintsadze, Alipi (Kote), 93-97
Tukhachevsky, Mikhail N., 220, 233
Two-and-a-Half International, 29

United Opposition, 164, 204, 205
USPD. *See* Independent Social Democratic Party

Venizelos, Eleutherios, 152, 233
Versailles, 152, 233
Volkova, Zinaida L., 201, 233
Vollmar, Georg H., 132, 233
Voroshilov, Kliment Y., 185, 218, 233
Vorwärts, 132, 233
Vyshinsky, Andrei Y., 172, 173, 233

Webb, Sydney, 131, 233
Weimar, 23, 157, 233
Wells, H.G., 55-63
White Guards, 22, 73, 233
Wilhelm II, 16, 233
Wilson, Woodrow, 33, 233
Witte, Sergei Y., 83, 85, 87, 233

Yagoda, Henry, 173, 188, 206, 233
Yegorov, Aleksandr I., 220, 233
Yenukidze, Abel S., 174-188
Yenukidze, Simon, 175
Yezhov, Nikolai I., 188, 233
Yudenich, Nikolai N., 80, 233

Zaria, 34, 42, 233
Zasulich, Vera I., 39, 41-47
Zinoviev, Grigori Y., 20, 164-73, 180

BOOKS AND PAMPHLETS BY LEON TROTSKY*

Against Individual Terrorism
The Age of Permanent Revolution
The Basic Writings of Trotsky
Between Red and White
The Bolsheviki and World Peace (War and the International)
The Case of Leon Trotsky
The Challenge of the Left Opposition (1923-25) (incl. The New Course, Lessons of October, Problems of Civil War, and Toward Socialism or Capitalism?)
The Crisis of the French Section (1935-36)
Europe and America: Two Speeches on Imperialism
Fascism: What It Is and How to Fight It
The First Five Years of the Communist International (2 vols.)
The History of the Russian Revolution (3 vols.)
In Defense of Marxism
Lenin: Notes for a Biographer
Lenin's Fight Against Stalinism (with V.I. Lenin)
Leon Trotsky Speaks
Literature and Revolution
Marxism in Our Time
Military Writings
My Life
1905
On Black Nationalism and Self-Determination
On Britain (incl. Where Is Britain Going?)
On China (incl. Problems of the Chinese Revolution)
On the Jewish Question
On Literature and Art
On the Paris Commune
On the Trade Unions
Our Revolution
The Permanent Revolution and Results and Prospects
Portraits, Political and Personal
Problems of Everyday Life and Other Writings on Culture and Science
The Revolution Betrayed
The Spanish Revolution (1931-39)
Stalin
The Stalin School of Falsification
The Struggle Against Fascism in Germany
Terrorism and Communism
Their Morals and Ours (with essays by John Dewey and George Novack)
The Third International After Lenin
The Transitional Program for Socialist Revolution (incl. The Death Agony of Capitalism and the Tasks of the Fourth International)
Trotsky's Diary in Exile, 1935
Women and the Family
Writings of Leon Trotsky (1929-40) (12 vols., to be completed in 1977)
The Young Lenin

In preparation:
The Challenge of the Left Opposition (1926-29) (incl. The Platform of the Opposition)
Kronstadt (with V.I. Lenin)
On France (incl. Whither France?)
The War Correspondence of Leon Trotsky

---

*This list includes only books and pamphlets by Leon Trotsky published in the United States and in print as of 1977.